FIRST COMES LOVE.
THEN COMES MARRIAGE.
AND THEN COMES . . .

THE DANCE - AWAY LOVER

& Other Roles We Play

"Fun . . . and a goodly amount of pactical advice."
—**Dallas News**

"Highly readable . . . constructive . . . and lively."
—**Publishers Weekly**

"Thought-provoking . . . aims to help couples push themselves towards lasting love."
—**Penthouse**

"Perceptive analyses of the roles we're caught in . . . Anyone who can't recognize himself (and everyone he knows well) in at least one of the ten roles, either can't see—or isn't willing to look."
—**Kirkus Reviews**

THE DANCE-AWAY LOVER

And Other Roles We Play in Love, Sex, and Marriage

Daniel Goldstine

Katherine Larner

Shirley Zuckerman

Hilary Goldstine

BALLANTINE BOOKS • NEW YORK

Library of Congress Catalog Card Number: 76-54928

ISBN 0-345-29763-6

This edition published by arrangement with
William Morrow & Company, Inc.

Manufactured in the United States of America

First Ballantine Books Edition: July 1978
Third Printing: September 1981

Acknowledgments

We gratefully acknowledge the permission given us by publishers and authors to reprint passages from the following works:

from *The Savage God: A Study of Suicide* by A. Alvarez, copyright © 1970, 1971, 1972 by A. Alvarez. Reprinted by permission of Random House, Inc.

from *Collected Poems, 1951–1971* by A. R. Ammons with the permission of W. W. Norton & Company, Inc., New York, N.Y., copyright © 1972 by A. R. Ammons.

from "Clepsydra" from *Rivers and Mountains* by John Ashbery. Copyright © 1966 by John Ashbery, reprinted by permission of the author.

by W. H. Auden: "O who can ever gaze his fill" ("Death's Echo") copyright 1945 by W. H. Auden; "Precious Five" copyright 1950 by W. H. Auden; "As I walked out one Evening" copyright 1940 by W. H. Auden, renewed 1968 by W. H. Auden; and "Lay your sleeping head my love" ("Lullaby") copyright 1940 and renewed 1968 by W. H. Auden. Reprinted from *Collected Shorter Poems 1927–1957* by W. H. Auden by permission of Random House, Inc.

from *Lyubka the Cossack and other stories* by Isaac Babel, translated by Andrew R. MacAndrew. Copyright © 1963 by Andrew R. MacAndrew. Reprinted by arrangement with The New American Library, Inc., New York.

reprinted from *Light from Heaven; Love in British Romantic Literature* by Frederick L. Beaty, copyright © 1971 by Northern Illinois University Press. By permission of the publisher.

from *Virginia Woolf: A Biography* by Quentin Bell. Copyright © 1972. Reprinted by permission of Harcourt Brace Jovanovich, Inc.

Reprinted with the permission of Farrar, Straus & Giroux, Inc., from *The Blue Estuaries* by Louise Bogan, Copyright © 1923, 1929, 1930, 1931, 1933, 1934, 1935, 1936, 1937, 1938, 1941,

1949, 1951, 1952, 1954, 1957, 1958, 1962, 1963, 1964, 1965, 1966, 1967, 1968 by Louise Bogan.

from *Alice in Wonderland and Through the Looking Glass* by Lewis Carroll, illustrated by John Tenniel. Illustrations, copyright 1946 by Grosset & Dunlap, Inc. Reprinted by permission of Grosset & Dunlap, Inc., Publishers.

from *A Personal Record* by Joseph Conrad. Used by permission of Doubleday & Company, Inc.

from "Marriage" by Gregory Corso, *The Happy Birthday of Death*. Copyright © 1960 by New Directions Publishing Corporation. Reprinted by permission of New Directions Publishing Corporation.

from *Complete Poems 1913–1962* by E. E. Cummings. Published by Harcourt Brace Jovanovich, Inc. Reprinted by permission of Harcourt Brace Jovanovich, Inc.

from "Adultery," copyright © 1966 by James Dickey. Reprinted from *Poems 1957–1967* by permission of Wesleyan University Press.

from "The Love Song of J. Alfred Prufrock" by T. S. Eliot from *Collected Poems 1909–62*, copyright 1936 by Harcourt Brace & World; copyright © 1963, 1964 by T. S. Eliot. Reprinted by permission of Harcourt Brace Jovanovich, Inc.

from "Upon the much-to-be-lamented decease of the Reverend Dr. John Cotton, late Teacher to the Church at Boston N. E. who departed Life 23 of 10 (16) 52" by John Fiske from *America A Prophecy*, edited by Jerome Rothenberg and George Quasha, copyright 1974. Reprinted by permission of Random House, Inc.

from "To Earthward" from *The Poetry of Robert Frost*, edited by Edward Connery Lathem, copyright 1923, © 1969 by Holt, Rinehart & Winston. Copyright 1951 by Robert Frost. Reprinted by permission of Holt, Rinehart & Winston, publishers.

reprinted from *Between Parent and Teenager* by Dr. Haim Ginott, copyright © 1969 by Macmillan, Inc. Reprinted by permission of Dr. Alice Ginott, executor.

"Those Winter Sundays" reprinted from *Angle of Ascent, New and Selected Poems* by Robert Hayden. By permission of Liveright Publishing Corporation. Copyright © 1975, 1972, 1970, 1966 by Robert Hayden.

from *Something Happened* by Joseph Heller, copyright 1974. Reprinted by permission of Alfred A. Knopf, Inc.

from "At the Winter Solstice" in *The City of Satisfactions,* © 1963 by Daniel Hoffman (Oxford University Press). Used by permission of the author.

from "The Leaden Echo and The Golden Echo" by Gerard Manley Hopkins, reprinted from *Poems of Gerard Manley Hopkins,* copyright 1967 by The Society of Jesus and Oxford University Press. Reprinted by permission of Oxford University Press.

from "Hedda Gabler" in *Six Plays by Henrik Ibsen,* translated by Eva LeGallienne. Copyright 1953 by Eva LeGallienne. Reprinted by permission of Random House, Inc.

from *Knots* by R. D. Laing, copyright © 1972. Reprinted by permission of Random House, Inc.

from "Talking in Bed," in *The Whitsun Weddings,* copyright © 1964 by Philip Larkin. Reprinted by permission of Faber and Faber Ltd.

from "Lament for Ignacio Sánchez Mejías" by Federico García Lorca, translated by Stephen Spender and J. L. Gili. From Federico García Lorca, *Selected Poems,* edited by Francisco García Lorca and Donald Allen. Copyright 1955 by New Directions Publishing Corporation. Reprinted by permission of New Directions Publishing Corporation.

reprinted by permission of the author and G. P. Putnam's Sons from *Advertisements for Myself* by Norman Mailer. Copyright © 1959 by Norman Mailer.

from *The Prisoner of Sex* by Norman Mailer. Copyright © 1971 by Norman Mailer. Reprinted by permission of the author and the author's agents, Scott Meredith Literary Agency, Inc., 845 Third Avenue, New York, N.Y. 10022.

from *In a Man's Time* by Peter Marin. Copyright © 1974 by Peter Marin. Reprinted by permission of Simon and Schuster, Inc.

from *Winnie-the-Pooh* by A. A. Milne. Copyright, 1926, by E. P. Dutton & Company; renewal, 1954, by A. A. Milne. Reprinted by permission of the publishers, E. P. Dutton & Company, Inc.

from *The Bell Jar* by Sylvia Plath. Harper & Row, Inc. Reprinted by permission of the publisher.

from *Three Women: A Poem for Three Voices* from *Winter Trees* by Sylvia Plath published by Faber and Faber Ltd., London, copyright Ted Hughes 1971. Reprinted by permission of Olwyn Hughes.

from "Oblation" by R. M. Rilke, from *Rilke: Selected Poems* with English translations by C. F. MacIntyre. Copyright © 1940 by C. F. MacIntyre. Reprinted by permission of the University of California Press.

from "The Wraith," copyright 1953 by Theodore Roethke, "The Lost Son," copyright 1947 by Theodore Roethke, "The Dying Man," copyright © 1956 by The Atlantic Monthly Co., "Her Becoming," copyright © 1958 by Botteghe Oscure, "I knew a Woman," copyright 1954 by Theodore Roethke; all from *The Collected Poems of Theodore Roethke* by Theodore Roethke. Used by permission of Doubleday and Company, Inc.

from *Pygmalion* by George Bernard Shaw. Reprinted by permission of The Society of Authors on behalf of the Bernard Shaw Estate.

from *Beyond Monogamy*, edited by James R. Smith and Lynn G. Smith © 1974, The Johns Hopkins University Press. Reprinted by permission of the publisher.

from "Not Waving but Drowning" by Stevie Smith, *Selected Poems*. Copyright © 1962, © 1964 by Stevie Smith. Reprinted by permission of the New Directions Publishing Corporation.

from the book *From Time to Time,* copyright © 1973 by Hannah Tillich. Reprinted by permission of Stein and Day Publishers.

from *Anna Karenina* by Leo Tolstoy, newly translated and with a Foreword by David Magarshack. Copyright © 1961 by David Magarshack. Reprinted by arrangement with The New American Library, Inc., New York.

from "The Ivy Crown" by William Carlos Williams, *Pictures from Brueghel and other poems.* Copyright © 1955 by William Carlos Williams. Reprinted by permission of New Directions Publishing Corporation.

from *A Room of One's Own* by Virginia Woolf, copyright 1929 by Harcourt Brace & Company, Inc. Reprinted by permission of Harcourt Brace Jovanovich, Inc.

from "A Prayer for My Daughter" from *Collected Poems of William Butler Yeats* (Copyright 1924 by Macmillan, Inc., renewed 1952 by Bertha Georgie Yeats.)

Preface

THE ANCIENT POETS tell us that Venus, the goddess of love, was born in a chill and effortless moment of self-procreation from the foam of the surging sea. Poets also tell us that she took, as her most illustrious lover, Mars, the god of strife.

This is a book about love and strife, and about the fruitful and necessary interaction of desire and struggle. It is a book which, as will be evident, acknowledges the ability of poets and poetry to register the complexities and simplicities of relationships.

Yet Mars and Venus do not establish the paradigm of this book's applicability. Our discussion is based on work with clients in a large variety of settings: a private, nonprofit clinic, a county medical facility, a university. And while the great majority of the couples we have seen were heterosexual, to the limited extent that we have worked with homosexual couples, we believe that our conceptual and therapeutic framework has proved itself applicable to them as well. Although we have also worked with low-income couples, this book addresses itself primarily to the stresses and aspirations of men and women whose situations afford them the luxury of separating emotional and economic needs, men and women whose relationships are not fundamentally or crucially exacerbated by the struggle for economic survival.

Moreover, this is a book about love, whose origins could not be more radically different from the chill and isolated birth of the goddess of love. The book resulted from interchanges that involved a much larger group of individuals than a glance at the title page would indicate. Not that the title page doesn't list a larger contingent than usual—three therapists and one writer. As co-authors, we bear and share all responsibility for the defects in this work. What strengths it possesses are due, in an important sense, to the others whose contributions we want to remember here.

The most extensive debt we must acknowledge is to the men and women we've come to know as clients. This book is based on the peculiar process known as therapy, an experience that casts one participant in the role of professional and the other in the role of client. This distinction often conceals the fact that the process is mutually instructive. As clients ourselves, we have learned from our teachers and therapists, but as therapists, we have learned far more from our clients, and we give them, in return, our respect and our gratitude.

This book emerges, specifically, out of the work that Daniel Goldstine, Shirley Zuckerman, and Hilary Goldstine have done over the last five years at the Berkeley Therapy Institute. The B.T.I. is a nonprofit private clinic located in Berkeley, California. Daniel Goldstine is the chief psychologist of its staff. He graduated from the University of California, Berkeley, in philosophy, and received his Ph.D. in clinical psychology from the same institution. He has taught at Bennington College, and served as staff psychologist at the Contra Costa County Medical Services Facility. In 1970 he began to work with Shirley Zuckerman, who was employed then as the chief social worker of the Day Treatment Services in Contra Costa County. She graduated from the University of California, Berkeley, with a degree in history, and received her M.S.W. at the Smith College School for Social Work. She is now the chief social worker at the Berkeley Therapy Institute. Hilary Goldstine is a graduate of the University of California, Berkeley, in psychology. She has received her Master's degree and her Doctorate in Clinical Psychology at the California School of Professional Psychology and has done considerable work as an intern at the Berkeley Therapy Institute. In addition to their work at the B.T.I., for five years Daniel Goldstine and Shirley Zuckerman have served as co-directors of the Sex Therapy Program at Cowell Memorial Hospital, University of California, Berkeley; Hilary Goldstine has worked in this program as well.

By now it is commonplace observation that the field of psychology has tended to focus on deviance. We have concerned ourselves not with deviance but with the question of how people in the mainstream face normal life situations and how they go about sharing life and love with a partner. Our perspective on these issues bears the firm imprint of role theory, which considers the social positions that individuals find themselves in with respect to each other. We want to express our special gratitude to Ted Sarbin, mentor and friend, for the invaluable work he's published on role theory, and for his willingness to explore the implications of these ideas informally as well as formally. Systems theory, as developed by Bateson, Jackson, Watzlawick, Weakland, and Fisch at the Mental Research Institute in Palo Alto, has influenced our thinking, as has the work of Salvador Minuchin, Frieda Fromm-Reichman, and Jay Haley. We have also been influenced by the genius of Milton Erickson. We wish to credit Eric Berne, from whose writing we derived the concept of the "Victim" and the "rescue" and whose notion of scripts is closely related to role theory. We owe appreciation to Margaret Singer for her insightful exploration of family structures and her inspirational example as a truly great clinician. We would like to thank Frank Beach for the benefit we've derived from his extensive research into and his profound understanding of sexuality, especially his insistence upon the interrelation of behavior and context in a naturalistic setting.

We are obliged to thank not only our clients and our teachers, however; we must also thank our colleagues. We have been privileged to work with a group of remarkable individuals: Michael Evans, Charlie Pollack, Vicki Galland, Karen McLellan, Arvalea Nelson, Jacob Herring, Jeremy Jacobs Gordon, Richelle Jacobs, Bob Dolgoff, Fred Behrens, Nina Ham,

Marcia Perlstein, and others who have at various times been part of the Berkeley Therapy Institute and the University of California Cowell Program. All therapists should be blessed with such thoughtful and convivial associates.

This experience of doing therapy and talking about therapy produced a mass of ideas, many of which were fragmented. The credit for turning them into a book belongs to the writer Katherine Larner. She received her B.A. in history from Swarthmore College and her M.A. in American Studies from Brandeis University. It was she who elicited sense and even made sense of thoughts that were often inchoate. It is her style that informs this book.

The process of rewriting involved many of our friends, most particularly Linda Tillich, Joe Juhasz, Arvalea Nelson, and Florence Goldstine. There are no more gifted or generous people anywhere. Jim Landis brought enviable capacities for patience and encouragement to bear on our behalf, and his skill and dedication as editor shepherded us through a difficult process.

Fanchon Lewis and Erica Stone turned tapes and squiggles into the kind of beautiful manuscript every author covets, and we thank them for it.

Finally, we thank the family members and friends who bore with us through this effort. We owe our deepest debt to these people: Josh and Maya Goldstine, Edgar and Regina Goldstine, Harold and Harriet Brady, David and Rosalind Zuckerman, Hugh and Dorothy Larner, Mary Larner, Stephen and Florence Goldstine, Stephanie Bennett, Donald Catalanello, Peter Dybwad, Judy DeVries, Noel Day, Anne Bernstein, Meta Kauffman, Steve and Julie Pittel, Carolyn Craven, Stephanie Bennett, Sala Steinbach, Denny Abrams, Donald Stanford, and Judith and Jeffrey Klein. Without their support and their criticism, their affection and their tolerance, we could never have commenced or completed this undertaking, this attempt to reconcile and accommodate love and struggle, Venus and Mars.

CONTENTS

Introduction

WE STARTED OUT to write a book about sex. We ended up writing a book about couples. Others who have tackled the topic of sex have wound up with studies of physiology (what happens in the human body when it responds sexually) or works of sociology (what kinds of sexual behavior are prevalent among what kinds of people). Some have depicted sex as a form of sensual specialization with techniques that can be mastered; others have analyzed it as a kind of performance that can be remedied if inadequate. An individual's ability to function sexually has been portrayed as a legacy from his childhood relationships, and as the consequence of broader socio-cultural conditioning.*

The literature on sex has grown to be vast and diverse, but overall, nonliterary treatments of this theme have failed to reflect one crucial aspect of human sexual behavior: that most of it happens between two people, and that most of the time, those pairs of people have a relationship that extends beyond sex. Most couples don't just go to bed together at night; they get up together the next morning and confront a whole range of shared concerns—children, household responsibilities, money, friends, and so on.

* The monuments to which these extremely general comments refer are, in order, *Human Sexual Response*, William Masters and Virginia Johnson; *Sexual Behavior in the Human Male* and *Sexual Behavior in the Human Female*, Kinsey, Pomeroy, et al; *Sexual Behavior in the 1970's*, Morton Hunt; *The Joy of Sex*, Alex Comfort; *Human Sexual Inadequacy*, William Masters and Virginia Johnson, and *The New Sex Therapy*, Helen Singer Kaplan; *The Female Orgasm*, Seymour Fischer, and *The Sexual Revolution*, Wilhelm Reich.

Our work as sex and couple therapists has taught us to examine a couple's sexual trouble in the context of their entire relationship. As one client observed, "It's amazing how being angry will ruin your sex life," and infrequent or unenjoyable sex is often the signal that other grievances are simmering.

For example, one male client who was married to a sharp-tongued woman found himself progressively less willing to make love with her. When she complained about the dwindling ration of sex, he replied, "If you just stopped bitching so goddamned much. Constantly bitching—about the stupidest things—and then you want me to turn on to you at night."

Sex can also become a problem for a couple if one partner uses it to obtain reassurance that he's cared about, if he turns making love into a test of love. Nervous eating can happen in solitude, but most forms of sex cannot, and the person who uses sex to allay his anxiety is likely to pressure his partner into obstinate refusals.

Sex can be used as a weapon, or a way of being close, or a lure.

> (cccome? said he
> umm said she)
> You're divine! said he
> (you are Mine said she)*

In order to understand the meaning sex has for a couple therefore, it's necessary to know what functions it fulfills for them emotionally, as well as what physiological dysfunctions it obliges them to contend with.

Just as a couple's inability to get along in other areas is apt to have repercussions on their sex life, so sexual disappointment is likely to have adverse effects on the rest of the relationship. One husband, whose sexual advances frequently met with rejection, said, "I feel somewhat vulnerable when I make an overture to Maggie. When it's obvious that I want to make love

* e. e. cummings, # 38 from *100 Selected Poems*.

and she doesn't, I feel she's rejecting me emotionally. Then I sort of withdraw, so she also loses *me,* because I'm not there any more." He added, "I realize that people can have different levels of desire for sex, but that's just an intellectual awareness. It doesn't help when I want sex. I can look at it, and explain what's happening, but I can't deal with the emotions I have."

The feelings stirred up by a person's inability to perform to his own or his partner's sexual satisfaction are often even more threatening. A serious sexual dysfunction can undermine a person's confidence in his adequacy and shake his faith in the future of his relationship. The nonorgasmic woman often succumbs to the Magic Penis Syndrome: *If only I had a man who could do it right, I'd be fine.* The impotent man wonders, *Would I have this problem with somebody else?*

As people's sexual expectations rise, so does the significance they attach to failure. One man said stiffly of his wife, "If we don't have a successful sexual incident, she assumes something in our relationship is wrong." In fact, the long-term consequence of a serious sexual dysfunction is apt to be that something does go wrong emotionally.

Frustration can be one consequence. A woman said of her husband, who prematurely ejaculated, "When we go to bed, he goes to sleep. He says, 'Who says we have to make love all the time?' And if we do make love, I get all excited, and then in two seconds he comes and it's all over for another week or so."

A person's inability to achieve arousal or orgasm on the proper schedule often registers on the partner as rejection. Be it misperception or actual fact, rejection causes pain. One man who was married to a sexually aversive woman said, "I touch her and she stiffens up. It always tickles or it hurts or something. That makes me feel really bad. If you won't have sex with somebody, you can't possibly love them."

Sexual disappointment makes a breach in the physical intimacy between two people that often jeopardizes their emotional intimacy as well. The presence of sex —potential, actual, or remembered—is a defining characteristic of a couple relationship. The "unison of affection and desire"* that allows two people to become 'one flesh' is what differentiates a couple from two individuals who simply care about each other.

Not that the mere existence of a sexual relationship between two people guarantees them much. Each person who grows to sexual maturity discovers that "good, betimes, as it [sex] may be, there are dead small corners for which he is not prepared, and responsibility he never knew. Nothing in the life of his fantasy prepared him for tenderness, for war, for the tragic need of sex to move into love or be chilled to something less."†

Perfunctory sex often leaves a person in the position one client described sadly, "I have always wanted him to love me, and he never has. He says he has, but I've never felt it." A sexual relationship that's alive and mutually pleasurable isn't enough to ensure a couple happiness, but it does seem to be a necessary element of a fully satisfying, fully committed couple relationship. To be a couple without being lovers is to be only partial partners.

Sex, in turn, can serve as a metaphor that sheds light on the way a couple relationship works overall. Sex raises many of the crucial problems inherent in such a partnership: how to respond to conflict, failure, excessive familiarity, and a sense of obligation; how to secure pleasure, and how to give it. A sexual interaction can serve as a paradigm for a couple interaction, providing a framework for a sprawling and complicated phenomenon.

Until recently, the unit of the couple has suffered a curious neglect. Theoretically and therapeutically, psychology has concentrated primarily on the individual on the one hand, and the family on the other. It is

* Mary Wollstonecraft, in *Letters to Imlay*.

† Norman Mailer, *Advertisements for Myself*.

clear, however, that a couple relationship is usually the deepest involvement an adult has. The couple is the nucleus of the family; the partners are together before their children come, and after their children leave.

Our interest in couples led us, as therapists, to focus on sex therapy and couple therapy. This work led us to the recognition that people predictably choose certain strategies in certain sexual situations. The person who wants to give his partner sexual pleasure is apt to offer her the kind of stimulation *he* enjoys.* The woman who caresses her husband very lightly is apt to prefer a feathery touch on her own body. Likewise, when people want to please each other in other ways, they tend to offer each other what they want to be given, or what they feel comfortable giving, and to translate their own preferences into a prescription for what the other ought to want.

Conflict over sex often triggers a control battle between the partners. One man asserted, "If I'm not aggressive, sex gets pretty few and far between." But when he tried to cuddle with his wife during the commercials in their TV watching, she pushed him away, saying, "One kiss will lead to one more kiss, and then you'll want to go to bed." Driving in the car, he touched her knee with his hand as he changed gears, and she moved her knee away. He proposed sex in bed at night, and she disposed of the idea dourly. She explained, "I feel pressured to have sex, and it's like something inside me says, 'Don't do it. Don't give in to him.'" He began to demand sex and she continued to withhold it.

Avoidance is often the strategy people choose when they're faced with sexual failure. A man who had trouble keeping an erection said of his disinterest in sex, "In many ways, Amy has lost appeal to me, because of the anxiety. I don't like hassles, and if we're

* We have met the pronoun problem and been defeated by it. Since we don't have the necessary impersonal singular pronoun, we use "he" to refer to "a person," as well as "a male person." We regret the implications of this expedient.

going to get into a big teary scene about it, I'd just as soon not get it on at all, sexually." Amy concurred, "There's something really heavy about those bad times." Reluctant to risk another possible failure, they began to avoid each other sexually, pretending that their bodies somehow had become excess baggage in their relationship.

We can describe the way people react to nonsexual situations in these same terms, in terms of the strategies they adopt to get what they want and to protect themselves from what they fear. Avoidance is sometimes a couple's solution to financial failure. One man who was deeply in debt "wouldn't admit to my wife that anything was wrong. I would react very defensively when things were brought up." Even after bill collectors had begun to call, his wife hesitated to ask what was going on, for fear that the crisis would be harder for him to weather if it were brought out in the open.

Failure often hooks a couple into mutual avoidance. Conflict can polarize them into demanding and withholding. One classic nonsexual struggle occurs over the issue of togetherness. A wife pesters her husband to be with her, and he stubbornly refuses to give her his attention. We have found that we can describe many different kinds of interactions in terms of the way each partner tries to control the outcome. Each of the strategies we have identified—pleasing, avoidance, withholding, blame, and so on—secures particular gains and entails particular losses for the person who employs it.

Paradoxically, people often rely on strategies that are self-defeating. In *Alice's Adventures in Wonderland,* the King of Hearts tried to force the Mad Hatter to calm down by telling him, "Don't be nervous or I'll have you executed on the spot."* We understand many of the difficulties couples experience as the consequence of the ways they try to exercise power over each other.

* Lewis Carroll, *Alice's Adventures in Wonderland.*

Strategies adopted for self-defense often interlock into systems of behavior that are self-perpetuating and self-destructive.

It's difficult for a person to break out of a system like mutual avoidance, because usually he believes that his behavior protects him, and he believes, furthermore, that that behavior is the only possible response he can make to the situation.

We can describe individuals in terms of the strategies they rely on consistently in relation to a couple partner. Choices of strategy are rarely considered consciously, but however instinctively or automatically these choices are made, different people clearly do respond in different ways to the same kind of stress. In *Winnie the Pooh*, when a flood threatened the forest, Piglet reflected that among his friends, "Christopher Robin and Pooh could escape by Climbing Trees, and Kanga could escape by Jumping, Rabbit could escape by Burrowing, and Owl could escape by Flying, and Eeyore [the Donkey] could escape by—by Making a Loud Noise Until Rescued."* Most people, likewise, have characteristic ways of looking after themselves and responding to each other.

A given strategy tends to be buttressed by a predictable pattern of perception and emotion that altogether creates a role. The first role we recognized was that of the Dance-Away Lover, the partner who gets going when the going gets rough. Nine other roles subsequently emerged, each of which reflects an internal logic that knits expectation and response into a way of being that's taken for granted by the person who adopts it. Broadly, a role depicts a style of loving. Narrowly, it represents a way of responding to anxiety and resentment.

Some of the roles we describe—the Dance-Away Lover, for example—are characteristically male; others, like the Anxious Ingenue, are characteristically female, and there are social strictures against deviation from these norms. In deference to these cultural

* A. A. Milne, *Winnie the Pooh*.

realites, and to minimize the pronoun confusion, which can become quite troublesome in the discussion of couples, we describe the role as a single-sex phenomenon. We refer to the Dance-Away Lover as "he" and to the Anxious Ingenue as "she."

Each of the chapters in the first half of the book is a composite portrait of a type, not a description of a particular individual. The unfootnoted quotes are statements made by clients in tape-recorded therapy sessions, and the names and identities of these clients have been relentlessly concealed.

Our purpose in delineating these roles is to help people gain perspective on their own behavior, and to gain the insight into their partner's conduct that comes from the understanding that, as one of Jean Renoir's characters says, "In this world there is one awful thing and that is that everyone has his reasons."

We do not postulate a single "healthy" approach to love. We don't believe in this notion. We are pointing out the problems inherent in each of a range of approaches we see people adopt. Our object is to help people realize that in most situations there are alternatives in terms of behavior, and some of these alternatives will serve them better than others. Someone whose partner has just refused him sexually can entreat ('Oh please'), or blame ('You're frigid'), or throw her on the bed and start tickling her. Clarity about the options that are available to him can help free a person from the mistaken belief that he has to do what he always does.

In doing therapy, we've observed that there is a customary sequence of stages in a couple relationship. An individual has a life cycle, a family has a life cycle, and a couple relationship has a life cycle too.

At the point in their relationship when two people discover that they love each other and wish to become partners, they tend to experience a harmony and mutual delight that we call Stage I. They are happy,

for love are in we am in i are you*

This phase of a relationship is characterized by openness, optimism, and mutual engrossment. But it doesn't last.

To a couple's distress, real life gradually impinges on their relationship. Conflict surfaces, failure intrudes, and boredom casts its pall. Stage II arrives. The bright illusion *We are one* fades into the bleak conviction *We are hopelessly different.* Each partner begins to register only the other's misdeeds; each perceives the pain he is subjected to and not the misery he inflicts in turn. The result is a state of estrangement and mutual coercion that makes both partners unwilling to change lest they somehow lose by yielding.

At this point, people frequently resort to affairs to retaliate against their partners, or to fill the gaps left by their couple relationships. As often happens, however, people's solutions to their difficulties become problems in turn.

As therapists, we see a great many people who believe that their couple relationships have failed and that this failure leaves them only two possibilities: to split up, or endure misery in perpetuity. The trend toward divorce as a solution for couple trouble doesn't seem to have peaked yet. The life of the average marriage has dropped to 7.2 years, and the stigma attached to ending a marriage is fading into irrelevance.

In fact, a kind of moral backlash seems to have set in. Divorce isn't just being sanctioned now, it's virtually being sponsored. A profusion of books and articles is making the argument that lasting commitments aren't viable, that the risks involved in splitting up are manageable, and that people's personal selves are likely to thrive on departure.

Obviously, there are people for whom this is true. Obviously, there are couple relationships that ought to be ended. But we've seen many more couples for

* e. e. cummings, # 96 in *100 Selected Poems.*

whom splitting up is not only miserably painful, but pointless and destructive.

We believe in lasting couple relationships, and we want to fortify people for the struggle against the difficulties that are inherent in a long-term partnership. Couples can outgrow their alienation, and create the mutual acceptance that are the hallmarks of Stage III.

Our purpose in writing this book is the object we pursue in therapy: to help give people perspective on their experience of and their expectations for their couple relationships, and to aid those relationships to reach a Stage III accord. It's a difficult but not an impossible task to transform mutual attraction into lasting love. Painful struggles in a relationship don't make it a failure, and

> ruin'd love, when it is built anew
> Grows fairer than at first, more strong, far greater.*

* William Shakespeare, Sonnet 119.

CHAPTER 1

The Dance-Away Lover

THE VIRTUOSO OF INFATUATION, the Dance-Away Lover conducts an affair like Roethke's lover, who

> played it quick, played it light and loose.*

Once his interest has been piqued, the Dance-Away Lover brings a prodigal charm to bear on the woman he's drawn to. He knows how to involve himself completely in the moments he shares with her, and his peculiar gift is his capacity to be stirred by her manifest charms and her secret specialness. He courts her with his appreciation of her, instigating adventures and framing moments of intimate communion.

He's more proficient, however, at creating relationships than at sustaining them. Having wooed successfully, he displays as sharp an eye for the defect as he originally showed for the asset, and he's apt to tire of a lover as quickly as he gave himself to her some weeks or months before. As constraints and obligations impinge on him, disenchantment is likely to set in, and he is likely to take flight, leaving his partner wondering what went wrong.

One woman said about her affair with a Dance-Away Lover, "As fast as that relationship started, and as high as it went, it ended just like that. I have no

* Theodore Roethke, "I Knew a Woman."

11

idea to this day why it ended. We were doing crazy, wonderful things together and being really outrageous. Then the phone calls stopped and the letters stopped. I was tearing my hair out trying to figure out what the hell I had done. But all he would say was, 'I'm too busy to talk to you.' 'No, you haven't done anything,' and 'I'll see you.' And I never really saw him again."

However puzzled the ex-partner, the Dance-Away Lover has no trouble explaining to himself what happened. Arthur said, "Most of the women I've gone out with, I get to the point of knowing them, and I feel like I would be selling out to continue the relationship. They didn't have all the things that I wanted."

The Dance-Away Lover believes that relationships and their participants ought to fulfill the demanding specifications of his ideal. One aspect of that ideal requires that the Dance-Away himself exhibit only the most desirable properties. He must be vital, sexy, experienced, assured, entertaining, and so forth.

Sometimes, he believes that he is. Arthur, for example, found a checklist in the Sunday newspaper supplement that defined any child as gifted who possessed twelve or more of the qualities the article enumerated. Arthur read through the list and decided that he satisfied all thirty-one criteria. "I was bred to be a racehorse or a mandarin," he said.

Arthur was the possessor of impeccable social skills, "on" under all circumstances—dispensing ease, making contact, and ensuring that his presence made the occasion enjoyable for the people who mattered to him. But in a reflective moment he said, "The picture I have about myself is of being charming and seductive, but not following through in any way; becoming more and more an attractive object that I think is sort of trivial when you get right down to the substance." The Dance-Away fears that underneath the sparkle he's shallow, chilly, and destructive to other people. Afraid to be discovered, afraid that his real inadequate self warrants rejection, the Dance-Away Lover terminates relationships before propinquity can betray him.

Since he's self-doubtful, the Dance-Away Lover discounts the worth of anyone who would be willing to accept him. He assumes that someone who would love him either hasn't seen through his facade or is no great shakes herself. Half of the Dance-Away Lover's pervasive ambivalence makes anyone who would be willing to pair up with him unacceptable.

The arrogant side of the Dance-Away's ambivalence also deters him from pledging himself to a partner. He does not want to saddle himself with someone who is less than totally desirable, and settling for some current candidate might mean that he would have to forego some altogether superior prospect in the future. "Perhaps I take commitment too seriously. I want to keep every option open. It's maybe a form of greed."

The Dance-Away Lover is prone to perceive the partner he possesses as a liability. If he's worried that perhaps he doesn't have what it takes to succeed, he's apt to experience this as fear that his partner will somehow make it impossible for him to succeed. For example, when Ralph was invited to a prestigious fund-raising dinner, he felt a momentary impulse to leave his wife at home. He said, "Joanne is not good at that kind of thing. I wouldn't feel proud of her if she were there. I would prefer to be an individual with no ties."

The Dance-Away Lover converts fears about his own inadequacies into fear about the consequences of his partner's inadequacy. With each potential mate, the Dance-Away Lover stands in front of a mental mirror, trying to gauge how the outside world would assess him if he faced life with her beside him. Will she detract from me? Will she embarrass me?

In the first flush of infatuation, the answer seems to be "No." But as the relationship wears on, the Dance-Away Lover discovers a multitude of blemishes in his partner. He also discovers that the relationship doesn't offer him the kind of freedom that means safety to him. What he would like is "to have both parties have an option to terminate the contract at any point, or not even enter into a contract." Instead, he finds that his partner is becoming dependent on him, and he begins to get "this smothered feeling that I'm being expected to fill this great vacuum." Anxiety and resentment foster an emotional aversion to his partner. He becomes increasingly displeased with her and increasingly dubious about his involvement with her.

Given the level of the Dance-Away Lover's expectations, it's not hard for him to find grounds for his disgruntlement. He believes the partner should be compatible in all particulars and that their relationship should be richly rewarding, but exact no costs. He envisions the ideal relationship as a kind of slot machine that pays off with every nickel that's inserted. A relationship should afford its participants complete intimacy and complete freedom, he believes—contradictory demands which ensure his disappointment.

The Dance-Away Lover's fine eye for a flaw guarantees that he'll find cause for disillusionment with his partner. His dissatisfaction with her focuses on the characteristics she doesn't have that he wants, and the characteristics that she does have that set his teeth on edge.

Arthur said of a woman he dated, "I can't figure out why it was that I got turned off so quickly. She had a lot of the things I want, and it didn't work. I just noticed something fundamental about her that didn't appeal to me . . . she's got bad posture. She's a little overweight. She seemed to sweat uncommonly." Such slight shudders—she talks too much; she's too bourgeois; her table manners are bad—lead the Dance-Away Lover to turn a cold shoulder to his partner. Her sins of omission and commission seem to justify his distaste for her and to explain the fear and guilt the relationship causes him. It's not that he's uneasy about intimacy, in other words, it's that she's unworthy of it.

His criticisms aren't expressed out loud. The Dance-Away Lover silently indicts his partner and convicts her of unacceptability. Little by little he turns her into a caricature of herself, all defects, with no awareness about the anxiety about himself that gives those defects such crucial significance to him.

The Dance-Away Lover's faultfinding is one kind of blame. This form of blame is not intended to control or to punish his partner. Instead, it's intended to legitimize his need to distance her. In various ways, he tries to establish that he doesn't belong to her. She now looks to him like a loser.

The Dance-Away's repeated romantic disillusionments are the consequence of his discomfort with the intimacy and commitment love entails. The Dance-Away Lover is preoccupied with the fear of being trapped. He clings to his independence lest, in her eagerness to possess him, someone succeed in sucking him into a web of obligations and responsibilities. "In a way, I want to be totally self-sufficient. Because if there is no basic need involved, then there is freedom of choice."

"I can trust if I don't need," thinks the guarded Dance-Away. So he strives for his complete self-reliance. He conceives of having needs as being faintly undignified. Asking for things means acknowledging that he isn't complete in himself, and it makes him vulnerable to rejection. Furthermore, the desire to be given to entails the duty to give in return, and such reciprocity means mutual dependence.

Arthur said, "What freaks me out is the other person needing me and being weak." No amount of evidence can reassure the Dance-Away Lover that his partner is not, in fact, insatiably needy, and an actual request buttresses his conviction that she is a parasite who wants him and wants from him too much for his peace of mind.

Sometimes he imagines that she wants more from him than she actually does. For example, after Arthur had slept with a new acquaintance several times, he stopped calling her because he began to worry that "she would make demands on me. She would begin to expect me to be there every night or every other night." This despite the fact that "all her public statements say 'I don't want anything heavy.' "

The Dance-Away Lover is prone to see his partner as demanding and prone to be grudging in the face of her needs. He feels, however, that he ought to be willing to make her happy. "I feel like I *should* be able to relate to her. I *should* be able to express affection for her." But when he's prompted by a sense of obligation rather than by a positive desire to give to her, the taint of obligation is apt to betray itself. If he's not acting spontaneously, the Dance-Away Lover can't give generously or graciously. He may comply with her request (for affection, for example), but his manner conveys the resentment he won't avow openly. He gives churlishly, his chilliness or boredom bespeaking perhaps more plainly than he realizes the Dance-Away Lover's displeasure that his partner should encroach thus on his autonomy.

One day when Joanne asked to borrow a pair of sunglasses, Ralph lent them to her reluctantly. He said later, "The feeling that I had was of wanting something to be mine, all mine. My pens—don't touch them. They're always gone, in her purse, whatever . . . I feel like she's invading me piece by piece. Bit by bit she's taking me over. Everything that was me is slowly being stripped away and changed and altered."

The Dance-Away Lover feels pressured by his partner's needs because he is unable to say no to her. He doesn't feel entitled to tell her, "Cut it out, that bothers me," or "I want some time to myself." Instead, he yields sourly and resents her for asking.

Sometimes the Dance-Away Lover blames himself for his stinginess. Ralph said to Joanne, "I don't feel like I love you fully, deeply, the way you want to be loved. I'm not there for you all the time or even a lot, and it makes me feel guilty."

This guilt estranges the Dance-Away even further from his partner. The tension, the recriminations, the "cold turkey till you Sit Down and Talk About What's Wrong with Us," all increase the Dance-Away Lover's desire to "just be left alone."

As much as the Dance-Away blames himself, he is equally likely to blame his partner for his discomfort. If she wants to be with him more than he likes, he believes that she's too dependent. If he resents a request she makes, he concludes that she's too demanding.

Maneuvering to avoid the crushing jaws of intimacy, the Dance-Away Lover is apt to become unavailable to his partner. Feeling that he ought to say yes to her requests but wanting to say no, he makes himself scarce for fear he'll be asked. He throws himself into his work; he comes late for a date and leaves early in the morning; it slips his mind altogether to call her. Joanne said sadly, "With Ralph, I never feel he's with me. Even when we walk together, he somehow always manages to be at some distance from me. He always ends up talking to other people, or running around while I have to take care of the kids, in some way making sure we're separated."

The Dance-Away begins to withhold himself emotionally from his partner. He won't be warm with her or open with her. Frequently, he begins to withhold sexually as well. In Stage I of a relationship, the Dance-Away Lover usually delights in sex. But some form of sexual diminution seems to characterize almost every long-term relationship he establishes. Ralph said of Joanne, "I would know that Joanne wanted to have sex, and I just had no desire for her." Joanne said in her turn, "I guess he's just not the type of person who would want to make love every night. He's afraid it would get humdrum, like work. Like he would have to come home every night and make love." The Dance-Away Lover's rationale for his lack of sexual enthusiasm is likely to be, "You just don't turn me on," but the real issue is apt to be closeness. He often shies away from the sexual embrace because he's threatened by the emotional connection it represents.

The Dance-Away Lover is remote in the present and vague about the future. The more eagerly his partner plans for the two of them—to take a vacation together, to have a baby together—the more the Dance-Away Lover begins to suspect that she's a mistake. Her enthusiasm for him feeds his doubt about her and his interest in other potential candidates for the position of partner.

Unavailability and ill humor both serve him as alternatives to saying no. Both are apt to undermine his partner's self-esteem and her security in the relationship. She's liable to begin scrambling, clutching at him for some reassurance that he really does care about her, to counteract her fear that he's edging away from her.

The Dance-Away Lover often wins his partner initially by means of his ability to make her feel cherished, and she's usually unwilling to relinquish the closeness they once had. She's hopeful that the tenderness can be restored, and she's apt to pester him with the demands for affection and attention that make him feel suffocated.

Usually, she's anxious to give to the Dance-Away Lover, because his happiness would afford her some security. She tries to ingratiate herself but discovers that "he's so changeable, it's really hard to please him." If she realizes that the main thing that would please him is to be free of her, she's likely to be overwhelmed with hurt. Joanne began to cry after a party where Ralph had ignored her relentlessly. She said, "He didn't want to dance with me, just with everybody else. I never see him happy with me. He only has good times without me."

Almost invariably the partner personalizes the rejection she encounters. Like the Dance-Away Lover, she assumes that she's to blame, that he has stopped caring about her because of her shortcomings, not because of his ambivalence about involvement.

Ironically, his dancing away exacerbates the very dependence that repels him. It isn't just the Dance-Away Lover who aspires more intensely after the person he can't have. Rejection also makes his partner hunger more keenly for his love. Joanne said, "There's this sense that Ralph is the only man that I could care about. I can imagine being less unhappy with someone else, but I can't imagine that somebody else could have the same specialness. The only people I know who have that same fascination are bigger bastards than he is."

"Where were you?" Susan said frantically to Arthur when he showed up at her house two hours late one day. He described the scene as "a real downer, and there was something dreadfully familiar about that. I hate the heaviness in the air, the pall. Every time I pick up the phone to call Susan it's a risk. I always feel like I'm opening a can of worms."

The Dance-Away Lover usually won't acknowledge that he wants to be rid of a partner who's become troublesome. Hoping to avoid tears and recriminations, he tries to slip away unnoticed. It's rarely that easy, but an escape that's eventually successful leaves him breathless with relief. "After breaking up with Ann, I felt suddenly light and suddenly free, like a swimmer risen to the surface and breaking into light . . . It was that simple. All feeling went out of it, or rather it got pushed so far down that now I see it only by the cold spots, the places in myself I cannot go."*

The relief appears to prove the wisdom of his departure, and Stage I of a new love seems to clinch the issue altogether. New love cleanses the Dance-Away of guilt, dispels his loneliness, and fills him with hope.

Up again for a spell, the Dance-Away Lover is bound to come down shortly. In fact, his relationships follow two basic patterns. The more common: he is

* Peter Marin, *In a Man's Time*.

attracted to a woman; he becomes infatuated with her; he succeeds in eliciting infatuation from her in return. However, as soon as he realizes that she wants him and needs him, he begins to feel uncomfortable, bored and burdened. He contrives to end the relationship, to repossess his freedom, or to possess some new lady who's caught his eye.

Alternate pattern: The Dance-Away Lover becomes smitten with someone who's unavailable to him, either by dint of her circumstances (i.e., a husband) or her indifference to him. This kind of relationship doesn't involve enough intimacy or enough dependence to become threatening, so his passion grows. The only love that doesn't quickly tarnish for the Dance-Away Lover is unrequited love; the only partner who remains desirable is the partner who rejects him.

Until he's whiled away a number of years in this fashion, the Dance-Away Lover is unlikely to spot the recurrence of these patterns. He thinks of himself as involved in a continuous search for the right relationship and the partner he'll feel no impulse to leave, a quest which has led to a number of dead ends thus far. In fact, the Dance-Away Lover's course is not a journey toward anyplace. He's caught in a pendulum swing between desire and disillusionment. The faces change, which gives him an illusory sense that he's covering ground, but in fact he merely oscillates between approach and avoidance, bound at all times to a fixed point—his fear of intimacy.

When the Dance-Away Lover does perceive the arc he is describing between drawing close to someone and pulling away, he is likely to succumb to despair. Arthur said, "I always see the end now. I always know it's temporary, good for a few months. Then it's on to the next person. I have this feeling now that another year has passed and I have filled it with just another few affairs that didn't amount to anything."

As flings become tedious and his hopes dim, the Dance-Away Lover may begin to worry that perhaps he's incapable of loving and therefore destined to loneliness. He shies from that prospect, however.

> But there's got to be somebody!
> Because what if I'm sixty years old and not married,
> All alone in a furnished room with pee stains on my underwear
> And everybody else is married! All the universe married but me!*

The wish for a lasting relationship with someone may lead the Dance-Away to shift his tack eventually. He may decide to make a commitment on the basis of practicality instead of passion, hoping that if he doesn't foster the customary romantic expectations, he won't encounter the familiar disappointment. For example, in his late thirties, Ralph decided to settle down. He said, "It wasn't super love. Joanne feels I shopped for her for qualities A, B, C. I did in some sense. I married her for very rational reasons. I thought it made sense. I had confidence that I could grow to love her."

The fact that the Dance-Away Lover decided intellectually to secure a mate doesn't prevent him from feeling trapped once she's installed in his life. Sooner or later his abiding discomfort with closeness and responsibility leads him to dance away from the partner who was nominated by rationality as he did from the lovers who were sponsored by fancy.

The Dance-Away Lover believes that relationships ought to be harmonious and consistently gratifying. Ralph said, "When things are right, it's so simple. It's when they're bad that they get complicated." The tensions and difficulties that others would take in stride are proof to the Dance-Away Lover that things have gone wrong.

A disciple of spontaneity, the Dance-Away Lover measures each experience by the "does it feel good?"

gauge. If it doesn't feel good—and long-term relationships never feel good all the time—then he assumes that his discomfort is a signal that it's time to leave. The Dance-Away Lover will gladly expend enormous amounts of energy to create a relationship, but he won't struggle to make an ongoing relationship viable for himself. At bottom, he doesn't accept the necessity for emotional discipline. He lacks the familiarity with intimacy which teaches people that they have to endure some unpleasant stretches in relationships and have to forego some satisfactions they crave in return for solid benefits. The Dance-Away Lover doesn't want to make such tedious short-term sacrifices, and he doesn't trust that relationships reward such deliberate perseverance.

The only kind of energy the Dance-Away Lover trusts is the voluntary, unconstrained energy which flows from desire. He shuns what he sees as the "cold morgues of obligations."* In fact, however, the steadfast, patient energy that stems from resolve yields satisfactions as sweet and as true as those that flow from impulse, and not until he's capable of responsiveness as well as spontaneity can the Dance-Away Lover come to rest.

* Gregory Corso, "Marriage."
* Theodore Roethke, "Her Becoming."

CHAPTER 2

The Anxious Ingenue

THE ANXIOUS INGENUE enters into a new relationship with hope and fear in her heart, eager to believe 'this is the man for me,' apprehensive that somehow she'll blow this opportunity.

The Anxious Ingenue longs to be loved. She looks to a couple relationship to bring joy and meaning to her life and to establish her worth as a person. In comparison with her desire to install a man at the center of her life, friendships and family ties seem peripheral. She may be pursuing a flourishing career, but its rewards can't offset the shame of her status as an unattached woman. Marty said, "I've had experience being successful at work. I know how to come into a situation, figure out what's happening, and pull things off. I haven't failed with work; I've failed with me."

Spinsterhood means more than failure to the Anxious Ingenue—it means obliteration. The solitary woman in our culture has long been eyed askance. If no man will have her, the assumption has been that defects in her have made this outcome appropriate. Ironically, the women's movement has deposited a new layer of censure on top of this long-standing prejudice against the single woman. The mid-seventies Anxious Ingenue feels that if she were healthy, she would be able to "feel really whole and centered in

23

myself without a man." Since she can't, her loneliness and her hunger for love become evidence to her of her neurotic dependence. The contemporary Anxious Ingenue condemns herself from two vantage points: that of the traditional woman's, which labels her a failure for not having a man, and that of the liberated woman's, which labels her a failure for needing to have a man.

In order to get a man, the Anxious Ingenue polishes her appearance to a bright sheen, tending her figure, her complexion and her wardrobe, with the same solicitude an investor devotes to his stock portfolio. Her style varies. Marty said, for example, "I don't try to look gorgeous. I try to look natural." But the Anxious Ingenue is always mindful of her physical allure.

She views her personality as another means of establishing her desirability. Just as she doesn't let her lover see her in a bedraggled housecoat and curlers, so she conceals the loneliness or the depression that sometimes steals over her. "I always try to be cheerful," Marty said. "I think Tim accepts part of me. But the part of me that's weak and needs taking care of he doesn't like. He recoils from me the minute that I feel insecure and start putting pressure on. So I try to stuff those needs down inside myself. I try to live up to his ideal."

For the Anxious Ingenue, lovability equals an absence of demands. She construes her wants as a liability, which will lead her partner to consign her to the 'difficult' or 'burdensome' category. To avoid antagonizing her partner, to avoid becoming a headache to him, she doesn't trouble him with requests of any sort.

She does this partly because she doubts the legitimacy of her wants. A successful person is a self-sufficient person. If she wants to see her lover regularly, she interprets this as clinginess, which she can't countenance in herself, and which she certainly can't ask him to accommodate.

For example, for eight months Helena had been

having an affair with a co-worker. One day she asked him if they would be seeing each other the next night after their staff meeting, as they always seemed to. "He just grinned back at me. He didn't say anything. It was a weird response, and I totally freaked myself out thinking he didn't want to see me and I was forcing myself on him. I thought, 'Should I call him and say forget it?' I wanted to call him and say, 'Forget I ever said anything.' I felt like I was fourteen again."

The Anxious Ingenue can't muster up a "no" any more easily than she can manage a "please." Marty said, "I don't want to make myself available all the time, but somehow I always do." Afraid to lose any opportunity to be with her partner, and hopeful that compliance will endear her to him, the Anxious Ingenue doesn't refuse him. She doesn't allow herself to complain for fear her display of anger or hurt will alienate the man she's trying to land. The Anxious Ingenue plays her hand close to the chest, hiding both positive and negative emotions from the man who arouses them. She envisions all men as Dance-Away Lovers who want freedom and adventure, who want easygoing relationships with beautiful, together women.

She believes, nevertheless, that a man can be inveigled into a close attachment to a woman. He initiates a casual relationship; she fosters love within it, and beneath the level of his awareness, affection comes to tie him to her. A relationship is a woman's creation, therefore her responsibility, and a test of her adroitness. If she psychs out her prospective partner astutely enough, and controls herself stringently enough, the illusion of conquering her will beguile him into surrendering to a commitment to her.

Until she's secured that commitment, however, the Anxious Ingenue struggles to keep the lid on her avidity. One woman dreamed that she asked her lover as they went to bed one night, "Can we get married?" He replied, "We'll talk about it in the morning." The dream ended with her awakening to find the bed empty, the suitcase gone, her lover bolted. For fear of some such outcome, the Anxious Ingenue obeys the injunctions, 'Don't let him know how much you want him' and 'Never be the first to say "I love you." ' She neither asks for affection nor displays her own feelings for him. Marty explained, "I'm real careful about acting too loving toward him. The way to blow it with Tim is by choking him. So I try to look like I'm real independent."

The Anxious Ingenue's attempt at casualness is intended to persuade her partner that her expectations are as minimal as her demands. But by cherishing hopes she won't ask her partner to fulfill, the Anxious Ingenue sets herself up to be disappointed. Marty, for example, planned a surprise birthday party for Tim, expecting that he would celebrate the occasion with her. That afternoon, however, he called to tell her that something else had come up and that he would see her in a few days. Too embarrassed to protest, Marty was forced to confess to her guests that Tim couldn't make it after all.

The Anxious Ingenue will tolerate behavior that offends her or wounds her without objecting to it. Marty had originally met Tim in a bar and one night she reminisced about the 'karma' that brought them together. He replied, "When I met you, you were just a pick-up, a piece of ass." She tried not to flinch at the insult. Since she's unwilling to assert her wants, to say "no" when she'd like to, or set limits that would protect her, the Anxious Ingenue lays herself open to her partner's thoughtlessness, or worse, his exploitation. The Anxious Ingenue won't defend herself outwardly. Instead she tries to defend herself inwardly. Marty said, "I don't want to let it bother me."

The Anxious Ingenue's strategy isn't a simple matter of manipulation therefore. To succeed, she not only has to cloak her intentions and her emotions from her partner, she also has to conceal them from herself. One aspect of this self-deception is denying to herself how much she wants her man. To the extent that she can tell herself she's just out for a good time, she can salvage her pride and obscure the lopsidedness of their relationship. The Anxious Ingenue tries to brake her fall into love, tries to protect herself by limiting her attachment to her partner. Rebecca said, "I don't risk. It used to be as soon as I started to care, the guy would disappear. Now I'm real protective. I just don't let myself get into anybody very heavily."

The Anxious Ingenue often slips into magical thinking. 'If I admit to myself how much I want him to love me, then I'll hex it, and I'll lose him altogether.' In terms of R. D. Laing's *Knots,* the Anxious Ingenue's mental process goes:

> I tend to not get what I want
> So
> > To get what I want
> > I pretend not to want it.

The Anxious Ingenue tries to ignore her hunger for affection and security, but in a moment of introspection, Marty said, "I'm always filled with dread that maybe it's disintegrating, that it'll all come tumbling down around me. I'm sure I'll blow it, and that terrifies me." Most of the time, however, the Anxious Ingenue construes her anxiety—the way it rattles her when he finally telephones—as evidence that she's really excited about him.

Likewise, she will tell herself and others that she's happy with the sporadic and uncertain relationship she's got. Helena said, "I choose to see Alf once a week or so. I have a good time when we're together." Similarly, she doesn't allow herself to grasp that her partner drinks too much or lies to her. Because she idealizes whomever she's in love with, she tries to block out whatever shortcomings in him would jeopardize her respect for him and her trust in him. In order to live with the situation as a whole, the Anxious Ingenue denies the anxiety and hurt it causes her.

She simply cuts herself off from emotions that, experienced full force, would make the relationship unbearable for her.

Explaining away untoward episodes is another mechanism the Anxious Ingenue uses to render her position tolerable. If her partner only sees her fitfully, she ascribes it to his crowded schedule. If he always calls her at the last minute for a date, she tells herself it's because he likes to do things spontaneously. If he never tells her he loves her, she says to herself, "That's the way he is. He's just not an affectionate person." The Anxious Ingenue ignores evidence that should alert her to trouble, and she interprets danger signals as harmless idiosyncracies. By rationalizing away unpropitious events, she spares herself the pain that those events, rightly interpreted, would cause her.

Self-blame is another refuge the Anxious Ingenue flees to. If her partner stands her up, she tells herself, "I must have gotten the day wrong." If her partner criticizes her for being too dependent, she humbly concurs. Their joint conclusion becomes: he's not to blame for not filling her needs, she's to blame for having them.

In addition to denial, excuses, and self-blame, the Anxious Ingenue utilizes obsession to distance herself from experiences that would otherwise throw her into upheaval. If her partner suddenly turns chilly, she asks herself, 'What did I do?' She pores over the details of their recent interactions, examining his behavior for clues as to "Where Tim is at . . ." and how best to respond to that. Again and again, she rummages through her impressions, attempting to find some perspective from which her position will be acceptable, trying to arrive at a version that will put it all to rights. The more assiduously she scrutinizes the relationship, the more she dissociates herself from the humiliation, the fear, and the anger that would otherwise grip her.

Obsessing is particularly effective insulation when it's shared with a friend. The Anxious Ingenue's friends serve her as allies who console her and hearten her for the struggle. Frequently, the Anxious Ingenue discharges through her friends the anger that she's too ambivalent to vent more directly. They ridicule the man who mistreats her; they urge her to dump the cad and find somebody who's good enough for her—anger by proxy, which is only slightly better than no anger at all.

On her own, however, the Anxious Ingenue doesn't make the logical deductions from her partner's behavior. She avoids candid discussion with him about the the status of their relationship. She doesn't ask a question like 'Do you love me?' which might elicit an upsetting answer. Her rationale for this hesitance is likely to be that posing such a question would put pressure on her partner, thus making him uncomfortable, thus jeopardizing their relationship (a kind of emotional Heisenberg Uncertainty Principle). In fact, her reticence protects her more directly. A straightforward question might bring a straightforward answer, probably in the negative, which would shatter the illusion that there's love between them.

The resource the Anxious Ingenue draws on most heavily to mitigate the rigors of the present is hope for the future. Marty said, "Even if he doesn't care about me now, he'll come to love me. We get along so well. We have such good times together." The Anxious Ingenue accepts a relationship on whatever terms it's offered to her, partly out of pessimism—fear that if she grumbles, her partner will vanish altogether, and she'll be left with nothing. Her other motivation is optimism—the hope that, given time, those terms will evolve into some more congenial form. One young Anxious Ingenue said, for example, "I've been seeing this man for a couple of months. Apparently he isn't in love with me. I've been sort of hanging in and trying to keep it cool and go easy, hoping that maybe he'd fall in love with me. It hasn't happened yet . . . but I want to see if I can lower my expectations and flow with it, see where it goes, see if it builds to where it will work." The Anxious Ingenue subsists on the hope that as time goes by an attachment will take root if only she doesn't pull the seedling up to see how it's doing.

The Anxious Ingenue perpetrates a fictional self, unconsciously assuming that once she's secured a commitment from her partner, she'll somehow be able to switch selves on him without detection, that she will be able to metamorphose back into her real self without jeopardy. Likewise, that he'll be transformed into a newly giving and accepting individual—equally improbable assumptions. In fact, the Anxious Ingenue's blurry golden fantasy about the happiness she will enjoy once the pledges have been vowed is as flimsy as the false front with which she bids for his approval. The Anxious Ingenue characteristically underestimates the difficulty involved in papering illusion over reality. Only rarely can she avoid betraying her real feelings in assorted unconscious ways. She may respond with a shade too much eagerness when he telephones her or she may pause too long when he says, 'I have some things to do. I won't be around for a couple of weeks,' before she replies carelessly, 'Oh, that's fine. I'll be busy too.'

The Anxious Ingenue is usually unaware that she's giving her partner a double message—overt nonchalance versus covert desperation. The cultural stereotype of women as grasping, marriage-mad creatures lends credence to the covert message. And confronted with this kind of conflict between an explicit statement and a manner that belies it, the partner instinctively trusts the evidence that seems to have been supplied inadvertently. The partner is likely to respond to these uncertainties, these suspicions, with fear about the real extent of her needs. He is liable to ask himself, "What does she want?" and to surmise, "Much too much." The partner who's glimpsed an Anxious Ingenue's dependence may well become worried about being trapped in a network of obligations and expectations. He may distance himself to forestall that outcome. He may become brusque to her, so she can't construe friendliness as love. He may become guarded, careful not to talk about the future in terms which imply that it might be shared. And he may see her only sporadically, to avoid the two of them being considered as a couple.

Her ambivalence allows him to maintain a limited relationship with her; to have sex with her even though he doesn't like her much, or to have fun with her even though he doesn't love her. He can act as if only the explicit verbal message is operative, refusing to heed her wordless plea for commitment.

He's likely to feel guilty, however, knowing he's using the leeway she gives him to exploit her. Aware that he's extracting short-term benefits from the liaison without paying the long-term cost engenders a bad conscience. Feeling guilty, he's liable to become even more prone to incivility. He may rationalize his "sharp-toothed unkindness" along the line of "never give a sucker an even break." Or he can call up his resentment at her machinations to excuse his own.

The Anxious Ingenue's manner often leads her partner to discount her worth. The readiness with which she detaches herself from her own context and blends into his often persuades him that she doesn't have much of a life of her own to give up. She intends her tolerance and compliance to testify to her good nature. Usually, however, they lead her partner to the more brutal conclusion that she submits to bad treatment because she's used to it or because necessity forces her to accept it.

The Anxious Ingenue nevertheless contrives to make the best of her position. She luxuriates in whatever good times come her way. She lingers over the memories of what he said, what they did, and the way he touched her. She hugs to herself the times he speaks of "us."

But trying to be someone you're not for someone who isn't there for you becomes a dispiriting business, and it rarely breeds lasting love. The Anxious Ingenue tries to perpetuate even the most vestigial relationship because, "I'm too afraid of not having anybody." When it does come, an ending devastates her. Rebecca said, "I felt like I had just . . . I had lost somebody who I thought . . . I just didn't want to get up out of bed the next morning. I felt like I had no reason to go on."

Once a relationship has expired, the Anxious Ingenue may feel bitter. She's often sorry that she went so far and gave up so much. Rebecca said, "I think, 'Fuck, what did I do that for?'" And after Alf had left her Helena said, "It's amazing to me that I liked him so much, that I was living such a fantasy. I didn't realize how empty and cold and awful it was until later."

The Anxious Ingenue counts on ending as a failure, and blames herself for it. She reruns her memories to figure out where she went wrong. Helena explained, "I was too demanding. If I had just gone into it with the attitude of seeing him and having a good time, that's what it would have been. But it became this love trip in my head. If I just hadn't cared, this never would have happened."

Sometimes she thinks that this new cynical perspective will enable her to see her ex-lover again, to just enjoy being with him without hoping for anything more. Her disillusionment will protect her, she thinks, from becoming emotionally involved with him again, so that now she will be able to use *him* instead of being used by him. Another variety of 'If I don't want him, I'll be able to get him.' This illusion lands her back in the same powerless place she occupied originally.

The Anxious Ingenue may worry, with good reason, that the next relationship she enters into will follow the same formula. Helena said, "I am so afraid of this pattern I have of getting involved with men who don't care about me. It reinforces all the bad feelings I have about myself. All the time I was with Alf, I felt so threatened and so inadequate . . . but now I feel totally isolated. I don't think I'll ever find anybody who will love me."

The assumptions the Anxious Ingenue brings to a relationship are not conducive to the growth of love, but they are assumptions that can be altered. She must begin to assert her right to be treated decently, no matter what the scope or the nature of the relationship in question. Her willingness to tolerate bad treatment doesn't reflect credit on her, it diminishes her worth in her partner's eyes and it undercuts her own self-respect, since both parties assume that if she deserved to be treated well, she would be.

The Anxious Ingenue must learn to take responsibility for herself. As she acquires confidence in her ability to take care of herself, she'll be better able to inspire love, and to believe in that love when it's offered to her.

CHAPTER 3

The Disarmer

"WHAT ATTRACTS people to me more than anything else is that I am understanding. I really am, and it's a part of myself that I like. They know they aren't going to get hurt by me." As a Disarmer, Dorothy knew that her friends, her children, her partner could trust her to be accessible to them and accepting of them. She valued in herself the consistent warmth she offered others. "If I'm in a room, I always know who's uncomfortable. I know where other people are at. I become involved in their lives really easily. I like to take care of people." This concern for others' well-being manifests itself most clearly in her couple relationship and the need she pays to her partner's happiness.

The Disarmer is only fully herself when she's enfolded in a love relationship, part of a solid "us," not a solitary "me." Once she's established a couple connection, the Disarmer defines herself through it. In the same way that her partner's career molds his personality, her status and her obligations as 'his woman' shape hers.

The role of Disarmer embodies our traditional vision of womanliness, and the forces in this culture which shape women's identities to conform to the feminine ideal are pervasive and powerful. Accordingly most women internalize at least a dose of this conditioning as they are growing up. To the extent that they don't embrace the role as adults, they are often reacting against it—defining themselves in contradistinction to it.

The Disarmer knows she wants her partner, knows she values him, and allows herself straightforward dependence on him. She empowers him with the ability to protect her and to fulfill her, and she achieves significance in her own eyes by means of the contributions she makes to his well-being. Maria said, "One of the really great pleasures I get—I don't like to say 'doing things for Simon'—but it gives me joy to see him happy. I get goodies from 'Simon has done well,' and part of the reason is because I've done this and this . . ."

The highest priority for the Disarmer is to be responsive to her partner. Dorothy said, "I see myself in general being available to Lou whenever he needs me —making sure I'm sort of there for him." She adapts to her partner's choice of a life-style, a circle of friends, a political persuasion, guided, not by her own preferences, but by her reading of his predilections. Maria said of her ten-year marriage, "I never thought about myself. I thought about what would be best for Simon and the kids. My whole world was Simon and his music. Just being for him what he wanted really made me happy."

The Disarmer assigns her own wants a tenuous, second-best importance. Maria said, "I want Simon to be pleased more than I want to be pleased myself. First and foremost I'm concerned about him—making him look good and making him feel good." Her cooperation and the contribution her submissiveness makes to harmony will bring her, she hopes, a longterm satisfaction that will transcend the value of any immediate gratification she might forego.

The Disarmer isn't comfortable initiating activities independently or making her own decisions. She prefers to pass the ball to her partner so that he can determine whether to dribble or shoot. Simon told Maria at one point, "I would say, 'Make a decision,' and you wouldn't want to. You just don't enjoy making decisions so you have given me that role and I have taken it on, to the extent that when you don't agree, you say 'Oh, go ahead.' "

The Disarmer wants to be spared the responsibilities and the risks of decision-making. One such woman said, "I'm not used to doing things by myself." If a situation makes her anxious, her response is to turn to her partner and say, in effect, 'You take care of it.' If he isn't eager to do so, she's likely to pester him to take the steps that she's unwilling to venture herself.

For example, Lou and Dorothy's house developed serious roof trouble at a time when Lou was heavily involved in his work. Dorothy asked repeatedly, "Are you going to call the roofers today, Lou?" Preoccupied with his other concerns, Lou finally burst out, "Call the roofers yourself, for God's sake!"

The Disarmer's unwillingness to act independently is partly a function of timidity. Fear of failure deters her from learning to do things that are difficult or unfamiliar. The result is apt to be that "Most of our life together I've let him do everything. That's what my father did—just kind of took care of me and I never learned to do anything. I'm a marshmallow."

She may also be a nag. Dorothy admitted to Lou, "I rarely just go ahead and do something. Instead I sit around bugging you to do things—which you don't do . . ." When she's anxious and resentful, the Disarmer becomes insistent. She cajoles and pesters, convinced that the more pressure she applies the more likely her partner will be to move in the right direction. He may give into her demands. Often though, he "forgets," or "doesn't have time," or otherwise defaults on the agreement he made only under duress.

In exchange for her dependence and her demands in some areas, she offers her partner compliance in others. She accommodates to him partly because she dreads conflict, even though the outcome of the conflict might prove favorable to her.

The Disarmer can indulge her partner with less consciousness of the cost she's paying if she's a little fuzzy on whether she would have favored another outcome. Dorothy said, "I've never even said to Lou, 'I don't want to do it but I'll do it' that I can remember. I've just tailored my wants to his."

Since her highest priority is keeping track of what her partner feels and adjusting her reaction to that, she has relatively little attention to spare for registering her own preferences. Her inward longings rarely get the microphone, since her public-address system is too busy amplifying what her partner has on his agenda.

The Disarmer is giving as well as yielding. She offers her partner double-barreled support; she does the practical backup work that's required to make his life run smoothly and she nurtures him emotionally. She believes in him and tells him so. As his loyal ally, she backs him up against all opposition. She comforts him when he's troubled and reassures him when he's doubtful. The Disarmer will spring to the defense of someone she cares about, and she will attempt to buffer her partner from any difficulty or defeat that life metes out to him. Dorothy, for example, was married to an ardent tennis player. They didn't play together often because she didn't usually test his mettle enough to be an interesting opponent, but in one game she beat him. "It was a rare occurrence," she said. "At one point I lost track of the score so I whispered over to him to get it because I didn't want to embarrass him. He shouted at me, 'Don't whisper.'"

Empathy is one element in the protection the Disarmer offers her partner. One Disarmer said, "I'd do anything for anybody to the detriment of myself. I don't like to hurt people's feelings. I don't like to make anybody feel bad." She assumes that reference to a failure might make her partner feel very bad indeed.

The protection the Disarmer offers the partner reflects not concern for him, but fear for herself. "It really scares me to see him shook up," said Maria. She protects, in part, to spare herself the realization that he is not interposed, like a bulletproof vest, between her vulnerability and the depredations of the outside world.

When she perceives that her partner is worried, she is likely to be frightened, and to feel an urgent need to make things better for him. The sense of responsibility she feels for his emotional well-being may begin to weigh on her.

> How long can I be a wall keeping the wind off . . .
> How long can my hands
> Be a bandage to his hurt and my words
> Bright birds in the sky, consoling, consoling?*

The performance pressure of feeling 'I've got to do something' may trigger the formalities of reassurance, while fear prevents her from communicating the calm understanding that would be of value to him. Once when Lou faced business troubles, he decided to confide in Dorothy. He felt that her response was "to pat me on the back, saying, 'It's going to work out fine. It'll all be okay.' I was trying to talk about it seriously, but she seemed like she was brushing it off."

In fact, protection can shift into avoidance. One Disarmer was upset because she felt her husband paid too much attention to other women at parties, but she said, "I didn't want to hurt his feelings or embarrass him and I decided it wasn't that big a deal; I could just let it go."

Trained to avoid negativity and confrontation, the Disarmer has difficulty asserting herself and she's unable to express anger on her own behalf, even if it's richly deserved. "I almost never feel plain angry," Dorothy said. "I feel hurt, or helpless, and I start to cry."

In the Disarmer, love can't coexist with anger. She's apt to swallow such resentment as she feels. For ex-

* Sylvia Plath, "Three Women: A Poem for Three Voices."

ample, for a while Lou held two jobs and Dorothy recalled "I didn't see him much. I remember feeling bad when he wouldn't be there, but I didn't say much. He didn't need any pressure from me. He didn't need me hassling him." The Disarmer hates to cause a fuss so she keeps her troubles to herself, squelching her loneliness or disappointment or resentment with an outward success that may lead her partner to conclude, like Lou, "I think you probably hide quite a bit."

She may hide altogether too much. Since she's not the selfless creature she feels the role calls for, she may eke out her accommodation, support and protection, with dissimulation. She is likely to profess to be delighted with her husband's promotion even though it means moving the family from the house she loves. She will admire the haircut that she privately thinks is quite a bit too short. She fudges, avowing the enthusiasm she doesn't feel, and hoping her partner won't notice the forced smile with which she's boarding the bandwagon. When she votes the party line rather than her conscience her self-respect dwindles. When she hides behind a kind of nurturing persona, she forecloses the possibility of real intimacy with her partner. The Disarmer does not realize that idiosyncracies of tastes and hopes and beliefs are the elements from which identity is compounded. Her flexibility and her compliance can make the Disarmer an easy person to get along with but they can hinder her from evolving a firm, fully articulated self to share with her partner.

The insecure Disarmer is apt to have some trouble figuring out who she is and to doubt that her partner knows or cares much either.

> You take Sally, I'll take Sue,
> Ain't no difference twixt the two.*

If she realizes the irresistibility of the approval and acquiescence she offers him, she may begin to feel like Eva: "I have to play a certain role for him to love me.

* Traditional Blues.

Over the years I've completely hidden whole parts of my personality from him—things that I've felt and thought about that didn't fit into my role. I've always thought if I was really myself doing things the way I wanted to, I'd lose him." She may suspect that the tie that binds her partner to her is more self-love than love of her; believe that he married 'a pretty face' instead of a person he genuinely valued.

Often, the Disarmer feels that her dependence is responsible for her fuzzy sense of her identity. "Chuck has loved me more than anything else in my life and I have loved him, but I've totally turned myself over to him and not had anything of my own," said Eva. The Disarmer may begin to feel like a retread version of her partner—someone who can discuss his job, state his opinions in slightly jumbled form, and display an acquaintance with his interests—but not much more.

Domesticity and dependence don't tend to be conducive to individuality, and a Disarmer like Dorothy often doesn't "have my trip together in terms of earning money or relating to the outside world. I don't have a way of fulfilling myself outside of the homelife kind of thing."

The role dictates that if the Disarmer works outside her home, her job must remain subordinate to her involvement with her family. If she's employed, therefore, she's likely to work for the money alone and not for stakes of authority or achievement or status. Usually just the lower echelons of the job world are accessible to the pure Disarmer, who can make at best a limited commitment to her work, who must respond first to her family's call on her resources.

The isolation and mechanization which have stripped the satisfaction from others' occupations have drained homemaking of much of the sense of accomplishment it once could offer, and the Disarmer's domestic tasks often feel to her like an endless succession of trips to the grocery store. Dorothy complained that she no longer had anything to talk to her husband about when he came home from work. "I can tell him where I drove the kids and what room I cleaned, but aside from that . . ."

Whether she works inside or outside the home, the Disarmer is apt to feel guilty about siphoning off time and energy from her family to devote to interests of her own. When Eva got involved in a local political campaign, she wanted "to go out and do things at night, but it made me feel guilty. Chuck would tell me, 'If I get irritated by it, so what? If you want to go, go. Just let me be irritated.' But I got pretty hung up on worrying—how does he feel if I'm not home?"

Her reluctance to initiate the pursuits that would give her pleasure may mean that, "I don't seem to get enough satisfaction from what I do to keep me going." Often, she can neither validate herself nor enjoy herself through her activities, and her self-image shows it. Dorothy said, "I just don't feel confident doing things. I don't think I've ever felt confident."

The Disarmer wants to be able to look up to her partner, but when she compares herself to him she may well conclude that she's not the appropriate one step behind him, that she's straggling unsuccessfully in the rear of his expedition, and that at some point he's likely to disappear from view altogether.

The Disarmer is apt to look to her husband to provide the appreciation and enjoyment that are otherwise lacking in her life. Intimacy with him and romantic gestures from him would lift her spirits and her self-esteem, she believes. "I feel like I'm always saying, 'I need to be with you. I need your closeness.' I wish he were more into me," Maria said sadly. Simon rejoined, "When I'm totally with her, she's great. We have a marvelous time. But I can't be with her all the time. I can't give her constant attention and support."

Dependence makes the Disarmer vulnerable and she needs a great deal of reassurance that she's wanted. Preoccupied with the need for her husband's approval, she is acutely aware of and susceptible to such doubt or criticism as her husband may register.

Her insecurity may lead her to anxiously monitor the state of the relationship. Maria said, "I really feel conscious of us all the time. 'Are things good? Are we getting along?'" When her emotional needs make her anxious, the Disarmer responds as she does to her practical needs—she pesters her partner to allay her fears. "Do you love me?" she queries. Her husband may find her uncertainty oppressive.

In some sense, the Disarmer knows the price she pays for her anxious demands. She knows that she can force her partner to do a lot of things he doesn't want to do, and she knows, or believes she knows, that some part of him loves her less because of these demands. The Disarmer construes a request as a form of coercion. Her reasoning process is:

—If he is willing to give to her,
  then he will do it of his own accord.
—If he's not doing it,
  it's because he doesn't want to.
—And if she asks him to do something he doesn't
  want to do, he'll resent her.

Dorothy wanted her husband to spend more time with her. She realized, she said, that she could pressure him to give up other activities to be at home more. "What's that going to get me, though?" she asked. "Somebody who's here because I'm demanding it. I don't want him to be with me because I'm doing this drama to force him to stay . . . I don't want to see myself as trying to control what he does." Maria said that when she asked for agreement from Simon, "I'm left with the unpleasant feeling that I'm imposing something and I don't really know how he feels. I look for any sign that I shouldn't have done it." Rather than antagonize him, she often doesn't ask for things she wants, and she discounts what she gets if he hasn't offered it to her spontaneously.

One Disarmer and her husband struggled for many months over the question of whether he would relocate with her if she were to be accepted at a graduate school in some other part of the country. She was afraid to ask him to accompany her if he didn't really want to move. She said, "I feel like I've done a lot for him, and I resent him for a lot of those things. Or I feel like he wasn't aware of what I was doing for him, so maybe I'm afraid if he says, 'Yeah, I'll move to wherever so you can go to school,' that then I don't have any protection against his getting real mad at me."

The Disarmer is controlled by her fear of her partner's resentment, and if she's self-doubting she's likely to perceive resentment even where it may not exist. A Disarmer like Dorothy, who isn't gainfully employed, may be prone to think that, "Deep down, no matter what he says, Lou must resent me. He's never said anything, but that's what I fantasize. Like I'm not pulling my share. Like I'm a burden on him."

To reduce that burden, to protect herself from the resentment she anticipates, the Disarmer discounts her own wants. If 'It's just for me,' she decides, like Dorothy, 'No, I can't justify it in my mind. It's just too selfish.'

The Disarmer often deals with her sexual wants in the same reticent fashion. Eva said, "Let's say I don't have an orgasm when we make love. So I ask him to rub my clitoris because I'm still turned on, and I get an orgasm. But somehow it's like getting the booby prize. Asking for it isn't as good as it happening naturally . . . I like it much better when he offers."

When she wanted sex, one Disarmer sometimes "would hint that this is a good time. He would go from there but usually I didn't let him know how I felt, I just hoped." This makes the Disarmer powerless to obtain satisfaction if it doesn't appear unbidden. Her hesitance to assert her own wants means that she often doesn't get what she would like. The gap between the scale of her giving and the scale of her getting may leave her feeling exploited.

Her partner, on the other hand, may feel pressured to give her more than comes naturally to him. Chuck said of Eva, "I know my schedule is rough on her. She likes to spend a lot of time with me and I'm in a demanding work situation. It takes more than eight hours a day to make it go and that causes friction. I'm always driving home knowing she's going to be upset because I'm late." His lateness meant to her that he was indifferent to her. She would never keep *him* waiting. She said, "I'm very low on your priority. It's hard for me to believe that you love me when you ignore me."

The Disarmer who feels unloved is likely to become sexually withholding. "Love and sex—I can't separate the two. I have to feel love to feel sexual," Maria said. Her unwillingness to make love is rarely a conscious tit for tat retaliation against her partner, but turning off sexually is the Disarmer's characteristic warning signal that all is not well with the rest of the relationship.

The Disarmer assumes that if she loves her partner, she will be willing to give openhandedly, and go without cheerfully. But this approach is apt to mean that she gives more than she gets, and, over the long term, her dissatisfaction with this arrangement can't be wished away. Resentment cuts off her warmth and she begins to believe not only that he doesn't love her but that she doesn't love him.

Unexpressed anger eclipses her affection and she's left with "this kind of nothing feeling. I can be civil to him but I don't feel anything about him." That "nothing feeling" is often the prelude to departure; abandoning the relationship becomes her solution to dissatisfaction with it. She doesn't struggle; she leaves.

The role of the Disarmer is no longer viewed with the wholehearted (if somewhat condescending) favor once accorded it. The women's movement has thrown into sharp relief the toll that conventional femininity exacts from a woman. This role force-feeds capacities like patience and sensitivity, attributes that are valuable, but that do not by any means exhaust the range of human capabilities. The Disarmer's excessive reliance on her emotional skills may leave her unbalanced, handicapped by the relative pinching off of her cognitive faculties and her will.

But the Disarmer's role offers far more scope for self-realization and makes a far more valuable contribution to human relationships than the women's movement is inclined to admit. The movement has urged women to cast off the dependence to which they've been confined, but the Disarmer's dependence is not incapacitating per se. The inability to allow oneself to feel dependent on another person is as disabling as the inability to achieve a healthy measure of independence.

The task for the Disarmer is not "To get so strong that I never need anybody," as Eva put it. The objective is to begin asserting her wants, and taking responsibility for her own well-being, on a gradually widening front within the relationship.

She can discover that there is a happy medium between silence about her wants on the one hand and a din of anxious demanding on the other—asking for what she wants. She can begin to accept and express the negative feelings—anger, disappointment, and so on, which invariably accompany the positive features of a love relationship.

The Disarmer assumes that a failure or frustration is a necessarily destructive experience. In fact, failure can teach a person his limits or goad him to surpass himself. The Disarmer often ends up supporting her partner's excuses for and evasions of a reality that he would do better to confront. For her sake as well as for his, the Disarmer must realize that the best service to her partner may be to challenge him to rise above his weaknesses and fulfill his strengths. The best service she can render herself is to recognize that her wants are as legitimate as his, and that she's entitled to ask for the same consideration she offers him, to learn to be straight with him, and loyal to herself.

CHAPTER 4

The Provider

FOR THE PROVIDER, love means responsibility.

> Sundays too my father got up early
> and put his clothes on in the blue-black cold,
> then with cracked hands that ached
> from labor in the weekday weather made
> banked fires blaze. No one ever thanked him.
>
> I'd wake and hear the cold splintering, breaking.
> When the rooms were warm, he'd call,
> and slowly I would rise and dress,
> fearing the chronic angers of that house,
>
> Speaking indifferently to him,
> who had driven out the cold
> and polished my good shoes as well.
> What did I know, what did I know,
> of love's austere and lonely offices?*

The Provider's love bespeaks itself in actions. Uncomfortable avowing his love verbally, the Provider expresses it instead with unassuming gestures of thoughtfulness, on the one hand, and yield from his in-

* Robert Hayden, "Those Winter Sundays."

dustry on the other. Karen said of her husband, Tom, "He's not the type to go around saying 'I love you' all the time. When he does say it, he really means it. But he shows his love to me in other ways, like having the garage door open for me when I come home at night, things like that."

The Provider sublimates much of his love into his work. He works diligently and fosters the family's fortunes cautiously, to fulfill the obligation he feels to his partner—to keep her snug in the present and to give her a shield against the future's uncertainties.

The Provider knows "it's a mean old world" and he takes life seriously. As Tom said, "My father taught me—in order to survive, you must know how to work." The Provider endures such frustration and tedium as his work entails and enjoys whatever benefits it offers him. "I like the security," Tom said. A pragmatist, the Provider takes what he gets, rather than demand more and allow his expectations to make him vulnerable to disappointment.

Bringing home a paycheck, keeping the insurance up-to-date and the car lubricated—taking care of business in other words—means to the Provider that he's fulfilling the requirements of adulthood. By executing such responsibilities punctually and precisely, he achieves a kind of peace with himself.

Caution serves as a way of allaying the anxiety that the Provider often experiences. He worries about external circumstances (whether the auto plant where he works will be laying off employees), and he's prey, as well, to apprehensions about his personal adequacy. The Provider dreads being wrong, dreads failing, dreads feeling that he's made himself ridiculous. To protect himself, he consults common sense and tradition as a distillate of wisdom that offers him the best available prescriptions for achieving success and avoiding failure. For further protection, he encloses himself in a structure of habit. Routine doesn't strike the Provider as a rut. He experiences it as a comfortable, well-polished groove.

He strives for self-control and the preservation of rationality. Tom said, "I always try to be objective about things. If you can't be objective, you're wasting your time, the way I see it." The Provider views feelings as misleading, as obscuring his perception of the relevant aspect of the situation—its facts. The Provider moderates his enthusiasm. He views impulse and inclination as mere fancies, pleasure as a lure that will inveigle him away from the proper objective: to to do right by his responsibilities. He has learned self-discipline. He may regard his marriage the way Brooke did for years, "I'm doing what needs to be done. I'm not outrageously happy with this relationship, but I accept it. Things are working."

The Provider can subordinate the present to the future, can tolerate a painful process (like medical school or an internship, for example) in pursuit of a goal he deems important (becoming a doctor). His ability to disregard his immediate desires gives the Provider a long-term freedom which others may envy; for example, when his children's college education is being financed by a decade's cautious savings. The steadfast Provider can make an agreement and hold to it with a constancy that the Dance-Away Lover cannot match.

The Provider strives for composure, and distances himself as speedily and as completely as possible from feelings like fear and anger. Tom said, "I always assumed the way mature human beings handled emotions that were difficult was to pull themselves a little bit away from the situation and look at it objectively and rationally to resolve it. To constantly let everything hang out—involving yourself in those emotions —is childlike."

On rare occasions the Provider knows that he preserves his equilibrium by cutting off threatening feelings. Brooke said, "I have these very strong feelings. But when I have experiences which in some way I can't handle, I just divorce the emotional content from them. It's my basic defense against danger." This Provider won't allow himself to be sick or to feel weak. He feels obliged to maintain a stable unflinching posture vis-à-vis his partner, for fear of alarming her.

Fearful of being controlled by his feelings, the Provider cultivates an imperviousness to emotion that can leave him uncertain about what's going on inside him. Tom said, "I've buried my emotions so much . . . I think I have some problems now trying to figure out what I feel."

The Provider hesitates to express even the emotions he is clear about. "You don't talk about feelings. They just are," Tom said. The intellectual or technical competence the Provider possesses is often oddly incongruent with the awkwardness he displays talking about emotions. Brooke said, "I guess there's feelings in there, but I don't know how to express them . . . If it's feelings where I'm involved, I get that lost feeling."

When he's forced to express his feelings, he's liable to fumble them out with painful constraint, or to lapse into sentimental formulas. Sometimes liquor can untie the Provider's tongue, or he may use humor as an outlet for emotions he can't articulate directly. While his partner may long to be told outspokenly and imaginatively how much she is loved, the Provider's constraint can preclude the kind of verbal intimacy that is liable to mean real closeness to her. He also experiences difficulty perceiving what his partner feels. His lack of insight into his partner's frame of mind is sometimes but not always the result of inattentiveness. Often the Provider is positively reluctant to involve himself with his partner's emotions, no matter how plainly she displays them. He feels threatened by her desire for tenderness, and he's alarmed even more by her unhappiness or fear or anger.

The Provider can't draw on empathy to help connect him to his partner's distress, because his own response to a crisis is to distance himself from the emotions, rather than thrash them out with his partner. The Provider struggles to keep his problems and their emotional concomitants concealed beneath a "business as usual" facade. The resulting silences are likely to upset his partner, who feels relegated to the position of an outsider. "While I was still a kid, I learned to keep my own counsel," Brooke explained. "If I'm having some difficulty at work, I have to work it out as best I can by myself." Maureen replied, "I feel like I don't want to pump you about how you feel about your job, but I feel like you kind of withdraw and don't let me in on how it feels to you. I feel kind of pushed away a lot of the time." Brooke replied, "Sometimes I don't like to talk about it. Can't you just respect that?"

When the Provider is under stress, what he wants from his partner is warm acceptance and complete absence of demands. To disclose his painful feelings would mean a frightening vulnerability to his partner. He keeps silent the better to retain control of the situation. When he was having severe conflicts with his boss, Brooke said, "I want to go to sleep at night because I'm tired. Maureen wants to sit up and talk about the problem."

When she responds to her own troubles by asking for help, the Provider is apt to be at a loss. Tom said, "When Karen's upset, I feel bad about it, but I don't know what to do." The Provider usually chooses either to problem-solve on his partner's behalf, or to withdraw from the situation altogether. Brooke, for example, came home from work one summer day to find his wife sitting in tears at the kitchen table. When he asked what was wrong, Maureen sobbed that the kids were driving her crazy with fights and commotion and demands to be entertained. Brooke suggested that she get a baby-sitter so she could leave the house sometimes, and appended to that recommendation the reminder that if she had just agreed to send the kids to camp, the problem never would have arisen.

Problem-solving allows the Provider to express his concern in a practical, rational way that allows him to feel both responsible and efficacious. His commitment to logic as a response isn't prompted wholly by rational considerations, however. His partiality to logic also reflects his fear of emotional engagements with others. He doesn't know how to respond directly to emotions, how to convey sympathy and reassurance that the Disarmer instinctively supplies. Emotions are alien ground for the Provider, and he tends to back away from them to the cognitive realm that's home to him.

When the Provider responds to his partner's problems with advice instead of the sympathy she's likely to want, she's apt to feel rebuffed and to experience his calm as an implicit criticism of her turbulence. She's often too wrought up to engage with him in a reasonable discussion of her situation, which leaves him frustrated by her "irrationality." Frequently, they end up in a struggle over the merits of his advice.

Furthermore, a person who's being offered advice often perceives it as being tinged with blame, even when it's not. The overtone of 'if you'd only managed better you wouldn't have gotten into this predicament in the first place' puts the Provider's partner on the defensive and hooks her resistance to advice which may have sound content.

The other course of action the Provider may choose when he feels uneasy is to withdraw. Tom said of his wife, "She'll come out with such an emotional thing, and I'll just feel like it's an attack on me. And I'll sit there and say nothing. And she'll say, 'Won't you even talk to me?'" Feeling threatened by his partner's emotionality and her demand that he respond to it, the Provider withdraws rather than risk a response he's afraid won't suffice. His mind wanders; he thinks of something else he needs to do; he picks up the newspaper—insulating himself from the pain of the experience by removing himself from it emotionally and/ or physically.

He doesn't do so consciously. Usually the Provider loves his partner and he doesn't intend to leave her stranded amidst her tears, but he feels unable to be helpful.

His withdrawal usually gets read, however, as an unwillingness to help. Karen said to Tom, "It happens a lot that when I need to say things that are hard to deal with, you say, 'No, I don't want to get into it.' 'I'm too tired.' 'I don't want to talk now.' " She takes his unresponsiveness for rejection. Maureen said of Brooke, "He doesn't appear to be really interested in what my problems are. I practically have to beg him to listen to what I have to say."

The Provider's means of defending himself usually threaten his partner. As he extends the distance between them beyond her ability to endure it, she's liable to snap back like an over-stretched rubber band. Her response may be to pull at him, pleading for closeness; or she may pound on him, trying to provoke him into fighting with her. Her attempts to prod him into anger usually arouse stubborn passivity instead. Tom said, "I hate the screaming bit." Karen replied, "You're just stone-faced."

Such gloomy or hostile transactions estrange the Provider from his partner and erode his respect for her. In fact, however, both represent attempts on her part to break through his remoteness and to make contact with the Provider on an emotional level.

The Provider distances his partner in other ways as well, one of which is work. Work justifies the Provider's existence in his own eyes. Tom said, "I feel that I must produce something, do something, in order to be me."

The most obvious negative effect his work orientation has on the couple's life is the deficit of enjoyment it creates. The Provider systematically places practicality ahead of pleasure. For him, a sunset is a prognosis of tomorrow's weather, rather than a dimension of today's beauty.

The Provider may allow the obligations of his career to encroach on his private life so far that the couple has little time for recreation together. Furthermore, it may be hard for the Provider to turn off his tension enough to allow for enjoyment. Brooke said, "I'm under tremendous pressure at work, and I go into this high gear. I get all wound up like a spring, and I have a difficult time letting up—so difficult that sometimes it's impossible for me to relax and have a good time."

To have a good time with his partner can be a more difficult matter still, for the Provider often enjoys the company of men friends more than togetherness with his partner. Tom said, reminiscing about his youth, "As I was on a troop ship sailing out of San Francisco Bay, I remember feeling this enormous sense of relief that I wasn't going to have to hassle with that problem now [relating to women]. That burden was off my shoulders."

Some such uncertainty about how to deal with the opposite sex often lingers for the Provider even after he's experienced loving and living with a particular woman. He shares a sexual relationship with her, and he shares the responsibilities of daily life with her. But he is often unclear about how to talk with her and how to enjoy being with her. She may accept his interest and his circle of friends but often she feels left out. She mourns that 'We never do anything together.'

When he's around the house, the Provider is apt to relax by puttering, a form of activity that subtly excludes his partner. He waters the lawn, attends to the car, makes minor repairs around the house. Karen said of Tom with some amusement, "When he's done all the chores around our house, he goes next door to the neighbors' to see if they've got anything for him to do." Puttering consists of small-scale chores that are, by definition, manageable. The Provider can set his own pace while doing them and he can take satisfaction in having done them. But puttering also has another meaning for him: it's a way of legitimizing solitude.

Puttering allows him to be physically present in his

home but supplies him with immunity from the demands of others. Puttering allows him to say "No" without guilt, 'Can't you see that I'm busy? Go ask your mother,' so it gives him room to breathe. The Provider doesn't question whether his time would be better spent talking with his family than refinishing a secondhand end table for the family room. The Provider counts his puttering as work, not as the makework it may be closer to being.

On a small scale, puttering can enable the Provider to avoid his partner. On a larger scale, his career can serve the same purpose, i.e., allow him to stave off her demands for his time and energy. When the Provider retreats into work, he's able to refuse her without the guilt he would otherwise experience. His partner is likely to become painfully aware of the negative side of the mixed message 'I love you, but let me alone' that's implicit in the Provider's diligence.

The Provider's "austerity is not asperity."* He likes people, but he feels ill at ease with them. The taciturn Provider doesn't look for opportunities to "inject," as O. Henry says, "a few raisins of conversation into the tasteless dough of existence." Instead, he often chooses the role of a bystander. Tom said, "I like to be kind of an observer. I don't enter in as much as Karen thinks I ought to."

When the Provider's obliged to be companionable, he's apt to get anxious, and he's apt to interpret this anxiety as a sign that something is amiss with his practical responsibilities: he's behind schedule; he's wasting time he should be devoting to work, and so on. Quite unconsciously, Providers translate relationship anxiety into responsibility anxiety.

For example, one evening Tom sat at the table chatting, as he infrequently did, with his teen-aged son. He began to feel a bit uneasy after twenty minutes had passed, and he coded that anxiety as an awareness that the bank statement had arrived and he hadn't yet

* Daniel G. Hoffman, "At the Winter Solstice."

balanced his checkbook. He excused himself, therefore, and went, with some relief, to spend the rest of the evening tidying his finances.

Tom was fond of his son but he didn't know how to talk to him, and when they did talk he both enjoyed the experience and wanted to get it over with. The press of other commitments provided both an explanation for his disquiet and a legitimate excuse for leaving. In fact, the pattern of breaking off emotional interactions to go to work or to escape to the tranquil solitude of puttering intensifies the awkwardness the Provider feels when he does deal with people; the system of avoidance can escalate, trapping him into progressively greater isolation.

Often, however, there is a level on which the Provider can achieve intimacy with his partner. Through sex, the Provider can often express the love that he can't articulate verbally. Sex may serve him as a form of play and a source of reassurance, which creates the profound sense of connectedness that other kinds of interactions with his partner can't give him.

Sex may not have the same significance for the Provider's partner, however. Unaware of the multiple meanings that sex has for him, she may discount his desire for her as crude lust. If their love-making isn't mutually pleasurable, she may resent the sexual demands he makes on her. In fact, the Provider's emotional reserve tends to precipitate sexual withholding in his partner, who becomes averse to putting out for him since she feels he won't give her the closeness she wants.

Because sex is fraught with so many kinds of significance for the Provider, he's peculiarly vulnerable to his partner's "no." Sex may well be one of the only demands he feels he's entitled to make of her and her refusals may embitter him. One recently married Provider said of his partner, "In her eyes I'm the guy in the bar who's trying to hustle to get into bed with her. The image I have of her is the old maid who was told

'Sex is bad and don't let anyone take advantage of you.' "

The Provider may find himself in the position Norman Mailer described, aching "with that most private and tender pain . . . Never to know in advance when he shall be undesirable" to his partner. ". . . resent her as he must, be furious with himself as he will, there is not very much he can do about it."*

The Provider doesn't vent the anger he feels on this or any other score. Brooke said, "I have people yelling at me ten hours a day at my job. I associate anger with ignorance, and irrational impulse and counter-productive results." The Provider views the ability to control anger as a major aspect of maturity. Anger means loss of control, and loss of control means jeopardy to the Provider, who hates recriminations. Tom said, "I can't stand to argue." Karen agreed, "He's always so damned reasonable. He never yells."

Instead, the Provider's anger is liable to lead him to withhold cooperation from his partner in various ways. For example, Karen complained persistently about the lack of "communication—plain old talk" in their relationship. So, the couple agreed to take turns reading to each other out of a book that both found interesting. The third day of the reading program, Tom lost the book, and two weeks later hadn't managed to replace it. The Provider often isn't in touch with his suppressed resentment. He doesn't consciously intend to retaliate against his partner, but he can't find time to do the things she asks of him. He clean forgets things she tells him, and he can't muster up any enthusiasm for activities that excite her. He doesn't perceive the hostile component of his lethargy or his absentmindedness. But from his partner's point of view, it's more than ample reprisal. Karen said of this passive aggression, "Frustration is a mild word for what he does to me."

Perhaps nothing frustrates the partner more keenly than to want sex and to have the Provider withhold it from her. As more women begin to experience and

* Norman Mailer, *Advertisements for Myself.*

express a desire for sex, more men find themselves in the uncomfortable position of being pressured to respond. A man who has doubts about his sexual proficiency, or who feels uncomfortable with his partner's aggressiveness, or who cherishes resentment about other aspects of the relationship may turn sexually withholding.*

Rather than face a confrontation, the Provider puts up with resentment and disciplines himself not to complain. Tom said, "I'm after peace. Ignoring the situation is better than going through the hassle." But over the years, "ignoring the situation" can make the Provider's position in the relationship untenable. One Provider said about the marriage he had just ended, "We didn't have a bad life, but we didn't have a good life." Of his ex-wife, he said, "I didn't talk much to her. I never did. I just let things slide. She would do something that pissed me off, and I'd just say, 'Well, that's all right,' I did that for years, but I wasn't happy. Then all of a sudden, it cut loose all at once. I thought, 'The hell with this.'" The Provider's reluctance to struggle can allow his partner to drift into behavior that offends him. By the time he can no longer stave off his unhappiness, he has become so disheartened and so alienated from his partner that "it's too late" for him to salvage the relationship.

But escaping from that relationship doesn't bring the Provider to grips with his responsibility for its deterioration. By tuning out his feelings—his anger, his frustration, his anxiety—the Provider ignores the signals which would alert him to the fact that the relationship is going awry; it's failing to serve his needs.

Indeed, naked self-discipline can't make his position tolerable over the long term. The Provider has a responsibility to his partner and to himself to structure

* The Provider's withholding is apt to reflect resentment, or an anxiety about sex, rather than the ambivalence about commitment that usually provokes the Dance-Away's sexual withholding.

into the relationship the personal gains and personal pleasures that will enable him to feel a desire as well as a duty to stay with his partner.

Their relationship may not afford the Provider's partner any surfeit of satisfaction either. She may look to him in vain for the appreciation that would help her feel good about herself, for the openness about himself, and for the warmhearted interest in her that would enable her to feel that their relationship was a genuine union, not just a practical arrangement.

To ensure that she does things properly, the Provider may chide and direct his partner, reducing her to the status of a resentful subordinate. Maureen said, "When we got married, I would vacuum and Brooke would vacuum after me, because he didn't think that I had done a good enough job."

When it comes to his job, the Provider often assumes that if his wife doesn't complain, she's comfortable with the existing balance between the time he devotes to work and the time he spends at home. But in fact, she may feel guilty about making demands on him, especially if she doesn't translate his breadwinning or his sexual desire for her into love messages. She may find it hard to believe him when he says, "I keep telling you, the marriage is more important to me than my career." She may discount his genuine love for her because of his lack of expressiveness. As Karen said, "We never have talked to each other much. I think he's worse than I am that way." She may conclude, like Maureen, "From his point of view he loves me. He loves me as much as he can love me, but that isn't enough for me."

The Provider must learn to get in touch with his feelings and to share those feelings with his partner, whether they be tender, angry, or fearful. He must begin to struggle through difficulties with her instead of withdrawing when trouble arises. He must also learn to respect his own wants. He can draw on his partner for strength in adversity and share with her the daily weight of responsibility for their lives, and in so doing, forge a stronger, more equal alliance between them.

Apprenticed to discipline, the Provider needs to discover the validity of desire. Without self-control, spontaneity can fragment a person's energies, and lead to a series of fizzles instead of a series of accomplishments. But without the thrust that desire supplies, a person's life can harden into a mechanical structure of obligations. The Provider needs to learn to listen to his longings and his aspirations and to accept the risk of following them—at least a little. To trust in his heart as well as his head. To become

> That final thing
> A man learning to sing.*

* Theodore Roethke, "The Dying Man."

CHAPTER 5

The Prizewinner

"IMAGINE FOR ONE SECOND that you raise hell in public places . . . You're a tiger, a lion, a cat. You can spend a night with a Russian woman and leave her satisfied. You're twenty-five. If rings had been fastened to earth and sky, you'd have seized those rings and pulled the sky down to the earth."* Or as Andy said, "At some point you just know you've got it in you to do it." The Prizewinner trusts his judgment and his nerve. He possesses the energy that gets things started and the discipline that sees them through to completion. Under pressure, the Prizewinner stretches to his full reach. Like a bow and arrow, the greater the tension the more powerful the thrust.

The Prizewinner looks out for himself with resilient skill. Only truly comfortable when he's in command of a situation, he sits easy with the prerogatives and the responsibilities of power. He can make choices and take chances without collapsing into doubt. He operates strategically with an eye on the long term as well as the short term. He can posit the terms of his involvements—manipulating (structuring the range of options to his advantage, for example). The Prizewinner can exercise power effectively, partly because he's sure he's entitled to it. This conviction gives him the clarity and the self-assurance to set limits on the behavior he'll accept from others. The extent of his tol-

* Isaac Babel, *Lyubka the Cossack and Other Stories.*

60

erance varies, but when its boundaries have been sufficiently over-stepped, he squares off against the transgressor. The Prizewinner is too tough to be intimidated, too sure of himself to be immobilized by the guilt or self-doubt that erodes others' resolve. "There's no way I'm going to let people lean on me," as Andy phrased it.

By setting limits, the Prizewinner spares himself the vexation that a laissez-faire stance might expose him to. He ensures that an accumulation of resentment won't slowly curdle his relationships, as it may for the Disarmer or the Provider. The Prizewinner's willingness to call people to account for behavior that displeases him can rebound to their benefit as well as his.

People frequently cope with their troubles by avoiding coming to grips with the real source of difficulty. Anxiety is channeled instead into behavior, like blame, which exacerbates their predicament. The Disarmer's supportiveness often reinforces this kind of counterproductive response, and the Provider shies away from a showdown over it.

The Prizewinner, however, low on empathy and trepidation alike, trounces the person who's offended him. He specifies the terms which must govern the relationship and requires that the other person meet them, or else. This 'shape up or ship out' message can force a person to confront and take responsibility for behavior which serves him ill.

The Prizewinner's "get your act together" directive can bespeak respect for the unutilized potential he glimpses in the other person. Limit-setting, likewise, can testify to the Prizewinner's desire to work things out and salvage the relationship, instead of accepting the colder solution of casting aside the friend or firing the employee who's trespassed.

The objective of helping others to shape up remains secondary, however, to the Prizewinner's primary goal, which is to reinforce his own position. Aggressive and dominant, he is characteristically unable "to let things just happen to me . . . to allow other people to initiate and control situations involving me. I'm afraid I give people very little room to be in charge of a relationship they have with me," Jerome observed.

The Prizewinner seeks the upper hand in his undertakings. "I have a certain drive," said Martin, "a drive for ascendancy and for achievement." The Prizewinner judges others as he judges himself, by the stripped-down standard of performance: how well you do, how fast you finish. He sees losers as differentiated from winners by two factors: losers don't have what it takes and/or they don't try. Competition spurs the Prizewinner to excel, and his pleasure in victory isn't diluted by any remorse about the plight of losers. He strives for the laurels he wins. He feels his performance merits them, and at least some small corner of him feels contempt for the rivals he's outstripped.

The Prizewinner believes, "You either is or you ain't." But an occasional upset doesn't consign him to the "ain't" category. "I've experienced momentary setbacks," said Martin, "but I've never had a real failure." The Prizewinner views a reverse now and then as a challenge to his resourcefulness, not a cause for self-doubt; as a single episode in an ongoing process, not as the culmination to which that process has tended. As long as he acquits himself well enough often enough, a failure may break his stride, but it doesn't break his spirit.

The Prizewinner's self-assurance is usually built of solid stuff. Jerome said of his research in chemistry, "I love this kind of work. I want to do something. I want to accomplish something significant. I take great pride and pleasure in what I do. I'm good at it. I work on important problems, and do it in an interesting fashion. I feel very positive about myself."

The Prizewinner's robust self-esteem derives, in part, from his tendency to envision himself as the sum of his strengths. To the Prizewinner, the abilities that matter are those he possesses. He tends to dismiss his ineptness as irrelevant, and he avoids placing himself in a context where those deficiencies would render him helpless or foolish. Through this kind of selectivity he protects his image. And others, like his partner, who have a stake in his viability, tend to protect him also.

The Prizewinner filters out the emotions as well as the perceptions that might sap his morale. Andy said, "I really think that I like myself a lot. But I think that underneath I can't be any more free of self-doubt than anyone else. I must have the same anxieties about myself that other people have, but I have to a large extent masked them, suppressed them. I suspect certain things I do are to keep those things as far back from the surface as possible."

The Prizewinner quells threatening emotions. He simply refuses to yield to such feelings as pain, hopelessness, and uncertainty that he lumps together as symptoms of weakness, for fear that surrender to them might push him into the slow tumble down to mediocrity. He fears that others would cease to respect him if they saw him waver. So he strives for emotion-proof self-control. Andy said, "I don't mind getting angry as long as I have control. If I didn't have control, I'd start throwing things or hitting Gail. It's something that I dig about myself, that I keep control no matter what." The Prizewinner bluffs when his actual imperviousness wears thin to maintain his own equilibrium and to safeguard those who rely on him. "I don't let things get to me," Andy said. The Prizewinner uses fear to mobilize himself, but he can't fend it off altogether. His response to anxiety isn't to worry, like the Provider. Instead, he seizes the offensive. When anxiety stirs inside him, he codes it as a signal that "Somebody has screwed up." His response is often to don the hat of prosecuting attorney, probing the dimensions of the mishap and assessing accountability for its occurrence. The Prizewinner tends to hold others responsible for things having gone wrong, but he assumes responsibility himself for setting them to rights. The other role he's likely to assume is that of major general, barking the orders that he intends will salvage the situation.

To relieve his anxiety, the Prizewinner tightens his grip on the situation that threatens him. For example, Gail and Andy's small son had contracted asthma. When the boy suffered an attack, Andy would quiz his wife about what had precipitated the episode, call her down for what he perceived as failures in her mothering, and instruct her about the precautions she ought to be taking. Doubtful of others' ability to cope, the Prizewinner calms himself by checking up on them and superintending them. Andy remarked, "I make Gail sufficiently anxious so I don't have to worry about it anymore."

The spotlight of the Prizewinner's scrutiny usually unnerves the person it's trained on. Gail said, "Inside I feel truly competent, but when he walks in and starts grilling me, I begin to worry that maybe I'm not. I start to judge myself by his standards, and I turn into a nervous Nelly." Once her self-doubt was hooked, Gail became flustered and fearful that somehow she *had* bungled. The uncertainty she displayed fulfilled and fed Andy's suspicions that she couldn't be trusted to manage on her own. The Prizewinner, therefore, doesn't so much dispel his anxiety as deflect it to others. He perceives himself, however, as hammering the situation into shape, which he may well be doing —not as browbeating his associates, which he may equally well be doing.

Toughness defends the Prizewinner against his vulnerability, and his apparent immunity to fear can be enormously reassuring to people who feel wobbly themselves. Others are drawn to the dynamism and the strength they perceive in Prizewinners,

> those men of hard voice,
> Those that break horses and dominate rivers
> Those men of sonorous skeleton who sing
> The mouth full of sun and flint.*

* Federico García Lorca, "Lament for Ignacio Sanchez Mejias."

For his part, engrossed in real-world activities, the Prizewinner tends to eye relationships slightly askance, to be inclined to believe that

Most friendship is feigning, most loving mere folly.*

Nevertheless, on some deeper level, he often cherishes loyalty between friends and lovers as one of the ultimate values in life. This tension between cynicism and idealism often enhances his attractiveness, as does his aura of unavailability. The proud, charismatic Prizewinner often seems to dare women to possess him, and it's a seductive invitation indeed.

A relationship with a Prizewinner confers vicarious status on the woman he's chosen, and it often gives her entry into a far more exciting world than she could win access to independently. If she's a Disarmer or a Fragile, she's as likely to back away from power as the Prizewinner is to pursue it. So their couple system operates in harmonious "Jack Sprat" fashion. She admires him and defers to him and relies on him to protect her.

In many ways, however, a relationship with a Prizewinner can mean heavy sledding. His priorities usually place his pursuits ahead of his partner. The drama that stirs him is played out in the public sphere. And it's those challenges, those stakes, which arouse his interest. In comparison, domestic pleasures often seem relatively thin to him. Sooner or later, his partner may find herself obliged to come to terms with the fact that most of the time she's at the periphery, not at the center, of his field of vision.

The Prizewinner brings to his couple relationship the same 'me first' mode he employs in the rest of his life. He often visualizes the relationship in traditional terms as providing him a support system and a haven from stress. Andy said, "I want to go home to a woman who cooks my food, washes my clothes, and

* William Shakespeare, "Blow, Blow, Thou Winter Wind."

loves me." He wants his partner to minister to his needs, believing that the rigors of his exertions entitle him to this kind of special treatment.

The Prizewinner is not, however, particularly giving in return. The lack of conflict about his own needs, which is a significant source of strength for him, stems in part from insensitivity to the needs of others, which might impinge on him. Should he realize that a conflict exists between his own needs and his partner's, the Prizewinner expects to prevail. Norman Mailer said of himself, "He could love a woman, and she might sprain her back before a hundred sinks of dishes in a month, but he would not be happy to help her if his work should suffer. No, not unless her work was as valuable as his own."* Often the Prizewinner is simply oblivious of his partner's needs and the pain his unresponsiveness causes her. Gail said, "It seems that Andy is unable to think of anyone's feelings beside his own, to say please, thank you, or I'm sorry."

It's always, "He makes the decisions and I go along," said Gail. The combination of his aggressiveness and her compliance can allow the Prizewinner to exercise an inordinate degree of control over their lives. Since Andy claimed that he couldn't go to sleep without Gail beside him, she consistently yielded to his pressure. "When he goes to bed, I go to bed. When he turns off his light, I turn off my light. If he decides that's the side of the bed he wants, I take what's left." Over time, her forbearance drained, the Prizewinner's partner may feel a discontent with the leftovers, which crystalizes into a sense of exploitation. Susan remarked bitterly, "Martin enjoys his life. He makes sure he enjoys his life. He does everything he wants to do at the expense of everyone else in the family."

The Prizewinner's tendency to lean on people too hard may cause him an occasional spasm of guilt. Exacting and impatient, Martin found himself telling his wife how to dress, what to cook, whom to befriend. He admitted, "I have no right to order her around like

* Norman Mailer, *The Prisoner of Sex.*

that. She shouldn't take that shit from me. I know I do things that must be terribly fucking painful to her. I relate to her in ways I prefer not to but I find myself stuck with."

Able to set limits for others, the Prizewinner may be unable to curb his own excesses. He may experience a bit of relief, therefore, when people refuse to submit to his coercion. Martin said, "When somebody fights back, I have a good kind of respect for that. When somebody tells me to get fucked, I say to myself, 'You're right. It sure took you long enough to tell me off.'" But if his partner doesn't push back, the Prizewinner is forced either to master restraint or to suffer the consequences of his oppressiveness.

A formidable opponent, the Prizewinner is often one who "can fight clean and fight dirty, but who likes to fight."* He accepts conflict as an inevitable feature of activity in the marketplace, but he considers discord in his relationship a sign of his partner's untrustworthiness, her disagreement as tantamount to treason. To reestablish the order he perceives her as challenging, the Prizewinner implicitly threatens his partner with being demolished or being ditched. He has learned "how to get to people. I can hit where it hurts," Andy said. His full-borne assault, whether its particulars be remorseless rationality, abusiveness, or a withering caricature of his adversary, will quash any but another bulletproof Prizewinner.

The other weapon he wields is the threat of abandonment. Andy said, "I put it out in a very civil way. 'This is how it is. If you don't like it, hit the door.'" Sid dragooned his rebellious partner with the warning, "I am going to have it my way, and if it doesn't go my way, there isn't going to be any way. That's it." Part bluff, part real conviction that he doesn't need anybody, the Prizewinner's 'Take it or leave it' stance serves as a defense as well as an offense—a shield against his own fears of being manipulated or deserted.

"People don't come up and get me pissed off," Andy

* Norman Mailer, *The Prisoner of Sex.*

noted with satisfaction. The Prizewinner's partner is apt to be especially careful about provoking him. She usually lacks clarity about her wants and belief in their legitimacy, and she can't match his zest and skill as a combatant. Characteristically, she concludes, like Gail, "It won't do any good to fight about it," and yields to his wishes.

In time, however, each new concession may touch off a spurt of resentment that leaves her stewing. Gail concluded bitterly, "My life disappears for the sake of us. I don't even feel like a person when he's around." The Prizewinner's partner often feels helpless, however, to act on her own behalf. Susan said, "I take too much, but I don't know what to do about it." In fact, although the partner's too intimidated to retaliate openly, she is likely to resort to withholding and other passive-aggressive forms of reprisal. The cause-and-effect connection isn't visible to her, but frequently she loses interest in sex. She remains tepid when the Prizewinner wants her passionate, indifferent when he wants her appreciative. She may subtly sabotage—allow a look of distaste to cross her face when he begins a familiar story, or enlist the children in a tacit alliance against their father. She tries to reclaim sub rosa some of the autonomy she feels she's forfeited to the relationship.

This strategy places the Prizewinner in an awkward spot. He's liable to feel somehow thwarted and undercut, to be furious about his vulnerability to his partner and baffled about how to short-circuit her resistance. His grievance is likely to be her manner—too nebulous a complaint for vigorous prosecution. And he's usually unable to force her to confess the malicious intent he suspects, since she doesn't feel she's willing her behavior and its punitive component is usually hidden to her. The more stringently he tries to control her, the longer the shadow her disaffection is likely to cast over their relationship.

The Prizewinner characteristically attributes his partner's behavior to personality defects, not frustration.

"Susan's a very cold woman," was Martin's explanation of their couple troubles. The gap between his overt power and her covert power is so great that he doesn't acknowledge her as an honorable opponent. "You control me by being negative," Jerome groused. "You're always trying to bring me down." He may translate his displeasure with her way of fighting into disrespect for her person.

She is likely to occupy the status of an inferior in the relationship, and her ego may take a severe drubbing. She usually bears some responsibility for this. If she starts to measure herself against her mate—ability for ability, achievement for achievement—she may begin to doubt how much she has going for her. Wittingly or unwittingly, the Prizewinner is likely to scene steal, reducing his partner to the role of a bystander, while he commands the audience she might love to share.

Her self-esteem may also be bruised by the brusque (although not ill-intentioned) handling the Prizewinner gives her. He brings to the relationship a cast of mind that is more attuned to spotting weaknesses than reinforcing strengths. She may well interpret the shortage of approval she gets as a commentary on her inadequacies, not as a reflection of his bias.

When the Prizewinner thinks that his partner is managing poorly, he tells her so. When he perceives self-doubt in her, he pushes her. When Susan worried about her ability to get a job after ten years at home, Martin replied, "What are you talking about? You could persuade anybody to hire you if you just came on like you knew what you were doing. And they'd be lucky to get you." The Prizewinner feels that it's his responsibility to help his partner to upgrade her operation, but he usually underestimates the value of nurturing and overestimates the usefulness of bald assessment in these circumstances. His quarterbacking and his reprimands may rattle her at best, or humiliate her at worst, a consequence the Prizewinner doesn't perceive and consequently doesn't attempt to mitigate.

The Prizewinner is an elitist who ranks people on the basis of what they 'do' and how well they do it. If his partner devotes herself to the tasks of wife and mother, she's likely to disperse most of her energy among chores that offer her no real opportunity to distinguish herself in her own eyes or her husband's. Sexism compounds the problem. The Prizewinner measures with the traditionally masculine yardstick. He values traits like rationality, and doesn't attach equal importance to such conventionally feminine qualities as gentleness. So his appraisal of his partner is likely to be skewed to her detriment.

The Prizewinner acknowledges few as his equal, and his partner is rarely among them. Confident of his own worth, the Prizewinner assumes that he's entitled and equipped to pass judgment on others, and he often utilizes this judgmental stance to increase his leverage in the relationship. If his partner's self-esteem is shaky she may be anxious for his approval, and empower him with the same objectivity he ascribes to himself. Accordingly, he can reward her by granting her a nod of approval and punish her by withholding from her his respect or his confidence. The feebler her self-esteem, the more susceptible she is to this kind of manipulation, and the more painful and destructive the consequences it has for her.

In sum, the Prizewinner may roll over his partner like a steel-belted tire, flattening her personality and squelching her initiative; then yearn for a woman who possesses his own kind of vitality and self-assurance.

Ideally, a couple relationship operates like a relay team, with the partners spelling each other, knowing that they share the same goals and that pooling their resources will maximize the likelihood they'll achieve them. The individualistic Prizewinner, however, runs a solitary race. Confident of his own powers, he's fearful that his partner won't be able to pull through. So he chooses self-reliance over interdependence. One penalty of the path he chooses is isolation; loneliness and the pressure of knowing that there's no one to relieve him should his endurance run low. The Prizewinner's unwillingness to share responsibility with his partner often means that he carries a grueling burden of obligations, and she is never obliged to develop the strength that would stand them both in good stead.

The Prizewinner is characteristically far more willing to commit energy to, and to make sacrifices for, the pursuits that interest him than for his couple relationship. This reluctance to give of himself emotionally means that the relationship lacks the richness that only deep personal involvement can create.

The Prizewinner struggles for success, not intimacy, and he often doesn't recognize the dimensions of the loss he's incurred until disillusionment has tainted his pleasure in the possession of power. He doesn't realize how heavily the brunt of his impact falls on others, that he mortifies or intimidates them into the very hesitance and error and passivity that exasperate him. He doesn't perceive that his preoccupation with dominance blights other aspects of his relationship, and prevents him from experiencing the openness and trust of real mutuality.

The Prizewinner dismisses nurturing as coddling—blind to the fact that it can foster strength and competence as surely as his own uncompromising demands for excellence. He must learn to offer others support as well as limits. The necessary complement to taking charge is the ability to perceive others' perspectives and to respond to their concerns. He can learn, as well, the sense of potency and fulfillment that giving can create.

The Prizewinner can discover that, despite its value, toughness isn't a sine qua non for self-worth. Most critically, he can begin to acknowledge his own vulnerability. This will allow him to learn the acceptance and the compassion that will give flexibility to his strength.

CHAPTER 6

The Fragile

HELPLESS. For most people, the realization of helplessness is frightening. The Fragile woman or, less often, man, lives with a pervasive sense of helplessness and is not dismayed by that awareness much of the time. In fact, the Fragile uses helplessness to appeal for others' aid, and it's only when such assistance isn't forthcoming—when the Fragile is alone—that fear overwhelms her.

The Fragile is like a stranger newly arrived in the city where everyone else bustles about his business, guided by familiarity and interlocked into networks of relationships that bewilder her. Apprehension deters her from taking steps (like looking for a job) that would ultimately enable her to feel at home in her surroundings. Instead, she shrinks into herself, trying to become invisible.

Taking care of business is one major source of stress for the Fragile. Transactions like getting her car repaired or submitting an insurance claim can cause her an agony of apprehension. To those with more *savoir-faire* or more fortitude, the Fragile's fear appears to be out of all proportion to the actual difficulty of the task. To her, however, each such episode poses the risk of failure and humiliation. Adrienne was even afraid to go into a restaurant alone for fear that waiters would ignore her.

The Fragile is as intimidated by personal relationships as she is by impersonal interaction. She can't imagine that she can inspire genuine interest or affection in others or that her presence might add to their pleasure. In fact, she often can't believe they will even remember her face or her name. So, she's apt to resort to ritualized ways of earning her keep socially, sexual compliance with the men who take her out, or a zeal for washing the dishes after every dinner party she attends.

Sometimes people are so frightening to the Fragile, and her attempts to deal with them so unnerving that, as Adrienne said, "I go home from work and hide." The Fragile may retreat into isolation, filling her life with pets, or alcohol, or drugs, or sleep——substitutes for the human contact that it seems beyond her to sustain.

The Fragile feels too vulnerable and too helpless to involve herself much with others, or to participate actively in the situations around her. Instead, her desire for safety leads her to choose passivity. For example, Ruthie was afraid of boring people, or saying something stupid, so she chose to listen in on rather than contribute to conversation. Her acquaintances grew accustomed to the fact that she never opened her mouth, and gradually they came to ascribe her silence to emptiness. Ruthie's manner communicated her self-doubt so persuasively that others accepted her fears about herself as objective fact.

Almost any kind of stress means trouble for the Fragile. When Ruthie decided to go back to college, she found herself unable to fill out the application. "I just look at it and I think, 'I can't do this.' I get all sort of panicked," she said. The Fragile falters under performance pressure. Her mind goes blank during a crucial examination, or her hand shakes so badly that she can't hold a drink at a cocktail party. So she begins to back away from the situations that threaten her. She drops the course which daunted her; she stops going to parties, both excusing and disparaging herself with her plaintive 'I can't.'

When the Fragile can't withdraw from the situation altogether, she slips into avoidance. Letting things go is less alarming to her than confronting her difficulties and taking the steps necessary to remedy them. For example, Adrienne found it hard to keep her checkbook up-to-date, and she periodically lost track of her balance. She continued to write checks, however, anxious but hopeful that she would be able to cover them. When checks began to bounce, she couldn't bring herself to open the telltale envelopes from the bank, much less sit down with her backlog of statements and figure out the dimensions of her indebtedness. Such avoidance is apt to make the Fragile's life precarious, economically and socially, and this external instability contributes a good deal to her internal instability.

Adrienne said of her checkbook debacle, "I kept pushing it away and pushing it away and thinking 'It'll be okay. It'll work out somehow.'" Denial then, serves as the accomplice of avoidance. The Fragile shuts out her fear and ignores the indications of trouble, hoping that somehow cause and effect won't make their customary connection in this case.

Denial permits the Fragile to remain passive when she ought to act, or to act recklessly, blind to the consequences she's inviting. This defense mechanism, therefore, can have the paradoxical effect of allowing the Fragile to expose herself to hazards that those with firmer allegiance to common sense would shun. Adrienne, for example, had been given to walking the streets in downtown Atlanta alone at night. A beautiful woman, she was frequently accosted by men. She would allow them to drive her home and sleep with her, oblivious to the danger that this involved. Denial ('this isn't real') provides the Fragile with a counterfeit security which lowers her immediate anxiety to a bearable level, but it's as ill-advised as disconnecting the fire alarm when it's ringing, instead of extinguishing the flames.

Denial can't blot out the Fragile's fear altogether, so she continues to experience a general uneasiness that sometimes gives way to panic. Ruthie described herself as being seized sometimes by "this huge fear. I want to run away. I have this place in my mind, just going someplace—nowhere real that I know of—and just being totally by myself and not having to deal with anybody."

The Fragile may resort to drugs or alcohol to anesthetize herself to the pain her situation causes her. Adrienne said, "What I have to do is find a way to live so that I'm not always at the edge of financial crisis. When things get too heavy, like they're about to turn off the utilities or something, I think, 'Something will happen,' and I take a few drinks."

Adversities that would jar a more self-possessed person flatten a Fragile. "Things get to me real easy," said Margaret. "I just get knocked off my balance totally. I feel like I lose control." If her other defenses fail, the Fragile may unravel. Like the child Joseph Heller described, she seems "to come very close to completely falling to pieces, to crumpling like a frail, inanimate bundle of little boys' clothes, or to spilling out emotionally all over the room . . . with a frenzy of melancholy anguish that is at once petrifying and shattering . . ."* In one sense, the Fragile's fall-apart is inadvertent, the result of her inability to keep a grip on herself when she's under pressure. She starts to feel "completely overwhelmed. I begin to cry, and I can't stop," Adrienne said. Her pain puts her "beyond shame" and she yields to her despair, allowing it to spill over the wall of reserve that others maintain.

The fall-apart is not, however, just another aspect of the Fragile's helplessness. On the contrary, it's a powerful form of communication and a powerful

* Joseph Heller, in *Something Happened*.

means of coercion. The fall-apart is an implicit appeal for help. The general burden of the message is 'I can't stand it.' The specifics may boil down to 'Please do this for me,' 'Please don't do that,' or 'Please don't make me do the other thing.'

The Fragile's request isn't straightforwardly expressed, however. Instead, her plea is imbedded in a chunk of emotion-fraught behavior. The medium of the fall-apart is drama, not discourse. The Fragile doesn't say, in adult fashion, 'I feel anxious and I want to be comforted.' Instead, like a child, she signals for help through a piece of behavior—beginning to cry, for example.

In such a fall-apart, the Fragile sinks into a "world of tears which is so huge and beautiful that everything except those tears vanished from before my eyes."* The fall-apart is an experience of entire self-involvement. Fear suffuses the Fragile so completely that it obliterates all other perceptions—all other considerations. Childlike again, the Fragile demands total attention.

His attention engaged, the partner must draw the Fragile into conversation (via a sympathetic 'What's wrong?' for example) in order to discover how to interpret her behavior. Is she crying because she's in physical pain or psychological pain? The fall-apart attests to the existence of a need and to the urgency of that need, but does not specify the nature of the need.

When she's asked, the Fragile may be able to explain what's troubling her. But the more severe her fall-apart (e.g., hallucinations as distinguished from tears), the more confused she's apt to be about what's happening to her. After Adrienne had fainted a number of times in succession, she said, "I'm not really aware of anything that's wrong . . . I don't know why I'm feeling dizzy." In fact, the nature of the problem might be quite clear to a perceptive bystander. In this case, Adrienne was being considered for a long-

* Isaac Babel, *Lyubka the Cossack and Other Stories.*

overdue promotion, which she might or might not be given. But often, the Fragile's fall-apart is the culmination of a long process of denial, which leaves her blurry about what's really bothering her.

The Fragile who's experienced a series of fall-aparts may begin to experience fear of her symptoms in lieu of fear about the situation that provokes the symptom. For example, Adrienne kept watching for the telltale dizziness; she became preoccupied with the fear, "I'm going to fall down. They're going to see me." Instead of addressing the causes of her difficulties, the Fragile focuses on trying to ward off her symptoms. But this anxious self-monitoring is likely to raise her anxiety level and exacerbate her fall-aparts.

The Fragile is apt to need someone to help untangle the jumble inside her, as well as to help put her external circumstances to rights. The fall-apart can function as an intrapersonal communication as well as an interpersonal one. It can alert the Fragile herself to her failure to take care of herself, to the existence of crucial wants that she has neglected.

The fall-apart can also legitimize her wants in the Fragile's eyes. Her self-esteem tends to be so low that she dismisses her wants as trivial or illegitimate, nothing she's entitled to bother other people about. But in order to get by, the Fragile requires a great deal of assistance and a good many allowances. She resolves this conflict between the volume of her wants and her sense of their inadmissibility by converting wants into needs. Ruthie couldn't ask her partner to glue himself to her side at parties just because she wanted him to. But if, when he wandered off, she went stiff with fright, she could believe that she *needed* his presence, and the need justified the petition. The fall-apart, then, testifies to both the Fragile and her partner that she's gripped by genuine need, not by mere frivolous penchant.

The Fragile's deepest fear is the fear that she's

alone. Even a couple relationship offers her little re-
prieve from the fear that her partner won't be willing
to come through for her. So she resorts to the fall-
apart, a display of desperation, to overcome the in-
differences she anticipated would meet a prosaic
request.

On an operative, though not a conscious level,
the fall-apart is dictated by the awareness that a display of need often has more impact than a statement
of need. Insofar as a person can formulate a logical
statement about how an experience affects him, he appears to be in control of himself. The power of the
statement, 'I'm going crazy from fear,' is eroded by
the discrepancy between its format (business as usual)
and its content (a warning of crisis). When speech
is disordered by emotion, or is superseded altogether
by action (or inaction, as in catatonia), the covert
and overt messages interlock to proclaim an emer-
gency.

But behavior like hysterical babbling, which is extremely compelling, can be so obscure that others are
baffled about how to respond to it. Or a fall-apart can
be so disturbing that others back away from the threat
it poses, shifting the burden of response to a specialist,
such as a therapist, instead of involving themselves
directly. When the fall-apart lies between the bounds
of comprehensibility and bearability, however, it has
a resonance that a statement of need cannot equal.

Even when the Fragile is a stranger, her visible suffering can arouse compassion. To see someone sitting
on a bus, shaking with sobs, is a troubling experience.
When the fall-apart occurs in the context of a personal
relationship, it's apt to be far more moving.

One basic response to the fall-apart is support. A
partner can offer warmth and tenderness, and sufficient quantities of such reassurance may calm the
Fragile down. Alternatively, a partner can address
himself to the objective problem, instead of the sub-
jective aspect of the Fragile's situation. If someone
assumes responsibility for figuring out what needs to

happen, and takes the necessary steps to make it happen, the Fragile can fall in gratefully behind his leadership. When someone begins looking after her, emotionally or practically, the Fragile responds with overwhelming gratitude and whatever degree of cooperation she can muster up. She attaches no stigma to dependence on another. To her, dependence means protection.

The Fragile needs a partner whose strength and steadiness can ease necessity's sharp pinch for her. In return, she will reward him with boundless stores of affection. The Fragile pours almost all of her capacity to love into her couple relationship. Constant, undiluted closeness is her goal; couple's privacy the only state in which she feels completely comfortable. The man she's absorbed in can be warmed by the admiration and buttressed by the devotion she gives him.

In her own meek fashion, however, the Fragile often winds up making extremely heavy demands on her partner. She's apt to ask him to meet all the needs that other people satisfy for themselves through independent activities and auxiliary relationships. The weight of her demands (for companionship, affection, and so forth) may well become burdensome to him.

Furthermore, the Fragile frequently isn't able to come through for her partner in return, at the times or in the ways that matter to him. She's likely to be reluctant to meet new people and try new things, to entertain, to find a job, to develop interests of her own. If her partner shares needs or feelings that are troubling, it's likely to trigger so much apprehension in the Fragile that she falls apart and demands that she be given to first. In effect, the Fragile asks her partner to block out his own needs to protect her. She can't grasp his limitations or the impact her behavior has on him, and there's no more reciprocity between them than there is equality.

The Fragile doesn't feel powerful, and she certainly

does not command the kind of self-discipline, assertive power that the Prizewinner wields. Through her fall-aparts, however, she often exerts a remorseless control over her partner.

The partner is liable to be threatened by the craziness or the weakness or the fearfulness the Fragile displays. Ultimately he may protect himself from jeopardy by withdrawing from her emotionally. After he's seen a succession of fall-aparts, he's liable to discount her fits of desperation. He becomes proof against her tears. Margaret's husband said, "Formerly I think I was much more intimidated by her crying. I've gotten a lot more callous about it. Now I try to ignore it. I consider it indulging her."

As the fall-apart loses credibility, it begins to feel coercive. The partner may begin to interpret the fall-apart as a threat the Fragile relies upon to evade difficulty or to get her way. The more controlled he feels by the Fragile's fall-aparts, the more he's apt to resist responding to them, and the more he resents them. As he grows obdurate, the Fragile, in turn, is likely to escalate to progressively more extreme fall-aparts and to regressively greater isolation in herself.

The Fragile's pitifulness constrains her partner from venting his frustration. His resentment at having to pick up her pieces over and over again may be translated into the conviction that she's 'not trying' to manage and that her helplessness stems from self-indulgence. Alternatively, he can begin to see her as a kind of cripple. Either way, what he can't do and can't be with her is likely to gnaw at him. And he may become convinced that the relationship 'just isn't worth' what it exacts from him.

For anyone, the experience of being left by a partner is frightening. But being abandoned fills the Fragile with terror, leaves her feeling as if she were "being stuffed farther and farther into a black, airless sack with no way out."*

In fact, the Fragile has almost always colluded in
* Sylvia Plath, *The Bell Jar*.

her own undoing. She doesn't bestir herself on her own behalf, either emotionally or practically. Instead, she hides from the tasks that need doing and the people who cross her path. Rather than deal with her fear, she flees into avoidance or dependence. The former is a patently self-destructive response to adversity, but the latter has more covertly harmful effects.

The lonely Fragile yearns to confide total trust in others. Too needy to be careful, the Fragile is apt to accept anyone who comes along on whatever terms he offers her. She's too shy to initiate relationships herself, but when someone else seems to offer her friendship or love, the Fragile lowers her guard and makes herself abruptly vulnerable to whomever she's decided to believe in. Unfortunately, she often chooses to embrace someone on the basis of how acutely she needs love at the moment, rather than on the basis of how fully that person merits her confidence. It's frequently true of Fragiles that

> As like as not, when they take life
> over their doorsills
> They should let it go by.*

Since she doesn't feel entitled to assert her wants, and is too timid to stand up for herself, the Fragile can wind up in a very bad spot if she's chosen her partner ill-advisedly.

A friend or a member of her family or a therapist can rescue the Fragile from such a predicament. But the rescues the Fragile elicits are ultimately a mixed blessing for her. A rescue can reinforce the Fragile's tendency to give up when she expects trouble or encounters trouble. A rescue allows her to rely on others to salvage the undertakings she bungles and to pluck her from the ominous situations she becomes involved in. A rescue, therefore, can function like a wheelchair; it relieves the immediate stress on her body, but in doing so, it perpetuates the flaccidity of her muscles. The passivity, the avoidance/denial and the

* Louise Bogan, "Women."

fall-aparts the Fragile engages in all intensify her sense of her own inadequacy, and it's this self-image (of her weakness and incompetence) that makes the Fragile so susceptible to fear.

The highest priority for a Fragile who wants to strengthen herself is to make the kind of solid arrangements (a good living situation, a job she can handle) that will provide her some degree of security and some experience of her own personal adequacy. Within such a structured environment, the Fragile should begin to tackle the small-scale challenges, like learning to drive, or introducing herself to her neighbors, which will make her more comfortable and more self-sufficient.

The Fragile must also begin to acquire some perspective on herself. She must discover that she possesses resources as well as shortcomings, and that she's prone to excessive trustfulness as well as excessive fearfulness. She must realize that she doesn't have to collapse when the going gets tough and that she's capable of struggle as well as surrender.

At bottom, the crucial matter for the Fragile is the recognition that she can look to others as allies, but not as proxies, in the process of living that

> *is* in fact, a battle. Evil is insolent and strong; Beauty enchanting but rare; Goodness very apt to be weak; Folly very apt to be defiant; Wickedness to carry the day; Imbeciles to be in great places, people of sense in small, and mankind generally unhappy. But the world as it stands is no illusion, no phantasm, no evil dream of a night; we wake up to it again forever and ever; we can neither forget it nor deny it nor dispense with it.*

* Henry James, quoted in A. Alvarez, *The Savage God*.

CHAPTER 7

The Pleaser

THE PLEASER is the world's nice guy: caring, responsive, involved. He'll get up at four in the morning to come pick you up at the airport so you can save thirty dollars by taking the night flight, and he will say he was glad to do it. And he'll surprise you with a bicycle, even though the budget's tight and it means giving up poker. The impulse to help out, to give pleasure, is genuine and solid. The Pleaser wants the folks he cares about to have whatever he can give them, or do for them.

If people get what they want from the world by making others happy, we call them Pleasers. The Pleaser is primarily a male role, which departs conspicuously from the other two major roles that our society posits for men: the Provider and the Prizewinner. Unlike both of these, the Pleaser is involved with feelings. He engages emotionally with his partner far more than either the Provider or the Prizewinner does. He tunes in to her with a sensitivity that is foreign to them. Her happiness is the object of much of his effort.

Pleasers appear in two distinctly different guises, depending upon their relative self-confidence. The Self-Assured Pleaser feels truly capable and thinks he knows what to do for almost any problem; the

Anxious Pleaser tries to make his partner happy but is beset with worries and looks to her to tell him what to do. The two Pleasers have a very different impact on the world as well as on their partners, but it would be misleading to see them as two different species in the taxonomy of ways to relate. Actually, it is the same creature in different environments: one in which he's accepted and feels that what he is doing is right, and one where he's rejected and feels like he is not succeeding. The Self-Assured Pleaser, because of his confidence, is likely to relate to many more people and their problems than does the Anxious Pleaser, who is likely to be obsessed with somehow satisfying whoever is rejecting him.

The Self-Assured Pleaser

"He will really go out of his way for people. It's tremendously important for him to be a good person," a woman said of the Self-Assured Pleaser to whom she was married. He said, "Giving people a hand when they're in a bad way, it's kind of central to what I do. The process normally makes me very happy. I see myself as somebody after whom the other person feels better, their life flows a little more smoothly."

The Self-Assured Pleaser counts himself among the lucky ones; recognizing his own strength and resilience, he feels an obligation to use his power on behalf of those who are weak or needy. Often, he notices the subtle as well as the obvious clues that someone else is in trouble. The Prizewinner is generally too preoccupied with his own doing to lend an ear or hand to a person who's having a hard time of it. The Provider doesn't usually register the manifestations of need which people allow to escape them. But the Self-Assured Pleaser is both sensitive of, and responsive to, others' needs. Like a volunteer lifeguard he keeps a watchful eye on the heads in the water, and he may be the first or the only one to realize

I was much further out than you thought
and not waving but drowning . . .[*]

After he'd spent all Sunday afternoon helping some friends get their car to run, Andrew said, "I like to do things like that. There's lots of ego gratification in being able to introduce yourself into situations, help people out, make a positive contribution . . ." His generosity provides the Self-Assured Pleaser with ample altruistic satisfaction. Furthermore, a rescue affords him a kind of adventure—a chance to play the Lone Ranger, befriending the needy and protecting the besieged from the forces of wickedness or indifference. And like the Lone Ranger, he prefers to disappear without a thank-you. These sorties allow the Pleaser to experience himself as both powerful and pure.

His contribution is apt to win him others' admiration as well as their gratitude. Will's wife, Amy, said, "There are people who think he's wonderful—godlike. The people he works with, most of our friends . . . his faults are so minor and his good qualities are so overwhelming." His good disposition, his generosity, and so forth, establish the Pleaser as one of those who've got 'miles and miles of heart.'

He's also usually got a lot of ambition. He's apt to be keenly competitive and eager for the rewards success will yield. He tends to believe, "All ambitions are lawful except those which climb upward on the miseries or the credulities of mankind."[†] There are crucial limitations, however, and these scruples serve to differentiate the Self-Assured Pleaser and the Prizewinner. While the Prizewinner's desire for power is straightforward and unconflicted, the Self-Assured Pleaser must reconcile his ambition with his need to believe that he's a virtuous individual.

Characteristically, the Self-Assured Pleaser believes that his good deeds establish that he is a good person in whom power can be vested safely. Furthermore, he believes that his conduct establishes his right to the

[*] Stevie Smith, "Not Waving but Drowning."

[†] Joseph Conrad, *A Personal Record.*

prerequisites of success, but in order to keep ambition from leading him off the track, the Self-Assured Pleaser vocally espouses some set of moral principles.

His oft-proclaimed devotion to good may succeed in convincing others that he is, in fact, equipped with particular virtue. The Self-Assured Pleaser is prone to smugness, to adding up his plusses without reference to his minuses, one of the latter being his propensity for self-congratulation.

The Pleaser doesn't always get as much appreciation from the outside world as he feels he deserves. His rescues, for example, may not elicit cooperation on the spot and gratitude after the fact. After he graduated from law school, Will clerked for a prominent judge who possessed much common sense but little intellectual acumen. When the judge was asked to give the keynote address at an annual law school benefit, he turned to Will at the last minute to ask if the young man could rescue him from his predicament. Will proceeded to draft, and then to write, a brilliant speech with virtually no assistance from the judge, but contrary to custom the judge did not acknowledge his clerk's contribution or thank him for it. He read the speech at the banquet and published it in a legal journal, naming himself sole author to the embellishment of his reputation. Will was surprised and disappointed, but he said nothing.

A rescuer defines the problem he intervenes to relieve, decides what action should be taken, and oversees its progress. Frequently the recipient of the rescue feels a bit ashamed that he's been forced to call for help and he resents the subordinate status the rescue reduces him to. Deprived of the initiative, the recipient may assert his autonomy by withholding cooperation from the Self-Assured Pleaser and finding fault with his suggestions. To avoid feeling reduced to a cipher, the recipient converts himself into an obstruction countering each proposal with "yes, but" objections. This process can escalate into outright attacks on the Self-Assured Pleaser's motives and his competence.

The same antagonism can result if the Self-Assured Pleaser undertakes to rescue someone who only wants to be listened to and sympathized with. When he wants to help somebody, the Self-Assured Pleaser's tendency is to offer direction rather than the simple positive regard the Disarmer provides. He has trouble not taking charge of situations once he's become involved in them.

His confident assumption that he knows what's best for everybody may lead the Self-Assured Pleaser to make inappropriate choices on others' behalf. He often doesn't consult the wishes of the person he's ostensibly trying to please, and he may actually be deaf to suggestions from her about what would be suitable. For example, Richard had tried to persuade his wife to buy a fur coat for several years. After a particularly miserable fight, he decided to make up by buying her a fur coat himself as an expression of love. Sandy was not mollified. "I would have preferred to have some say in how that much money was going to be spent," she said bitterly.

The Self-Assured Pleaser doesn't accept the legitimacy of conflict between himself and his partner and he needs to believe that his actions are always unselfish. Uneasy with a want of his own that's nakedly selfish, he is apt to drape a few pleasing fig leaves around it to give it a more acceptable aspect. For example, when a Self-Assured Pleaser wanted to attend a professional convention, he suggested to his wife that they take their vacation in the city in which the convention was to be held at the precise time the conference was scheduled, without explaining why these particulars suggested themselves. The Self-Assured Pleaser tries to arrange for the outcome he wants by means that will persuade both his partner and himself that he's got her well-being firmly in mind. If she glimpses the self-interest crouching be-

hind what's theoretically concern for her, she's liable
to feel tricked.

The Self-Assured Pleaser is too susceptible to feeling guilty to give his partner a straight "no" in reply
to a request she makes. Instead, he tries to persuade
her that she doesn't really want what she's asked for,
and if that fails, he's liable to escalate to the argument
that it wouldn't be *good* for her to have it. He assumes
that he's entitled to decide what's in her best interests
and that if their judgments conflict, his is more valid
than hers.

The Self-Assured Pleaser 'avoids anything negative.'
He doesn't complain about his problems in general
and he doesn't complain about the problems she causes
him in particular. He is certain to believe that he
spares his partner his gripes and his demands out of
loving-kindness. In fact, he's also actuated by his own
motives—his desire to avoid appearing difficult or
feeling needy.

His self-esteem is based in part on his ability to
withstand stress. Will said, "I couldn't accept myself
failing, blowing it." And the Self-Assured Pleaser
learns to keep himself "aloof in a certain fashion"
from feelings that would threaten his equilibrium.
Richard commented, "I like ecstasy—the upbeat trips
—but I don't like sadness, thank you. I don't like
pain. I don't want that from me. I'll avoid them if
necessary." By blocking out feelings like anxiety or
loneliness or jealousy, the Pleaser spares himself pain
and safeguards his standing as one who gives comfort
rather than one who needs to be comforted.

The favorable balance of payments he maintains
may put his partner at a disadvantage. Amy declared,
"You put yourself in a spot where you don't owe anybody anything. That's not fair." In the back of his
mind, the Pleaser keeps a running tally of the good
deeds he's done. As he's dispensing favors, on some
level he's accumulating chips he can call in when he
wants something for himself. On the occasions when
he really does want his way, the Self-Assured Pleaser

feels that decency obliges his partner to yield to his request. Should she balk, he can summon up a powerful store of self-righteousness to prod her. "After all I've done for you . . ."

He may be able to control her through guilt, but she's likely to resent the retroactive tab she's been handed. To phrase a request as something he 'deserves' and she 'ought' to furnish is a form of manipulation. Over time the partner usually concludes that she would be happier if their relationship allowed her the freedom "to give without being coerced, to receive without being obligated."

The Self-Assured Pleaser has difficulty being on the receiving end of generosity and his *modus operandi* hinders his partner from giving him much. Amy said, "His whole number is he doesn't need anything, he's real strong." Furthermore, "A lot of time I don't even know what he feels like. It seems like either he does something to be accommodating to other people or because he feels it's what he should do . . . I can't pick up any signals as to where he's really at."

Furthermore, the Self-Assured Pleaser often isn't around enough for his partner to have much of a chance to give to him. As Stage II sets in, he's likely to become increasingly unavailable to her. Richard said, "I do put myself in a place at work where I'm indispensable and I'm there to deal with all kinds of emergencies. It's hard for me to say, 'No, that's not my job.'"

Other involvements crowd his schedule further. Amy told Will, "It threatens me when you're getting off on some project, when I see your energy totally taken up—when you don't have any time for me . . ." Like the Prizewinner, the Self-Assured Pleaser may keep his partner on sparse rations of attention.

The Self-Assured Pleaser tends to run on the "squeaky wheel" principle responding to the appeal that's loudest, the plight that seems the most serious. Since other people's crises are apt to be more dire than his partner's simple wish for companionship, he usually feels, as Amy said, "that somehow I should cope with the fact that he's gone so much. Sometimes I need him as much as those other people do."

Repeatedly, his partner finds herself shunted aside or forgotten, humiliations which he fails to apologize for because he's too busy to notice them. One Self-Assured Pleaser said, as he arrived two hours behind schedule, "I'm not late . . . I was busy . . ."

The Pleaser does possess a buoyance that more people than just his partner might covet. His imperturbability also reflects well on him. It may gall his partner, however. In *Anna Karenina,* Dolly Oblonsky thought of her husband, "Yes . . . He's happy and contented. But what about me? And that loathesome good nature of his, which people love so much, and for which they praise him. I hate it."*

Remembering a banquet where her husband was seated at the head table and she was relegated to the rear of the room, not for the first time, Sandy said, "I sat there thinking, 'Why do I feel so crummy?' I said to myself, 'I feel left out.' Like he forgot I was there completely until he came to find me at twelve-thirty to announce that he'd invited ten people back to the house. It's always been the pattern. I have to go seek him. 'Hey, remember me?' "

In an angrier vein, Amy charged, "I have to plead to get time together with Will. We never spend an evening together spontaneously. It's always got to be planned in advance. Half the time it falls through and I feel like I'm always fighting for it. I'm tired of begging him to spend time with me and begging him to love me." The Self-Assured Pleaser is likely to get tired of it as well. Will said, "Whenever I do anything I want to or think I ought to do, if it subtracts from my time with Amy, then there's hell to pay."

Feeling stinted herself, the Pleaser's partner is likely to become jealous of the people and the pursuits that rank higher in his priorities. She's liable to become envious as well. Amy said resentfully, "Everybody,

* Leo Tolstoi, *Anna Karenina.*

down to the corner grocery lady, tells me how lucky I am to have him. He seems to have it all together. I don't seem to have anything together. I'm mad at him in the sense that he's so self-satisfied, so self-contained."

"He never deigns to have a negative emotion," Sandy said. The Pleaser encourages his partner to share her troubles, but he never mentions his own. She allows unflattering feelings like fear and anger to overwhelm her, but his composure is never cracked; his vulnerability is never disclosed. She may feel that he distances her by suppressing all evidence of his woes, or he may begin to seem unwilling to admit that he's a real person with a real person's troubles and to cultivate instead the image of a paragon. The result is diminished intimacy.

The Pleaser's way of operating makes his couple relationship a subtly but profoundly unequal relationship. He's careful to give more than he takes, and he always imputes the most favorable motives to his actions. This pattern reinforces the Self-Assured Pleaser's belief that he's the stronger, the healthier, and the more admirable of the pair, and it exacerbates whatever insecurities trouble his partner.

Whether it's manifested in the form of hurt or anger, her discomfort with such a relationship is likely to provoke scenes at some point. Tears or accusations immediately engage the Self-Assured Pleaser's attention. She becomes the focus of his concern, concern that is, in part, genuinely empathetic. "I want her to be happy. I love her. I really care about her," Will said.

The Self-Assured Pleaser feels responsible for ensuring his partner's happiness as well as her safety, and he construes her unhappiness as an accusation that he's failed her. His reaction is to assert his innocence; in other words, his good intentions. Some misunderstanding has occurred and a clarification of what he really meant will clear the air. If his partner isn't satisfied, he escalates to self-righteous blame.

The Self-Assured Pleaser can't acknowledge that either his motives or his efficacy might not have been up to snuff, so if a transaction with his partner hasn't worked out well, he assigns the blame to her. Her conduct is responsible for whatever problems arose; the trouble could have been averted if she had acted differently. Amy said, "He always tells me that it's the way I approach him, that I don't ask the right way." She didn't ask the right way or she didn't ask soon enough or she didn't specify what she really wanted or she didn't allow him to help her.

When "some limit of negative vibration" is reached, the Pleaser's distress is likely to fuse into the feeling that he's being treated unfairly. Richard said, "I begin to feel very abused by her and very taken advantage of." Anxiety makes the Self-Assured Pleaser defensive, and he begins to proclaim, "I was so good to you," and starts rattling off the various forms and guises of his goodness over the course of the relationship. Under attack he becomes "very lofty and pious. You get into one of your self-loving little numbers, 'I'm so good.' It infuriates me," Sandy said.

Regardless of what condition he's in, the Self-Assured Pleaser feels an obligation to come through for others. He can't set the limits that would keep the commitments and his resources comfortably balanced. He can't acknowledge when stress in his own life makes a breather necessary. Consequently, he's likely to get overextended. Too many people learn to turn to him or a few begin to rely on him too heavily, and these obligations begin to weigh on him.

He doesn't consciously experience anxiety or resentment on this score, however. Instead, his discomfort is translated into the sense that others are taking advantage of him. He's doing more than could be expected, more than anyone else would do, and others are not doing their share. Blame discharges some of his resentment and relieves the Self-Assured Pleaser of some of the guilt it causes him to say "No."

The resentment that remains suppressed may lead the Self-Assured Pleaser to distance his partner. Characteristically, when the Provider is resentful he withdraws from his partner, cutting himself off from her by reading the newspaper or puttering out in the garage. When the Self-Assured Pleaser is resentful, he speeds up. He doesn't experience his hectic schedule as revenge against his partner, but she's liable to suspect there's an element of hostility behind "the days of tremendous distance." As Sandy said, "I know if somebody else came by to have a drink, Richard would have time, but he's too busy to talk to me."

The Self-Assured Pleaser needs to realize that his responsiveness to others may lead to neglect of his partner. He needs to realize that he's responsible for overestimating his capacities and agreeing to be in too many places at once. He needs to learn to say "No" straightforwardly and to accept the legitimacy of taking care of himself. D. H. Lawrence wrote, "The real way of living is to answer to one's wants, not 'I want to light up with my intelligence as many things as possible,' but 'I want that pound of peaches' . . . 'I want to kiss that girl' . . . 'I want to insult that man.' "*

To be forthright about his desires and to acknowledge his vulnerability will help the Self-Assured Pleaser to create a couple relationship that is more intimate, more equal, and thus more satisfying.

The Anxious Pleaser

Rejection may lead anyone, including the Self-Assured Pleaser, to adopt the strategy of an Anxious Pleaser. The Anxious Pleaser, who wants only to make

* D. H. Lawrence, quoted in W. D. Snodgrass, *In Radical Pursuit.*

his partner happy, frequently makes her cranky and guilty instead; longing to be embraced, he provokes rejection. The Anxious Pleaser is prone to espy rejection in any lack of enthusiasm he encounters.

His sense of his own vulnerability makes him a conciliator, a propitiator. "His impulse is always to be endearing. He wants no enemies, dislikes disagreements, and does not enjoy competition."† Tim said, "It seems like I'm always knocking myself out to keep everybody happy, so everybody likes me."

To win acceptance, the Anxious Pleaser tries to make himself useful and tries to make himself inoffensive. He always takes the most uncomfortable chair and he volunteers for grubby jobs that others are eager to avoid. He's reluctant to assume responsibility for fear that he might fumble it, but when he does he is loyal and diligent.

The Anxious Pleaser is attuned to any evidence of others' displeasure, any hint that he's done the wrong thing. His insecurity leads him to construe suggestions, even neutral information from others, as an adverse judgment on his performance, and criticism can throw him into a panic of self-recrimination.

The Anxious Pleaser converts anxiety into guilt. When his actions don't succeed he immediately assumes that he's at fault. Joshua said, "When she criticizes me, I always believe there's some truth in what she's saying and the some truth makes me feel bad. I always have the feeling—'God, I'm inconsiderate to have done that.' "

The Anxious Pleaser needs a prodigious amount of attention and approval from his partner in order to feel good about himself. He needs to know that she is contented, and then he is secure. He gets worried when he can see that she is clouded in, and characteristically he translates his apprehension into self-reproach.

The Anxious Pleaser personalizes his partner's moods. When she seems ill-humored, he queries, "Are

† Joseph Heller, *Something Happened.*

you mad at me? Are you sure you're not mad at me? You sure look like you are . . . Well, if you're not mad, how come you're just sitting there and not saying anything?" His partner may crossly deny that anything is amiss, in which case the Anxious Pleaser persists. Eli said to Louise, "I've been consistently picking up vibes that you were distressed, so I've asked you a bunch of times 'Is anything wrong?' And you keep saying 'No,' so I go through doubting. Is it my imagination or what? What's happening?"

Often, his partner isn't quite sure. If other aspects of her life have made her anxious or touchy, she rarely has the perspective to say 'It's just me. Don't let it bother you.' She's more likely to flare up at him and feel that he's to blame for provoking her. For his part, the Anxious Pleaser rarely has the good sense to realize that he doesn't cause all his partner's difficulties and he can't resolve all of them either.

Instead of leaving her alone, the Anxious Pleaser persists in his efforts to restore his partner's spirit and reassure himself that things are all right. Such behavior often makes people feel fussed over or 'pawed at.' Valerie said of her husband's anxious-pleasing, "If I'm on a bummer, which is not a rare thing, I can't stand to have people bother me; and he'll come over and I know he's trying to be really understanding and all, but he'll come over and he'll put his arms around me and I'll feel really lousy because I don't feel I can reciprocate that affection and then I get irritable and I'll push him off—either physically, or you know, there's lots of little devices for doing that kind of thing. 'Gee, I've gotta get a drink or go outside.' Something like that. And then I feel really awful. But if I tell him he's bugging me, he gets upset."

The Anxious Pleaser wants to make things better for his partner. He also wants to make them better for himself. He wants to be forgiven if he's done something wrong or reassured if it's not his fault. But his anxiety is likely to make his partner uncomfortable. His eagerness to please registers as the covert demand for re-assurance it is.

To the person who's on the other end of it, the Anxious Pleaser's giving often feels coercive because it entails an obligation to respond with approval and affection. The degree of intimacy that feels cozy to the Anxious Pleaser may make his partner feel "I am really being smothered." As Valerie said, "Sometimes I think all I want is a space." But if she pushes him away to get breathing room, he's sure to be troubled. Tim described one evening when Valerie "was sitting on the sofa and I went over and sat by her. She said, 'Don't sit so close.' Now I can move away someplace else, but it makes me feel bad. A time here and again, that's fine. But when it gets to be habitual, it really gets me down."

When the Anxious Pleaser encounters rejection, he tries to explain it away. 'She didn't mean it. She's just tired. She's had a hard day.' He refuses to recognize hostile intent, forgiving her as readily as he'd like to be forgiven himself while struggling to conceal the distress she's caused him. But the Anxious Pleaser is too thin-skinned to be able to hide his emotions. He wears his vulnerability on his sleeve and his partner is likely to feel guilty about the unhappiness she so clearly caused him. This failure of imperturbability differentiates the Anxious Pleaser sharply from the stalwart Provider, the Prizewinner, and the Self-Assured Pleaser.

The Anxious Pleaser's besetting weakness is fear of his own failure. His couple partner is apt to be particularly threatened by the fact that he can't simply say, "I'll handle that," and dispose adroitly of whatever difficulties they both encounter. Performance pressure rattles the Anxious Pleaser and under stress he's liable to falter. His inability to take care of himself, and of her, is likely to trouble his partner seriously.

The Anxious Pleaser is prone to hang back uncertainly. He would rather accommodate than commandeer, but since his partner isn't likely to volunteer what she wants at every turn of the road, the Anxious Pleaser usually has to solicit her opinion, in order to be guided by it. So he asks, "Do you want me to turn off the TV?" "What do you want to do tonight?"

The Anxious Pleaser is not just asking his partner to register her preference, he's asking her to make the decision for both of them. His anxious-pleasing isn't just intended to ensure that his partner gets what she wants; it's designed to buffer himself against the risks of assertion. The Anxious Pleaser is dependent on his partner for direction—what to do and how to do it, and for approval if he manages to do it. This arrangement is not likely to agree with her. A relationship with an Anxious Pleaser thrusts an unwelcome responsibility on a woman who would prefer to be taken care of. Her resentment at being forced to be the stronger of the two of them can make her short with him as he tries to pry answers out of her—'What shall I do?' She's apt to snap back, 'I don't care what you do.'

Tim said, "I feel very jeopardized by her anger. I have the feeling that her affection for me is so fragile that if I do the wrong thing I'll be out in the cold." The Anxious Pleaser's insecurities about his own worth translate directly into insecurity about the relationship. Eli said, "I've always been terribly threatened that Louise was going to leave me. Whenever I talk to her I'm always filtering what I have to say. I'm always there mentally juggling 'How is this going to affect her?' 'Is that going to put me in the dog house?' "

Usually, whatever the Anxious Pleaser does puts him in the doghouse because all that would really satisfy his partner is for him to become the kind of effective man he feels unable to be.

The Anxious Pleaser is usually unwilling to add to his partner's standing resentment the additional resentment that he believes conflict would create. He won't struggle with his partner because he's afraid to antagonize her. Eli, for example, had a child by his first wife whom his second wife, Louise, wasn't fond of. Louise didn't enjoy being present when Eli visited his daughter, but she felt left out if he went by himself to spend the day with her. Despite his fondness for his child, Eli gradually surrendered to his wife's jealousy. He spent less and less time with his daughter and he admitted, "I evade a kind of show-down conflict. I don't say 'I'm going to do this whether you like it or not.' I think that will make the situation even worse between us. I generally avoid conflict. I'm afraid of some kind of lasting disapproval or rupture."

The Anxious Pleaser will tolerate endless frustration and subject himself to immeasurable pain rather than draw the line and say, "Enough." Tim said, "I felt put upon by Val's demands but I didn't tell her. She's even asked me directly and I've said, 'No, nothing's bothering me.'" Such experiences, which the Anxious Pleaser is too timid or too naïve to call to a halt, are not only dolorous. They are invidious. Someone who repeatedly allows himself to be taken advantage of eventually begins to believe that he deserves nothing better.

Point-blank, or in a variety of ways, the partner is likely to express her disappointment that the Anxious Pleaser doesn't have more gumption. He hears the "be strong" message from her as an echo of her dissatisfaction with him and her discontent with the relationship. So ironically, it whittles away at his self-esteem and his security and increases the vehemence of his anxious-pleasing. He's liable to pressure her, apologizing for his shortcomings and asking for directions on how to win her approval, paradoxically perpetuating the abject behavior that alienated her to begin with.

In fact, when behavior is chronic, apologies for that behavior are meaningless. Furthermore, they're irritating because they constitute a demand for forgiveness. If his partner is provoked, she's likely to want a chance to vent her anger. The Anxious Pleaser's hasty apologies foreclose that possibility. The partner can't derive much satisfaction from denouncing him when he's denouncing himself even more severely and his collapse into pitifulness requires her to show mercy. So, she's left frustrated, stewing in resentment she can't decently discharge. The Anxious Pleaser's apologies and his visible suffering are partly sincere, but partly they're strategic; they're intended to protect him from others' hostility by portraying him as someone who shouldn't be picked on.

The Anxious Pleaser doesn't intend to manipulate his partner through guilt as we'll discover the Victim doing. The Anxious Pleaser induces guilt in his partner inadvertently, but induce it he does and control her by means of it he also does.

This guilt is apt to make her mean. Often, her response is to resent him and to reject him, discounting the merits he does possess for lack of that magic element—self-confidence.

The Anxious Pleaser must stop hoping he can win enough approval from his partner to compensate for his own lack of self-confidence. He must begin to say "I want . . ." instead of relying exclusively on "Do you want . . . ?" As he begins to accept the legitimacy of his desires and the responsibility for seeing that they're fulfilled, the Anxious Pleaser begins to develop some autonomy. It's only when he does so, when he "learns at last" the soul is

> self-delighting,
> self-appeasing, self-affrighting*

that he can begin to feel at ease with himself and secure in relation to the partner he loves.

* William Butler Yeats, "A Prayer for My Daughter."

CHAPTER 8

The Victim

THE SUFFERING OF A VICTIM, however authentic it may be, however real it may seem, is nevertheless a statement of retribution and reproach. It is a statement to whomever the Victim identifies as the *cause*. The dramatization of his own pain is the Victim's method of reproach, a method which may go dangerously, dramatically far.

With a three-day weekend coming up, one woman tried to persuade her husband to stay home with her instead of going hunting with friends. His response to her pleading was to ask her politely to come along with him if she wanted. She replied, "You know I hate hunting. You just ignore me." He then told her that no matter how she begged he was still going to go, and he left.

He returned Sunday night to find that his wife had overdosed on drugs Sunday morning, had been discovered by a neighbor, and was in the hospital. Her suicide attempt blamed him implicitly and her explanation of it—"I just couldn't stand your leaving me after I told you how much I needed you"—impugned him explicitly. In her mind, the only way out of the deadlock of feeling totally dependent on her husband yet abandoned by him was to turn herself into a literal casualty.

Sam had a job that he truly hated. It was the kind of sales job that paid well enough, but involved always having to wait for an opportunity to squeeze in a few seconds of sales pitch, and he frequently got the brush-off. Sam used to say that he would rather give enemas for a living than have this sales job. His Disarmer wife, Judy, was devoted to him and felt terrible that he was unhappy. At first she supported his hanging in there to get promoted. He didn't get promoted. Instead, he just got more money. The raises made it even harder for him to quit. Finally Sam agreed to Judy's suggestion that he start looking for more compatible work during his lunch hours. But he was so depressed by being unable to get a promotion that he decided to quit his job. Judy then went looking for work as a secretary, and luckily stumbled into an executive-training program for women in a large corporation. Things went exceedingly well for her and in a few short months she received a number of promotions. Sam became more and more depressed. To every suggestion of Judy's, he would counter with a "Yes, but . . ." His despondency grew as he failed to find work, and as Judy received more promotions. He became increasingly difficult to be around and began picking at his wife about trivial or nonexistent slights.

Nearly everyone, at one time or another, feels himself a Victim. He feels wretched and beleaguered, powerless to alter the circumstances that beset him. He sees someone or some thing as having brought him to this pass and as blocking his exit from it. The only power to relieve this plight seems to be located where the Victim locates the cause of his troubles: outside of himself.

There are, of course, both victims of circumstances, and self-made Victims. Victims of circumstances are people whose trouble is not of their own making—for example, the farmer who watches helplessly as his crop withers in a drought. But the self-made Victim isn't truly helpless. He has contributed significantly to his own difficulties although he usually neither recognizes nor acknowledges his responsibility. Yet while he might extricate himself from his predicament or mitigate it, he does not, because his attitudes and perceptions rule out this possibility.

Men are more frequently Victims in relation to their jobs while women are more frequently Victims at home in relation to their partners. In a couple relationship, the Victim is her own worst enemy. The essence of the Victim role involves using one's misery (consciously or not) to control and influence others.

The Victim is miserable partly because she is a prisoner of great expectations. She judges herself by the most exacting standards of emotional adequacy and professional accomplishment. She can never quite outdistance the fear that 'I'm a complete failure in every way.'

The Victim's low self-esteem may seem paradoxical, because her resources may be considerable. She focuses on what she lacks. Despite her considerable talents, Maggie, a female Victim, said, "I don't feel like I have anything to rely on in myself, that I'll ever have anything to give except superficially. I don't have any vitality, any strength, and I don't feel like that will ever change."

The Victim envisions the outside world as echoing the negative verdict she has reached about herself. Stephanie said, "I feel like people are always judging me, that I'm always competing and always losing."

The Victim is sensitive to the nuances of status and traumatized by competition. She discounts success and is devastated by defeat. If, for example, a Victim believes that she's the most notable guest at a party, she writes it off because nobody else worthwhile is there. If, on the other hand, she's a relative unknown among an illustrious company she feels crushed by her anonymity. The female Victim's perception of herself as an undesirable creature creates its own momentum. For example, a single woman in her early thirties feels rejected because former friends no longer call her or come to visit. She has, in fact, been dropped by a number of acquaintances because they found her friendship burdensome. She deluged anyone she considered a friend with invitations and allowed a refusal to visibly traumatize her. Since her conversation leaned to lengthy itemizations of all the slights she suffered, she made a taxing companion. When her friendships collapsed under this strain, she had more hard luck stories to tell.

The Victim is apt to become wary of people in general and to take refuge in quixotic idealism about intimate relationships. She considers that "one human being *entirely* loving me would not only have satisfied all my hopes but would have rendered me happy and grateful even though I had no friend on earth, herself excepted."*

The Victim anticipates that a partner will take care of her and make her feel good about herself, bringing out all that's finest in her and accepting her feelings tenderly. Each new infatuation bids fair to fulfill these hopes. The intense mutual involvement and mutual appreciation of Stage I exhilarates the Victim. Stephanie said, "What was so attractive about Don in the beginning was that he seemed so strong, so together. That seemed very impressive. Like he really knew where he was going and what he was doing and could take care of everything that came along." With her optimism up and her energy engaged, the Victim appears to best advantage as well. Don said of Stephanie five years after they'd met, "She seemed warm and accepting at first and I could talk to her. She opened up a whole world of feelings to me and she gave me a lot of insight into myself."

The advent of Stage II creates difficulties in every relationship. The Victim, however, is particularly hard hit by the evaporation of Stage I and especially ill-equipped to cope with the exigencies of Stage II. Other aspects of her partner's life bid for attention and the focus is no longer solely on her. She's likely to

* Samuel Taylor Coleridge, quoted in Frederick L. Beaty, *Light from Heaven*.

feel threatened by, and compete for, the energy her partner gives to his job or to other relationships.

The Victim feels that she needs to be taken care of. When her partner doesn't minister to her in the solicitous fashion she feels she requires, she uses her own misery as a retaliatory weapon.

Her partner's momentary desertion (or so she perceives it) has symbolic as well as practical significance to the Victim. She feels that love should entail complete attention and responsiveness to her own well-being. When her partner allows her to go wanting, the Victim construes this as proof that she is not loved. She can't accept her partner's love as a given; it's up for grabs at each new turn of events. 'Does he care about me? Will he be there for me?' She empowers her partner with the capacity to make her happy and each time she perceives his failure to do so, it triggers her fear that no one, no one would 'go the distance' for her. Once the Victim's fear is activated she becomes ever more wary, ever more focused on exactly how much her partner does and mostly doesn't do for her. This vigilance is defensive, designed to protect her from being caught off guard.

Her partner, feeling bad about her misery, responds by apologizing and trying to make amends. The Victim, instead of accepting reassurance as Fragiles do, feels her original complaint is validated by her partner's confession. She begins to see his apology as mere appeasement—it doesn't bespeak a real assumption of responsibility for her condition or represent sincere repentance of his misdeed. So she continues to hold her grudge.

Ed complained of Ruthie, "I bark at you. You're cool about it, but then an hour later I feel good about you and I go to hug you and I look at your eyes and there's the reflection back to an hour ago when I hollered at you. And I say, 'Why do you harbor these things? Okay. It's good now. Let's enjoy it. Why do you bring me back to yesterday, or whenever?' You kind of bring it up and you want to talk about it.

You want an apology, and more apologies . . ." In reality, apologies won't do. The Victim feels too resentful to make up. If they feel they've been unjustly criticized, some Victims will go to extraordinary lengths to get even. For example, Sharon decided to quit the secretarial work she hated and get a teaching credential instead. So she began to take courses at a nearby junior college. In the midst of a fight several months later, her husband told her that she wasn't paying her way and that she ought to earn some money. He regretted his statement almost immediately and apologized for being nasty. Sharon proceeded to quit school the next day, however, and sank into a grim depression.

Her husband tried to persuade her not to quit. She ignored him. He urged her to talk to her professors and at least to continue the French class she'd begun. Sharon refused. He suggested that she could enroll in another nearby junior college which was on a quarter rather than a trimester system, so she wouldn't lose so much time. To no avail. Sharon responded, "I don't think you're aware of how you injured me last week." When asked why she had to quit, she replied, "I was accused that I'm lazy. I can't remember when I felt so hurt."

Her suffering was clearly designed to punish her husband, and it did succeed. However, Sharon's recalcitrance cost her far more than it cost her husband. She wept, "I want to be somebody. I don't want to be just a secretary . . . Now I'll have to eat crow." She was sure she'd be humiliated in front of her friends after boasting about the step up in the world she was going to take. Having cut off her nose to spite her face, the Victim then laments her disfigurement.

Anxiety keeps the Victim from enjoying even the good times that come her way. If she isn't worried about her partner failing her, then she's worried about external circumstances undoing her happiness. Ruthie said, "When I really well up with a lot of feeling for Ed, I get afraid that something terrible's going to happen to him. I'm aware that it's very hard for me to let myself completely feel something good, hopeful. I draw back from it. It must frighten me. It puts me too out in the open and too vulnerable. I don't have very much faith in the future."

For the Victim, happiness is risky because it means lowering her guard. Her chronic misery is like a tattered pair of overalls. She feels at home in them. Garbed in these overalls, she doesn't have to worry about spilling on them or wrinkling them. The Victim would rather be spared the apprehension of wondering when she's going to ruin her best clothes, than savor the pleasure of being all dressed up.

A veteran at dealing with misfortune, the Victim concentrates on that instead. Sharon said, "I focus in on a problem. My theory is you get the problems out of the way, and then you can enjoy the pleasure. But when I get the problem out of the way, then I look for more problems."

The Victim is trapped in the internal contradictions of her stance. She looks to her partner for approval, to enable her to feel good about herself even as she blames her partner for making her feel bad. By focusing her energy on the input of her partner and ascribing her reverses to deficiencies in that input, the Victim keeps herself stuck. She stays locked in the system, not changing because she sees the locus of difficulty as external, not internal.

Blame provides the Victim with an explanation, albeit a specious one, of what has happened. 'I am unhappy because you are inconsiderate of me.' The Victim faults her partner for what has gone wrong, thereby absolving herself of responsibility. She does not feel able or obligated to act on her own behalf. She does not hold herself responsible for having permitted, contributed to, or having caused the contretemps that upset her. She assigns all guilt to her partner. Helpless and hapless she may be, but accountable she is not.

Not only does the Victim deny her own contribution

to her unhappiness, she often waits until it is too late to tell her partner what he's doing wrong. The Victim usually indicates dissatisfaction retroactively. When Sharon wails to Martin when they get home, "You left me all alone at the party," her blame makes an ex post facto request: "I wanted you to stick with me at the party."

The least obvious benefit that flows from blame is the reaffirmation of the relationship between the partners. Every blame is a statement of some form of need. Reproach particularly stresses the Victim's dependence on her partner and her vulnerability to him. The Victim's blame, therefore, simultaneously exerts power over her partner and bears witness to his power over her. It creates a highly emotional interaction that can knit the partners more closely into a network of expectations.

Yet the Victim's tenuous equilibrium endangers her alliance with her partner. Easily thrown off balance, she is too quick to accuse her partner of shaking the tightrope, instead of acknowledging the deficiencies of her own inner ear.

Sharon sighed, "I feel pretty depressed a lot of the time without being able to trace it to anything particular in the environment." Her dejection leeches out the energy that it would take for the Victim to break out of the miasma that envelops her. Sharon said, "I feel trapped. I can't seem to get myself out of this bad thing, and I just see it getting worse. There's something that prevents me from taking care of myself, especially when I feel bad. I sort of let my life take over rather than try to engineer a way out." The passivity masks unexpressed anger. Nothing seems enjoyable. Nothing arouses her interest. Nothing turns her on.

The standard sympathetic response to someone else's depression is, 'Cheer up!' This advice has the paradoxical effect of making the Victim feel worse. 'Look on the bright side' has the same unfortunate consequence of bringing to the Victim's mind other reasons why her depression is inescapable. Trying to look on the bright side just makes it worse for both of them.

When the female Victim asks, for example, 'Am I ugly?' her partner feels forced to say, 'No.' But she remains suspicious. 'Whatever I ask, you'll give me a positive response because you want to make me feel better'; the partner simply cannot respond in a winning fashion. Similarly, when a person responds to the Victim's blame with, 'I'm sorry,' the Victim is likely to doubt the sincerity of that response. "You're just saying that so I'll leave you alone," she thinks, and she redoubles her effort to get some presumably more 'real' response.

The Victim refuses to relinquish her grievance against her partner. She doesn't experience this process as 'I'm scared to forgive because I'm afraid to open myself up to another disappointment.' Her reaction to her partner's repentance and restitution is that it's 'not enough' to restore good faith. Like a telephone company after a phone has been disconnected several times for nonpayment of bills, the Victim keeps demanding larger and larger deposits from her partner to restore his credit and credibility.

Depression also cuts the Victim off from her positive feeling for her partner. Maggie said of her husband, "Since last week, I've been having trouble getting in touch with loving him, liking him. I can be civil to him, but most of the time I just have a kind of nothing feeling." When she's depressed, the Victim withdraws from involvement with her partner and withholds herself from him emotionally and sexually.

Like blame, depression serves as a covert outlet for the resentment that is denied. The victim sometimes realizes that she's irritable and full of an endless stream of complaints when she's depressed. But she rarely envisions this as the tip of the iceberg of antagonism within.

The Victim feels driven to blame, and feels reduced to depression. She doesn't perceive these as strategies, but they are, nevertheless, powerful means to control her partner. Her partner reinforces these behaviors every time he tries to make the Victim feel better. Pleasers are especially apt to be hooked by this maneuver.

Focused on her own misfortune, the Victim can't empathize with her partner (except, perhaps, when he's feeling down). She's often unable to grasp the meaning of her partner's behavior. She dismisses the constraints that may have affected him and attributes a selfish-hostile motive to action that he finds displeasing.

The Victim's competitiveness can cause her to perceive her partner as a rival and a threat rather than as an ally. 'I would like to be with a man who's better than I am. I don't want to be carrying someone along. It's a messed up place to be carrying someone along. So I don't want to do it. If anyone has to be carried, I want it to be me.' She wants to be with someone who's a success because that would reassure her of her own value. A man who was together and happy could include her in the charmed circle of his life, and she can't really envision getting to such a destination under her own power. Inevitably and paradoxically, at some point she begins to measure her life against her partner's, and feels eclipsed by his accomplishments, belittled by his stature. Her partner's success heightens her sense of inadequacy. Ed once stormed at Ruthie, "I want you to credit what I've done. It was good and got me high . . . Not feel jealous of it. But you can't do that because anything in me that deserves approval is threatening to you." Ruthie replied sourly, "That's because you're always mouthing off about how happy you are."

The Victim feels that she gets the worst of the relationship, but it's a close contest. Her partner doesn't have an easy time of it either. Feeling controlled, resentful, and guilty, the Victim's partner may suspect she would prefer to take her sorrows to bed instead of him. In fact, her grievance becomes a kind of passion of indignation, consuming and perversely satisfying.

The Victim has trouble grasping her partner's position, and counting him in. She has equal difficulty staying in touch with warmth. When she is feeling attacked or stabbed in the back, she finds it difficult to feel affectionate toward the person she holds responsible for her missing or mutilated extremities. Similarly, her own despondency curtails the reciprocal flow of warm feelings.

The Victim holds a grudge because of the massive resentment that churns inside her. Depression and blame allow a few drops of resentment to leak out, but they don't let the Victim 'get angry, get it over with' and purge herself of her negativity. She is oblivious to the wounds her negativity inflicts. Unacknowledged power is irresponsible power, and the Victim, accordingly, can wield her power with exceptional cruelty. Here we find the core of her problem: in some fundamental sense the Victim suffers from the withholding of anger, and the negativity that results is the embodiment of that withholding. The backlog of resentment makes it difficult to acknowledge appreciation for something thoughtful the partner has done. The partner is seen as having incurred so many debits in the past, that an occasional credit is, in comparison, too negligible to merit reward.

Gratitude is alien to a Victim on a fundamental level. The whole vision of her relationship to the world is predicated on the conviction that life (or one's partner, or one's parents) has 'done me wrong.' She ignores experiences that don't tally with that perspective.

The Victim has many contradictory impulses that cause her to reject the very help that she so desires. They encompass both the dependent yearnings of the Fragile and what in a later chapter will be called the counterdependent impulses of the Tough-Fragile; each serves to counteract the other. Like the Fragile, the Victim feels devoid of resources, so she hopes someone will rescue her, but her pride interferes with her ability to ask directly, or to accept, the help when it's offered. The Victim's negative energy is a sorry second to real aggression and assertion. The warmth and giving of the Fragile are also threatening to the Victim's sense of autonomy, so her role takes only the worst from each. The Victim manages to paint herself into a corner that others avoid. The Fragile's fall-apart is accompanied by the ability to take gratefully the hand she's reaching for. The Victim, however, rejects the hand and remains isolated—a prisoner of her own misery.

Like most of us, the Victim wants her own way. Like many, she uses guilt and blame to get it. This is a powerful strategy that works most effectively on those who love her. Friends and lovers come back time and time again to help. The real tragedy of the Victim role is that the hurt they experience is only effective and only has power over those who in fact do care. The recognition of this could free the Victim from what is a self-imposed isolation and a self-inflicted pain.

Over time, blame and depression deposit harmful residue in a relationship. Some kind of payoff has to be provided to induce a person to remain in a couple. Victims offer their partners several: first of all, like the Dance-Away, Victims appear to maximum advantage in the first flush of infatuation. A beginning summons up their talent, their goodwill, their appeal, of whatever flavor. It's as hard for a stranger to spot a chronic Victim as it is to recognize a Dance-Away. Then memories, and subsequent glimpses of the Victim's appealing original self, help keep the partner in a relationship with the Victim after the latter's demeanor has changed. A Victim bestows upon her partner two seductive kinds of power. She holds out the hope that if her partner only tries, he can make the Victim bloom. June said, "If Sander would only be supportive of me and affectionate to me, and wouldn't make demands, then I'd be fine and we'd have good sex together." In other words, the Victim invests her partner with potential Pygmalion-like power. 'You can free the glorious creature trapped inside me, if you only do exactly the right thing. You can rescue me!' Leaving the relationship means that the partner must renounce his claim to turn lead into gold, the alchemical ability that the Victim flatteringly attributes to him.

The partner derives another grimmer power from his relationship with the Victim. The Victim's blame makes plain how deeply the partner can wound her. The knowledge that you can make somebody else feel terrible may not be the greatest boon that a relationship can confer, but it counts for something, especially if your feeling of efficacy in the world is generally low.

The Victim elevates favored friends or a partner to a privileged status. She courts them, spares them the condemnation she rains on others, conspicuously allows them inside, while barring the rest of the world. Such highly exclusive intimacy may be delightful, but it's fleeting. By the very nature of the Victim phenomenon, good feelings sour, harmony disintegrates into despair and estrangement.

Over all, the Victim strategy yields a poor balance of gains to losses, for both the Victim and the partner. The suspiciousness encountered by the latter, the low motives that are attributed to him, the sabotage of his efforts to rescue, the accusations, the remorse, the pain—are the stuff of heartache.

The Victim can hook her partner into staying through guilt, but this existence they share becomes a yoke, not a union. This guilt may be oppressive to the Victim's partner, but it is also an effective way to bind him to her side; so much so that she may be reluctant to give it up. She knows that she can get a lot of conciliatory mileage out of beating someone over the head with her pain and is not likely to abandon this strategy until she realizes that her gain is at the cost of her own self-esteem and the respect of others.

The Victim's role is probably the most painful and

the most difficult one to alter. Some experience of hitting bottom may well be a prerequisite for major change. Once the Victim has realized that she has nobody to count on but herself, she can begin to deal with the fear that controls her and to turn inward to the strength and discipline she's heretofore neglected. The discovery that she can take care of herself reduces the demands she feels she must make on her partner and reduces the desperation that charges those demands.

The Victim can start to acknowledge other people's needs and feelings as well as to acknowledge the positive desires hidden in her own negative complaints. She must recognize and accept her own failures as just part of the common human condition. When a Victim can laugh at her own foibles and go after what she wants, knowing that everyone "wins a little, loses a little," she is on the road to maturity. She would do well to remember the adage, "Angels can fly because they take themselves lightly."

The Victim must dare to be vulnerable, dare to risk disappointment. Dare to admit that she makes her own bed. If she can't sleep, she may take her bed apart and start over again. But she should not look for the thief who robbed her of her rest.

As Howard Gossage, the wise man of advertising, said, "If you get a lemon, make lemonade."

The Victim can begin to figure out what she wants positively, instead of focusing exclusively on what she doesn't want. And she can begin to assert those wants in straightforward, present-tense terms. She can reduce her expectations to a more realistic level and begin to find other sources of supply (of companionship, support, and so on) beyond her partner. Most important, the Victim can shift the flow of energy she has poured into negativity by acknowledging the force of the recognition described by W. H. Auden:

> I could . . .
> Find reasons fast enough

To face the sky and roar
In anger and despair
At what is going on,
Demanding that it name
Whoever is to blame:
The sky would only wait
Till all my breath was gone
And then reiterate
As if I wasn't there
That singular command
I do not understand
*Bless what there is for being.**

* W. H. Auden, "Precious Five."

CHAPTER 9

The Ragabash *

THE RAGABASH is the romantic of work relationships. A quixotic idealist, the Ragabash clings to the belief that the right vocation exists, and his quest for it leads him, as Owen said, "through an odyssey—looking for something—looking for myself, I guess."

The Ragabash envisions "straight" America as offering him two alternatives: to grow up to be either a Provider or a Prizewinner. For the Ragabash, the prototype of the Provider is the civil servant; the prototype of the Prizewinner is the speculator. If the former seems to the Ragabash to be timorously moral, the latter seems brutally amoral. Stuart described his Prizewinner father as "a lawyer without a conscience," a man focused on obtaining power and wielding it without regard for others' well-being.

He sees the Provider, conversely, as having toiled to create security for himself and his family. A Ragabash raised on air raid drills in grammar school and a preoccupatinon with the draft in college usually can't imagine that the thin structure of financial security he might be able to create would actually shelter him or his loved ones come the holocaust. Real want, though, remains a hypothetical concern to him. The

* "An idle, ragged person," one of the "rabble," as defined in *Webster's*.

Ragabash sees the Provider's obsession with security as sadly comic. Furthermore, the scramble for stability in the future seems to doom the Provider to an anxious, joyless present. Jamie, son of a Provider, experienced his father as 'barely existing.' To the Ragabash, the Provider seems to mutter,

> I have married my hands to perpetual agitation
> I run, I run to the whistle of money.*

The Ragabash sees the Prizewinner as having demanded success as the reward for his labors. The Ragabash has discovered, however, at first hand or via the media, that wealth, power, fame, even greatness frequently do not bring happiness in their wake.

The Ragabash is determined to avoid being forced into either of these molds. His appearance, his political views, his diet, his pace, his pleasures, are all intended, in part, to differentiate him from the middlebrow, middle-class American mainstream.

The core of the Ragabash's sense of himself is his sense of being unlike his parents and their ilk. Stuart said, "I've been thinking lately about the long struggle I've had with my father . . . A friend of ours has sometimes described me as an upside-down version of my father . . . Something has made it really hard for me to accept the part of myself that's synonymous with my father." The Ragabash clings to his conviction that he's nothing like the older set. Jamie said of his family, "They're their way, and I'm different. I'm never going to fully explain myself to them or share my life with them—what I'm doing. They're never going to understand me. They just couldn't comprehend what I'm interested in." The Ragabash isn't comforted by indications that his parents understand him and sympathize with his position. On the contrary, he may positively chop down the bridges they try to throw across the generation gap. His career must buttress his sense of differentness and prevent him from metamorphosing into a duplicate of

* Theodore Roethke, "The Lost Son."

his parents. When Stuart fantasized once about returning to New York to work in his father's law firm, he worried, "If I ever went back, I'd disappear."

Fearful of distorting his identity with an inappropriate choice of careers, the Ragabash worries that an error might undermine his selfhood altogether. Jamie said, "I don't want to be just like anybody else. That's why I could never work for a company—a place where you'd lose your identity, where you'd have to give up that much of yourself."

Most legitimate careers, however, offer some point of contact with "straight" America, some danger to the Ragabash that he will blend back into the ranks of Providers and Prizewinners. A career that will elicit a parental blessing becomes particularly threatening. After Jamie spent a few months considering becoming a doctor, he admitted, "Medical school—I'm not sure I wanted to go, but I couldn't tell my parents I was thinking about it because I knew they would be happy." The Ragabash is controlled in reverse by parental approval. Their enthusiasm for a given alternative becomes the kiss of death—proof that the Ragabash couldn't use that career to demonstrate to them and to himself his estrangement from their values.

He usually sees his parents as people who have failed to find happiness with each other.

> You call that love—it should be called
> Civility and habit.

They haven't ripened into a rich, calm maturity. Instead,

> In headaches and in worry,
> Vaguely life leaks away.*

Ironically, as a youngster, the Ragabash was often his parent's bright hope. "I was supposed to be President Kennedy." The Ragabash seemed, early on, to

* W. H. Auden, "As I walked out one Evening."

possess the kind of conspicuous ability that made him a natural for achievement and leadership. "I was number one in my class in high school, which I liked —getting the best grades, student council, that kind stuff," said Stuart.

But at some point, personal experience or the increasingly audible voice of cultural dissent awakens the Ragabash to the realization that one person's win occurs in the context of another's loss. Owen reflected, "But I don't like to lose. Either I feel bad if I lose, if it's something that I care about, or if I win, I feel bad for the losers. And that's what's hard for me about winning—that I identify so much with the loser."

Alienation from a society which only respects victory fosters the conviction that "winners are the bad guys . . ." The Ragabash chooses sides against them, with the underdog, the helpless, the exploited. His premise becomes an equation of powerlessness with innocence, dominance with evildoing. Personal ascendancy becomes a troubling experience. Success means making a killing in a far too literal sense for his peace of mind. For the Ragabash, one penalty for success is guilt.

Success also brings vulnerability. Victory doesn't buttress his confidence in himself; instead, it increases the performance pressure on the Ragabash, who thinks down inside himself, "little do they know." When he has to repeat his feat, he fears that he'll expose himself as a fraud. He also fears that resentment will goad others into rivalry with him, into cutting him back down to the insignificance he deserves.

As he grows older, the Ragabash finds himself obliged to compete against a progressively wider field of opponents, so that victory becomes progressively more difficult. He often feels unprepared, finding the climb to the top growing steadily steeper. "I was spoiled when I was a kid," said Owen. "Things came easy. I hate that it's this hard now."

The inability of the Ragabash to make a vocational commitment or to come to terms with his performance anxiety means that the kind of work he considers most desirable (doctor, therapist, musician) is out of reach for him. The middle-reaches of the work world (the white-collar jobs) are anathema to him, so the Ragabash tends to end up in the least skilled, worst paid jobs available—handyman, substitute teacher, peddler. Owen said, "My parents were so much into doing well—being successful—that I really rebelled against that, rating people like that. My philosophy now is: it doesn't matter. A janitor is worth as much as anybody else." But when the Ragabash finds himself working as a janitor, he's likely to try to divorce his sense of self from the economic functions he performs. He may work hard at his job but he doesn't commit his loyalty, his ambition, or his brains to it. He views the 'shit job' as a temporary expedient, tolerable till he's managed to "get my trip together."

But the self-esteem issue is likely to remain a touchy one. Doing low-status, poorly paid dead-end work is likely to undercut a Ragabash's self-respect despite his belief that a person should be judged on the basis of the way he lives and not the way he earns his living.

His relationship, then, must sustain the burden of his frustration and his guilt about "how empty, how vacuous my everyday life is. There's nothing happening. I don't like knowing that my talents are going to waste . . . I'm just rotting away."

Ironically, the idealistic terms in which the Ragabash conceives a career make failure more intolerable for him than for the Provider or for the Prizewinner. A career is no practical arrangement for the Ragabash. He wants to fuse his identity with his calling, so that work becomes the arena in which he actualizes himself and expresses himself most fully. In return for his effort, the Ragabash demands the rewards that are the richest and the rarest—to be able to believe in the value of what he's doing and enjoying it.

This prohibition of failure creates extreme performance pressure for the Ragabash. When he's under pressure to produce (his Ph.D. thesis, for example), the Ragabash doesn't experience a straightforward localized fear around performance. Instead, his anxiety translates itself into pervasive gloom. As we will see in a later chapter, the Tough-Fragile converts anxiety into anger just as the Ragabash converts anxiety into unhappiness. Day after day he feels listless and forlorn. He assumes that he can't accomplish anything because someone or something is to blame: his job, society, or more particularly, his wife.

Unwittingly, the Ragabash takes the statement, 'If I could only work I would feel good,' and reverses it so that it becomes, 'If only I felt good, I could work.' Anxiety increases the demands he makes on others (for warmth, consideration, and so forth) and reduces his tolerance for disappointment and frustration. Since it's apprehension about work that puts stress on his relationship, and not the other way around, the Ragabash can't resolve his couple difficulties by tinkering with the relationship per se. In fact, just as a given quantity of tasks is apt to require every minute of the time allotted to them, so emotional crises are likely to balloon out, consuming all the energy that's available for them. The Ragabash's desperate effort to 'cool things out' in his private life simply make him more shaky and distract him from the real problem he faces: his fear that he won't be able to work successfully.

Emotions can work like a kind of shell game, with the unconscious executing the sleight of hand. For example, the Fragile doesn't express fear straightforwardly. Instead, her apprehension surfaces in the form of fainting spells or crying jags. The Ragabash's fear, likewise, can make its appearance in the form of a relationship crisis or a sudden irresistible urge for a love affair.

Departing is the Ragabash's other main response to difficulty. His departure from a difficult situation may be triggered by fear, but it may equally well be prompted by dissatisfaction of some sort. When a job fails to prove as interesting or as socially constructive or as personally harmonious as he anticipates, he feels cheated. He can't accept disappointment in a 'life's like that' spirit.

The Ragabash's recourse is to obsession, an attempt to think things into a more tolerable shape. What alternatives are available to him? Confrontation? Quitting? The Ragabash is hesitant to take action, but he resolves these questions over and over in his mind. He stews over the problem, hoping that some right solution will appear. His obsession is usually the prelude to departure.

The Ragabash often frames his exit as an act of conscience. He explains his departure as an inability to stomach the values that structure the situation, as a refusal to participate in cutthroat competition, or a rat race to get ahead, or the like. Alternatively, he attributes his exit to boredom. "It just doesn't turn me on anymore," said Jamie after a stint as a gardener. After a spate as a legal aid lawyer, Stuart admitted, "I no longer have the interest or the patience to deal with most of the problems that beset the lower classes in our social system . . . I am tired of staving off the landlord for more welfare mothers."

A complaint like, 'It's too competitive,' or 'It's not interesting anymore'—is intended not to force some change in the situation, but to legitimize the Ragabash's retreat from it. These are equivalent as alibis to the Dance-Away's statements, 'Your nose is too big,' or 'I just don't love you anymore.'

The Ragabash often invests an enormous proportion of his energy in speculation about what he might do. Most of his notions have the life expectancy of a soap bubble; others don't expire until after their shimmer has seduced him into a brief pursuit. Another fancy is usually ready at hand to console him for the collapse of its predecessor. Jamie said, "I just change my mind all the time about things. I blow hot about something, then cold."

The freedom to leave when he blows cold is the

Ragabash's protection against error. To him security doesn't lie in stability, but in mobility. Needless to say, this creates havoc for his partner.

Most rewarding careers in our society require a substantial down payment of energy in education or apprenticeship, and hefty installments of deferred pleasure. The Ragabash is reluctant to mortgage himself to the future in this fashion. He's also averse to hustling for opportunities, advertising his own worth, and safeguarding his own interests. "I've never been much of a fighter really," said Owen. Lacking the stick-to-itiveness of the Provider or the aggressiveness of the Prizewinner, the Ragabash is usually debarred from the deeply satisfying kind of work he dreams of —as a healer, a naturalist, a craftsman, and so on.

The Ragabash reconciles his work situation with the knowledge that he hasn't sold his soul to IBM for a houseful of fancy carpets and a handful of insurance policies. He espouses a peculiar brand of elitism—seeing himself and his confreres as free, cool, and loose in comparison to the bourgeois folk whom he disdains to join in their uptightness, materialism, and phoniness. However, the refusal to get it together around work creates great strain for his wife, who has been patiently waiting.

The Ragabash reverses the priorities the conventional male role establishes. He stresses the importance of private life as against professional productivity. He focuses on the present and he prizes pleasure. With Whitman, the Ragabash declares

> I believe in the flesh and the appetites,
> Seeing, hearing, feeling are miracles
> And each part of me is a miracle.*

The Ragabash is a gregarious sort for whom relationships count heavily. Stuart said, "My father was very successful in business and a failure in emotional relationships. I concluded that's crazy—to feel good

* Walt Whitman, "Song of Myself."

about yourself because you're a success in business and not feel bad about yourself because you're a failure in relationships." The conventional male role, which bids him to be cool, assertive, dominant, and rational, doesn't seem to the Ragabash to offer much potential for satisfying relationships. He tends to reject that way of being in favor of a style that has a more conventionally feminine quality, incorporating more warmth, openness, responsiveness, and gentleness.

His friendships with men reflect this altered stance. Stuart said, "I feel good about that. The men that are my close friends, we've gotten beyond some of the barriers about not showing emotions and not talking about personal things. I've got pretty strong relationships with some men that are supportive and interesting at the same time."

Since he values his ability to be playful and affectionate, the Ragabash can establish remarkably close relationships with children. The man who says, 'I don't want to be a grown-up, I still want to be a little kid,' often finds it easy to understand and enjoyable to involve himself with the pint-size people around him. Frequently he assumes far more responsibility for raising his children than other men do (partly because he has more time to devote to them), and children, in turn, become a real source of fulfillment to him.

On a day-to-day basis, however, the Ragabash looks primarily to his couple relationship to provide him with satisfaction and a sense of self-worth. The principal benefits he offers his partner are equality, on the one hand, and intimacy on the other.

The Ragabash doesn't monopolize the power in a relationship. Since he makes a scanty living at best, his partner usually contributes a fair share of the couple's wherewithal. The Ragabash's identification with the oppressed is likely to make him sympathetic to the women's movement. He is likely to share the housekeeping chores with his partner—to do some, if not a full half, of the cooking and the cleaning and the child care. The couple's decision-making process usually entails far more give and take than a Provider or a Prizewinner would accept. The Ragabash usually feels obligated to grant his partner the same rights he claims for himself—the right to take other lovers, for example.

The Ragabash shares himself with his partner more fully than other types of men are comfortable doing. He usually spends a great deal of time with her, so that the couple are companions as well as lovers. He'll talk lengthily and leisurely to his partner, disclosing his fantasies and his fears. He'll offer her a tender warmth when things are good, sympathy and acceptance when she's down.

Nevertheless, despite the value he places on openness, the Ragabash is by no means completely candid. The emotions he censors out as inadmissible are feelings of an angry or jealous ilk. The Ragabash can feel soft but will not allow himself to feel hard. He can accept the perception of himself as vulnerable but not as threatening.

To him, the healthy relationship is marked by accord. His utopian vision—enough for all—provides his working premise for relationships as well. With enough goodwill and enough effort, all parties can be accommodated, their interests reconciled. Conflict, then, becomes a symptom of selfishness or some other malfunction in the system.

The Ragabash can't assert his wants in the face of opposition from his partner. He can't tell her 'No.' His ambivalence (who to be? how to act?) makes him extremely susceptible to self-doubt and to guilt.

The Ragabash refrains from taking care of himself inside the relationship the same way he neglects to advance his interests in the outside world. To forestall unpleasantness, he bows to his partner's preferences. To minimize friction, he bends.

Fear of anger inclines the Ragabash to the strategy of passivity. He sees the angry man as a bully. So instead, the Ragabash backs away from a confrontation. 'Okay, if that's the way you feel,' he says, giving in. Stuart admitted, "The thing about anger you don't handle is—you end up resenting. I'm a silent resenter from way back."

The visible manifestation of that resentment may well be passive-aggressive behavior. He's late for his turn at baby-sitting or takes forever to return from the grocery store. Alternatively, resentment may settle into depression. When Jamie and Sophia backpacked into the wilderness, Sophia got frightened and asked to leave ahead of schedule, so they could spend the rest of their vacation in more civilized surroundings. Jamie agreed, but with disappointment. As they started to drive home he sank into a bitter depression that ruined the rest of the day for them both.

As unresolved conflicts and grievances accumulate, the Ragabash is likely to revenge himself on his partner unwittingly, by concluding, 'I just can't relate to her anymore.' The Ragabash may escape unobtrusively—by shifting his emotional center of gravity outside the relationship to a cause, to another lover, and so forth.

The Ragabash often feels that some version of open marriage ought to be feasible. Jamie said, "I think you can do it if you have the right relationship with the right person. Especially if everything's up front, if you're not doing it on the sneak." The Ragabash assumes that honesty will make infidelity acceptable. He can ascribe his partner's jealousy to possessiveness or some other such undeserving impulse. He can therefore dismiss her jealousy as a defect in her which she ought to overcome. It's more difficult, though, to shrug off the jealousy that her romantic and/or sexual entanglements bestir in him. The Ragabash who ventures into affairs to avoid problems in his primary relationship is likely to find that those original problems are aggravated by jealousy, and that friendships and couple relationships can be swamped with the furor that affairs create.

If one solution for the Ragabash is to distance himself from his partner, the other solution is to ditch her. The Ragabash often feels like Owen, "I don't see any relationship existing forever. I don't see a job existing forever. I don't see living in one place forever." His vow is of the 'as long as we love each other' sort, and not the 'forever no matter what' variety. When his relationship reaches a difficult pass, his mistrust of obligation and his stress on feelings as the touchstone of truth can interlock to persuade the Ragabash that he and his partner better choose separate paths. 'We just weren't in the same place anymore,' is not just a description of the situation that provoked his departure, it's a legitimization of that departure. While he can frame the end of a relationship as a necessary phase in his growth, in fact it's often a way of evading growth, avoiding working through the conflicts and the disappointments that relationships inevitably entail.

The meager income that he and his partner are obliged to skimp by on is another source of stress for the relationship. Cars that are forever breaking down, lumpy mattresses from Goodwill, no money to spare for an occasional movie—the discomforts and the anxieties of long-term poverty are likely to exhaust the buoyancy of the pair. The subsistence life-style that may have been acceptable to the Ragabash in his carefree twenties can weigh far more heavily on him when he's responsible for several growing youngsters. "I've got a ten-year-old daughter," one Ragabash worried. "She's going to need braces in a couple of years. How am I gonna come up with a thousand dollars for braces?" Owen admitted, "At first it's sort of good to let it go and hang loose and let it flow and pick up on all the nice things, but it can also make you very uptight if you don't have any structure, any security."

The Ragabash demands that his partner be flexible and tolerant of his carelessness about responsibilities in the present, and tolerant of his "que sera sera" sanguinity about the future.

Like the fellow Shakespeare described, the Ragabash

> doth ambition shun
> and loves to live in the sun.*

The lack of financial security is apt to be particularly difficult for his partner to bear. She's likely to become increasingly anxious for him to settle down, increasingly upset when he ups and quits another job and there's no money in the bank. One woman said of her husband, "I get really angry. I have to push him to care about me and the kids. I have to push him to get himself together so we can have a life together . . . There's no motivation in him. Everything has to come from me. I don't want the responsibility of saying, 'You have to go out there and do it.'" She's apt to be concerned for the Rabagash as well, knowing how much it bothers him that 'there's no money, and there's no direction.'

She nags and pleads for him to earn a steady living and disprove her fear that 'It's always going to be like this. You're never going to find anything in your whole life.' And he stubbornly continues to float from one interim arrangement to the next, offering her a lot of closeness but very little in the way of security.

Over the long term, this pattern of escape may itself entrap the Ragabash. His search for fulfillment leads him through a string of different relationships, a string of different jobs, a string of different places. In his thirties, the Ragabash may incline toward settling down. But to do so, he must come to terms with both his expectations and his self-indulgence. He must begin to recognize that his depressions and his boredom are a statement about himself as well as about the situation he's involved in, and he must learn to struggle through difficulties instead of just retreating from them.

* William Shakespeare, "Under the Greenwood Tree."

Furthermore, the Ragabash must realize that a couple relationship can't survive on intimacy. Until he learns to assert himself and assume responsibility for his commitments to others, the Ragabash can't count himself as actualized in either work or love.

CHAPTER 10

The Tough-Fragile

COMBATIVE AND COMPETITIVE, the Tough-Fragile wants to run her own show. When she's managing pretty well, the Tough-Fragile's gumption makes her a go-getter around work, and her high spirits and venturesomeness make her a delightful companion. When she's experiencing difficulty, however, the Tough-Fragile is prone to frantic fits of temper, which leave her partner walking on eggshells to protect himself.

The Tough-Fragile has her heart set on becoming somebody special. She longs for the success and the power that mean significance to her—to hold the center stage, not to stand in the wings. In essence, she strives to become a Prizewinner; to win recognition for her achievements and to occupy a position of strength and autonomy in her personal life.

Several years after they had married, John said to his Tough-Fragile wife, Carrie, "One of the things that I liked about you when I met you was that you seemed really strong and independent. It seemed like you did whatever you wanted to and didn't care what people thought. You ran your own life, made your own deals, made noise when things didn't suit you. I didn't have to worry about what you felt like all the time, and I liked that."

The Tough-Fragile lacks a prerequisite for independence: belief in herself. Carrie replied to John, "I came off as being a lot stronger than I really am." As much as she wants to make the grade, the Tough-Fragile worries that she hasn't got what it takes.

Accordingly, she needs ample quantities of support to fortify her. It is this very support that she is hesitant to ask for. It signifies weakness, and the Tough-Fragile does not want to give in to her weaker side. The Tough-Fragile yearns to have a partner whose invincibility can safeguard her against adversity and who can withstand the trouble that she is likely to give him.

She wants a relationship that is equal. She often fears

. . . that in spite of all the roses and kisses and restaurant dinners a man showered on a woman before he married her, what he secretly wanted, when the wedding service ended, was for her to flatten out underneath his feet like Mrs. Willard's kitchen mat.' *

The Tough-Fragile wants the status, the power, and the drudgery in the relationship to be divided right down the middle, and she patrols their relationship vigilantly for signs that her well-being is being subordinated to her partner's.

The Tough-Fragile's sense of her own value wobbles precariously. Keenly competitive with her partner in every respect, she's extremely sensitive to which way the breezes of external approval are blowing. Carrie reluctantly admitted, "The more success he has, the worse I feel." The Tough-Fragile is apt to probe her partner for the flaws which will reassure her that he's not so much better than she is, after all.

Given to "pick-pick-picking" at her partner, she is nevertheless extremely defensive about criticism that's directed at her. Rosa said, "Friday night Jerry gave

* Sylvia Plath, *The Bell Jar.*

me a taste of what I've been giving him for three years, nagging, bitching, mostly criticizing, and in five minutes I was in tears. It really hit me hard. I can give it, but I can't take it."

The Tough-Fragile channels much of her dissatisfaction with herself into discontent with her partner. Uncertain about who she is, the Tough-Fragile often defines her identity by opposing herself to her partner's values and preferences. She mistakes rebelliousness against his standards for independence. Likewise, she tries to compensate for the helplessness she feels by struggling with her partner for control of their relationship. Here, again, she mistakes pugnacity for autonomy.

Internal contradictions riddle the Tough-Fragile disposition. She wants to respect her partner, but the very superiority that allows her to admire him threatens her self-esteem. The Tough-Fragile derives security from the myth of her partner's unassailability, and insofar as she debunks that myth, she must relinquish the comforting belief that her partner is capable of rescuing her from any difficulty that besets her. When the Tough-Fragile runs aground and her partner does rescue her, she encounters the opposite difficulty. To accept his assistance implies that she needs him and that he can remedy a situation that has boggled her. These are humbling admissions the Tough-Fragile is loath to make.

In order to salvage her pride, the Tough-Fragile may sabotage her partner's rescue effort. For example, when Jerry advised Rosa on ways she could order her business finances, she rebutted each suggestion with "Yes, but . . ." objections. She attacked him for adopting a condescending attitude toward her and for allowing her to have reached such straits in the first place. Rosa said with asperity, "Jerry's involved in the store to the extent that I mess up." Although she depends on knowing that help is available to her, the Tough-Fragile can't accept it with grace because she interprets it as an adverse reflection on her own competence.

Unable to achieve self-acceptance, the Tough-Fragile needs a continual flow of attention and approval from her partner to reassure her that she counts. Frightened of failure, she needs support to fortify her to face the challenges life presents her with —going back to school, demanding a raise, facing health problems.

Nevertheless, the Tough-Fragile interposes a range of obstacles between herself and the caring she might elicit from her partner. She doesn't look like she wants help. She adopts a brisk 'don't mess with me' manner, and it requires real perceptiveness to grasp, as Jerry did, "Rosa's not as much piss and vinegar as she'd like to appear." The Tough-Fragile's bravado conceals from her partner, as well as from the rest of the world, a lonely, uncertain self. Rosa admitted, "I've got a lot of bitch in me, but there's another part, too. I want so much to have him put his arm around me, show me some love. I want so much to have warmth come from him. But I come on pretty strong, and it's like—he can't see past what comes out of my mouth."

The Tough-Fragile can't ask outright for emotional support. She usually suffers from the same fear of rejection which deters other kinds of women from asserting their wants. But the Tough-Fragile is debarred from asking for something by another, more crucial, stumbling block—her belief that she shouldn't need it. She believes that a sound relationship is structured on a 'you take care of you, I'll take care of me' basis.

The Tough-Fragile supposes that a strong person, like the Prizewinner, doesn't look to anybody for anything. She believes that she, too, should be able to manage her life unaided. In fact, the Prizewinner usually derives substantial advantages from his couple relationship, and he accepts his partner's contributions as his dues. In the Tough-Fragile's eyes, however, leaning on another person for support is akin to using a cane to get about.

Despite her efforts, the Tough-Fragile hasn't been able to rid herself of a deep dependency on others. She experiences this dependency as a defect in herself. She can't ask for her partner's attention, for his affection, for his approbation, because she interprets these desires as manifestations of the dependency she's trying to root out. Instead she resorts to counterdependence: when she feels weak, she acts tough.

She projects onto her partner the same dependence she fights off in herself. She hates the thought of being clung to. The Tough-Fragile fears an onslaught of demands from her partner because a guilt-free 'no' is as much beyond her means as a straightforward assertion of her wants. Afraid that she's a bad person for wanting to say 'No,' the Tough-Fragile declares instead that her partner is a bad person for asking so much (selfish), asking the way he does (manipulative), or asking at all the wrong times (inconsiderate).

Her defensiveness leads the Tough-Fragile to justify her refusal by means of blame and to enclose it in a push-away: 'Leave me alone. Stop hounding me.' She refuses angrily to relieve the anxiety it causes her to say 'No' and to deter her partner from asking next time around.

The Tough-Fragile deals with feelings that jeopardize her by transforming them into a feeling she's comfortable with—anger. The Fragile responds to stress by feeling helpless, the Victim responds by feeling hurt, but when the Tough-Fragile feels anxious or sad or uncertain, she gets angry. Carrie said, "It seems like the natural thing to do when something goes wrong—get mad." The Tough-Fragile lets fly with a burst of anger when she's distressed the way a cuttlefish squirts out ink, as a form of protection. She behaves in a way which defends her: she strikes an angry note to intimidate her partner, and she attacks him at a point where he's vulnerable, thereby diverting attention from her own vulnerability.

Carrie was a Tough-Fragile secretary whose husband worked nights as a bartender. The conflict in their schedules meant that she usually went to bed alone, and she had to tiptoe out of the house at seven-thirty in the morning to avoid waking him up. Carrie felt lonely, but she didn't avow her unhappiness straightforwardly. Instead, she pushed him away.

She told John that she wanted to move into the extra bedroom in order to "get my own space." Her underlying, unadmitted rationale was that she would feel better in a single bed in her own room than sleeping in a double bed that was half empty much of the time. She felt hurt that the discrepancy in their schedules bothered her but didn't seem to upset John. So, feeling unloved, she decided to restructure her life to reduce her husband's place in it—to punish him for not being there and to protect herself from the pain his absence caused her.

There's a nub of pain buried inside every such push-away. The Tough-Fragile may have fancied the slight or may have grossly overreacted to it, but what touches off the push-away is the Tough-Fragile's experience of being threatened. She is too proud and too counterdependent to acknowledge her hurt, however, or to display that hurt as the Victim does, compelling her partner to do penance for it.

Instead she appears to spurn her partner altogether. Her push-away says implicitly, "I don't even want your love. You're nothing to me." The push-away appears to constitute a rejection of the partner ('I don't even want to share a bed with you.'). In fact, however, the push-away's actual purpose is to maneuver the partner into moving toward the Tough-Fragile ('I don't want you sleeping in some other room. I love you, and I want you to be here beside me.').

To cover her vulnerability, the Tough-Fragile picks a fight around a false issue, which usually has some plausibility. The element of validity in the issue usually hooks her partner so that he accepts her accusations at face value. Carrie, for example, frequently complained that her husband considered her to be "just an appendage.' So he interpreted her push-away ('I want my own room.') as a variation on the 'I want to be me' theme.

By picking a fight around a false issue, the Tough-Fragile traps herself. If her partner capitulates around the false issue—for example, if John agrees that Carrie can have her own room—then the Tough-Fragile feels rejected. Carrie would take John's acquiescence as proof that he didn't really care about her because he didn't even mind if they didn't sleep together. Furthermore, if Carrie did move into another room, her contact with John would diminish even further, and she'd end up feeling even lonelier.

But if the partner struggles around the false issue, the Tough-Fragile feels he is trying to thwart her. For example, if John says, "I don't want you moving out of our room," then Carrie feels that he is trying to prevent her from making a change that she is convinced will improve her situation. Instead of dealing with the real issue (how to mitigate the loneliness she feels), the couple gets locked into a control battle over an irrelevant issue (whether it's acceptable for Carrie to have her own room).

Her partner is in a classic double bind. If he spots the pushaway for the cry of distress it usually is, he inadvertently humiliates the Tough-Fragile. For example, John might say, "I know that what's really going on is that you feel like you never get to be with me." He would be addressing the real issue, but he would be depicting Carrie to both of them as the kind of needy, dependent person she's determined neither to be nor seem. So the reassurance he offers her comes at the price of mortification, and the Tough-Fragile escalates to save face. She begins to blame even more vehemently to prop up her original push-away, or she shifts the grounds of her blame to a new false issue.

The Tough-Fragile believes, however, that her partner caused her anger in the first place and that he perpetuates it by doing the wrong thing in response to it. In fact, almost any response her partner could make would register to her as an attack.

Eventually the Tough-Fragile's rage is likely to push her partner into anxious-pleasing. He tries to propitiate her by apologizing profusely, and asking her what he can do to earn forgiveness. Anxious-pleasing throws fuel on the Tough-Fragile's fire. She sees his penitence as prompted by fear of her anger, not by a genuine assumption of responsibility for, and contrition for, the wrong he's done her. She interprets it, therefore, as an attempt to manipulate her into calming down, which makes her furious.

More crucially, the partner who anxious-pleases looks weak to the Tough-Fragile. He looks frightened of her, which makes her feel guilty; and he looks helpless to deal with her, which threatens her. The Tough-Fragile is scared by her sense of powerlessness, so she wants a partner who's unshakably strong—someone who stands there with his arms folded, while the darts she throws bounce off his chest. If he is intimidated by her bluster, then he's clearly, she thinks, a feeble reed who can't possibly support her when she needs somebody to lean on. In fact, the Anxious Pleaser looks to the Tough-Fragile like exactly the kind of weak, needy, clingy person she despises and fears she might become. So apprehension, a sense of repulsion, anxiety over her own destructiveness, and guilt combine to make the Tough-Fragile far angrier than she was to begin with.

If her partner displays a self-controlled rationality in the face of her rage, this restraint registers on the Tough-Fragile as disdain, as a kind of parental aloofness from a childish temper tantrum. Rosa said, "He tries to get me to discuss whatever it is, and I can't really discuss it at that point because I can't even get my breath. So then I'll walk away, and then he'll point the finger and say, 'See? You'll never get anywhere unless you discuss things.' " Her partner's refusal to show that the Tough-Fragile is hurting him may drive her into a frenzy. Rosa said, "I feel so impotent. I can't break him down. The coldness he shows, that obstinance—I'd like to get to him in a way that shows him what he's doing to me. He's really tearing me apart . . . and it doesn't seem that he's even affected." Carrie said, "I get crazy when I'm threatened, and John often threatens me. Sometimes every move he makes is a threat, an implicit criticism of the way I do things."

Easily angered, the Tough-Fragile is apt to get caught in a spiral of rage that just keeps building. Her anger may go no further than verbal abuse, screaming threats to leave, insults, and the like, or it may lead to physical destruction of property or an attack on her partner's person. The Tough-Fragile loses control. The hysterical quality of her onslaught often frightens her partner, and the damage done may dismay the Tough-Fragile after it's over.

Eventually the Tough-Fragile becomes exhausted, or somebody walks out, or the partner who's been trying to remain calm crumbles into fury or fragility.

The unpleasantness notwithstanding, the Tough-Fragile's anger brings her substantial gain. Most partners of Tough-Fragiles are deterred from saying and doing things they'd otherwise be inclined to allow themselves for fear of the horrible scene which might ensue. Her anger also guarantees that the Tough-Fragile's partner will take notice of her. A fight forces her partner to focus on her, and the Tough-Fragile prefers any kind of attention to being ignored. Perennially insecure about her partner's feelings for her, the Tough-Fragile also uses her tantrums to test his love. She derives a peculiar kind of reassurance from his willingness to endure these traumas.

Once her anger has been vented and her mistrust

allayed, the Tough-Fragile can experience a deep love for her partner. She can yield to the desire for tenderness and closeness that she normally keeps in check. The Tough-Fragile is able to be most fond and most endearing when she's making up.

Numerous gains, therefore, reinforce the Tough-Fragile's conniption-fit proclivity. These are short-term gains, won at the expense of major long-term losses.

The Tough-Fragile assumes that fighting with her partner for control of their relationship will build her strength. She usually does not have the clarity or the self-discipline to mount a sustained struggle for an equal relationship, however. Her belligerence is apt to produce a succession of fitful, desultory scuffles. In fact, the Tough-Fragile's incessant battles with her partner are likely to constitute an avoidance of a task that frightens her much more—struggling to establish herself in the outside world. Instead of confronting the real issues, she's likely to conclude that the relationship is oppressive, and her partner is to blame. A new partner, therefore, or no partner at all, seems to offer her the only avenue of escape.

Over time, the Tough-Fragile's behavior increases her self-doubt and exacerbates her insecurity. So it increases the virulence of the blame that's her solution to discomfort, thereby keeping the whole invidious process afoot.

The Tough-Fragile's *modus operandi* ensures that she will wind up looking like the bad guy no matter what kind of person she's paired with. Her hostility, her irrationality, and her selfishness cast the Tough-Fragile as the villain in almost any couple relationship. The outside world condemns such tactics particularly harshly in a woman. The guilt about such behavior besets the Tough-Fragile of either sex. Rosa said about her outbursts, "I always feel guilty afterwards. I feel terrible. I'm embarrassed that it happened, and I'm worried that I've really hurt him." Heavy on disparagement, skimpy on praise, the

Tough-Fragile is "one of the thorny kind"* of blossoms who's always pricking her partner in some sore place. John said, "I feel pretty helpless. I don't think I can do anything right. Every time I turn around, I'm fucking up again."

The Tough-Fragile's partner may well end up feeling like Alice, who found that the Queen of Hearts was always

> . . . in a furious passion, stomping about and shouting, "Off with his head!" or "Off with her head!" about once in a minute.
>
> Alice began to feel very uneasy. To be sure, she had not as yet had any dispute with the Queen, but she knew that it might happen at any minute.*

Jerry complained about Rosa, "I think that she overreacts to small things. She goes into big tirades then, all this fierceness over little tiny things, and turns them into huge things. She does a lot of name-calling, too. She calls me an ass-hole. I can't stand for people to put me down that way."

In fact, the Tough-Fragile completely loses touch with loving when a tincture of negativity colors her state of being. She lets fly with a hostility and a scorn that lead her partner to doubt her love. Jerry said, "It's hard for me to imagine she could care about somebody she has that image of."

Like the Victim, the Tough-Fragile underestimates the impact of her power. Always feeling on the defensive, she fails to perceive how much she wounds her partner and how deeply she threatens him.

She also fails to perceive how she uses her anger to control him. The Disarmer and the Pleaser envision warmth and niceness as ends in themselves, without recognizing the strategic utility of these modes. The Tough-Fragile distrusts warmth partly because she's so attuned to its manipulative dimension. But the

* Lewis Carroll, *Through the Looking Glass.*
* Lewis Carroll, *Alice's Adventures in Wonderland.*

Tough-Fragile is blind to the fact that her scorn can be fully as disingenuous and controlling as the Disarmer's amiability.

The Tough-Fragile woman on the road to liberation is apt to mistakenly view her relationship as the major threat to her identity and the major obstacle to her growth. One key to change is to realize that careers offer only one arena within which growth can occur, that a couple relationship offers equally real challenges which can be met with equal profit.

The Tough-Fragile can work toward independence by taking responsibility for herself and by confronting the internal obstacles to autonomy, which are apt to be at least as disabling as the external obstacles her partner or others in power create for her. The Tough-Fragile can strengthen herself by learning to assert her power positively (by initiating and asking for what she wants) and by taking responsibility for the negative power she exerts. She can learn to coexist with ambiguity—loving and being disappointed in her partner and herself at the same time, for example. She can learn to use her anger so that she controls it, rather than it controlling her.

She can learn, as well, to make her dependence work for her instead of against her. Often the Tough-Fragile feels like Rosa, that she can 'hold, not reach out.' She can take a major step toward maturing by discovering that love offers people the possibility of exchanging strength in a way that augments the endurance and the resilience of both.

CHAPTER 11

A Dry Interlude

IN THE PRECEDING CHAPTERS we've delineated ten roles people can adopt in relation to a couple partner on the one hand, and to the outside world on the other. Each role—the Dance-Away Lover, the Disarmer, and so on—incorporates characteristic interpretations and responses into a pattern that obeys its own peculiar logic and invites its own predictable consequences. A person who assumes a Fragile role clearly draws on a different repertoire of expectations, feelings, and behaviors than does someone who takes a Prizewinner role, and their impact on others is 'no more alike than an apple to an oyster.'

In order to differentiate the roles, we have described them as if each were a self-contained entity. In fact, however, beneath the level of diversity and discreteness lies a network of interconnections. We must therefore set about qualifying the dividing lines we've been at pains to establish among these models.

The Tough-Fragile role, for example, resembles the Prize-winner role in many ways. It is typified by competitiveness, ambitiousness, discomfort with vulnerability, and a retreat to hostility. The Anxious Ingenue and the Victim roles share in high, but rickety, hopes as well as a bedrock pessimism about how things will work out in the end. The Dance-Away role

—the tendency to shy away from an emotional commitment to a specific partner—is a first cousin to the Ragabash role—the tendency to shy away from commitment to a specific course of action, particularly in the world of work.

The Anxious Pleaser role characterizes a particular approach to relationships, one that nevertheless blends into the Self-Assured Pleaser approach at some points and merges into the Anxious Ingenue at others; some aspects of this role link it to the Fragile, others to the Ragabash, and so forth. Each role shades into the others, as in a natural environment,

> by transitions the land falls from grassy dunes to creek
> to undercreek: but there are no lines, though
>   change in that transition is clear
>   as any sharpness: but "sharpness" spread out,
>   allowed to occur over a wider range
>   than mental lines can keep . . .*

For the sake of clarity, we depicted these roles initially as if each represented a distinctly different kind of person. In fact, however, we believe that each individual self encompasses the potential for all these ways of being. Almost everyone feels and acts fragile at certain moments (in the presence of death, for example); feels hurt sometimes by what seems like others' unfair treatment (i.e., feels like a victim); and occasionally reacts to conflict with a disarming gesture of conciliation. These roles are best understood as options available to us all, options whose permutations help create the rich texture of the personality. Tolstoi wrote:

> . . . men are like rivers . . . every river narrows here, is more rapid there, here slower, there broader, now clear, now cold, now dull, now warm. It is the same with men. Every man carries in him-

* A. R. Ammons, "Corson's Inlet."

self the germs of every human quality and sometimes one manifests itself, sometimes another, and the man often becomes unlike himself while still remaining the same man.*

In our terms, this kind of fludity means that a person can shift from one role to another, depending on whom he's involved with, and what kind and what level of stress he's subjected to. For example, a woman can respond to her husband's worries about his job in Disarmer fashion (by supporting him and encouraging him), and respond in Prizewinner fashion when one of her children is injured (by taking immediate control of the situation and dictating what happens).

It is intuitively obvious that people are apt to become comfortable with particular roles or particular combinations of roles. For example, under normal circumstances, the giving man usually adopts a Provider or Self-Assured Pleaser style. Under greater stress, he may resort to the Anxious Pleaser mode. When, infrequently, he responds like a prickly Tough-Fragile, we note this departure by saying, "He's not acting like himself today." Therefore, we see consistency as well as flexibility in a person's approach to his relationships.

Over the long term, a person can shift from a preponderance of one role to a predominance of another. For example, an unattached woman who has tended to conduct herself in Tough-Fragile fashion ('I can take care of myself') may gradually shift into an Anxious Ingenue frame of mind ('Will no man ever want me?') as her thirties close in on her.

We reiterate: in describing someone as an Anxious Ingenue, we do not mean that that person invariably acts and reacts, and will always continue to act and react, precisely along Anxious Ingenue lines. We do mean, however, that more often than not, her as-

* Leo Tolstoi, as quoted in Haim Ginott, *Between Parent and Teenager.*

sumptions and feelings and acts within a relationship will display the disposition of the Anxious Ingenue.

To conceptualize relationships in terms like these is to run the risk of perpetrating a set of stereotypes which people will use to pigeonhole the others in their lives. This is a disagreeable prospect. We don't want to see through the "eyes that fix you in a formulated phrase."*

The danger implicit in any set of 'categories' is that it will be used to constrict and impoverish the perception of others. Our categories are certainly susceptible to such abuse. They can be hurled as insults to a person's face. 'You're such a Victim.' They can be used behind his back to demean his experience and to strip him of individuality.

There are, of course, inherent limitations on the worth of any such constructs. The idiosyncratic and mysterious workings of the human personality cannot be entirely rendered in the terms we are employing. A full and complete understanding of human relationships would obviate the necessity for the kinds of heuristic categories we are positing.

Nevertheless, to grant that models like ours have limited usefulness and that they can be used destructively is not to concede that this kind of undertaking is invalid. In our work with couples, we have observed that certain patterns of behavior occur over and over again. If these 'syndromes' weren't fraught with pain and loss for the people involved, there would be no particular need to note them or explore their implications. But, in fact, we have seen relationship after relationship blighted by the consequences of these patterns of behavior.

Personal experience in a relationship is usually

a page held
Too close to be legible.†

* T. S. Eliot, "The Love Song of J. Alfred Prufrock."
† John Ashbery, "Clepsydra."

We hope to put relationships in a perspective that is not too remote, but one that will enhance 'legibility.'

The patterns we've described in the first half of this book are one way of conceptualizing how couples interact. We've used the roles to describe certain constellations we perceive in the huge galaxy of human behavior. We don't claim to encompass the whole of that reality, or to have grouped the elements in the only significant pattern.

The astral constellations include only a handful of stars associated into arbitrary forms. But as familiar entities, they provide reference points by which we orient ourselves.

We believe that the patterns we describe possess validity and utility. Collectively, they create a framework within which feelings and behavior become more comprehensible and less threatening.

We intend each pattern to be a "Name form that whets the wits."* We are confident this method of description will enrich, rather than rigidify, the understanding of what it means to be a couple.

The ten roles may have relevance for all kinds of of dyads, (parent-child, friend-friend, employer-employee). We have only explored their potential vis-à-vis couple relationships, and we found them extremely useful for that purpose. But the roles themselves don't explain *how* a couple relationship functions. More than one level of analysis is necessary to come to grips with these complicated phenomena.

Until now, our discussion has been, necessarily, a one-sided affair. In the first half of this book, we described people in terms of the styles they adopt as individuals, the moves they customarily make within relationships. To convey the fundamental steps involved (the fall-apart, the dance-away, and so on) we demonstrated them solo at first (the Dance-Away

* James Joyce, quoted in Marshall McLuhan, *From Cliché to Archetype.*

Lover alone, his hands raised to enclose an imaginary partner); then paired him with an anonymous 'partner' (the Dance-Away Lover clasping a broom). Now it's time to observe the Dance-Away Lover in action with a particular partner to observe the couple relationship of which he's a member.

The Dance-Away Lover who's picked a Tough-Fragile will be pleased by her independence, and horrified by her penchant for anger. The Dance-Away Lover who's paired with an Anxious Ingenue is likely to appreciate the fact that she doesn't cause scenes, but he's apt to be alarmed about her desire to entrap him.

The Disarmer who's married to a Provider will benefit from his sense of duty and suffer from his remoteness. The Disarmer who's married to a Ragabash can have a surfeit of intimacy, but she's likely to pay the cost in terms of anxiety about the practical and financial dimensions of their lives.

The Prizewinner who's paired with a Disarmer will benefit from her support and her compliance 'Whatever you want to do.' But he will probably be unhappy about her amorphous identity. The Prizewinner with a Tough-Fragile will enjoy her spunk, but he'll resent her unwillingness to perform the function

> Women have served all these centuries, as looking glasses possessing the magic and delicious power of reflecting the figure of man at twice its natural size.*

Inherent in each kind of couple system are certain assets, and certain liabilities for both partners. A couple relationship is a joint venture. Each partner affects and, in turn, is affected by the other, and both share responsibility for the interactions that result.

In the first half of the book, we described how a Tough-Fragile differed from a Disarmer. We just touched, briefly, on the way the Disarmer and the

* Virginia Woolf, *A Room of One's Own.*

Provider as a couple are different from the Disarmer and the Ragabash as a couple. But the way a couple relationship works reflects the stage of the relationship, as well as who's involved in that relationship. A Disarmer and a Provider in Stage I, new to each other and powerfully attracted to each other, would have a significantly different relationship six years later, after Stage II had hit.

In the chapters to come, we'll describe how Stage I fosters systems of behavior that smooth away conflict and cushion a couple against failure. As the relationship wears on, however, people become less responsive to each other's needs, and more resistant to each other's attempts at coercion.

Feeling miserable, misunderstood, and trapped, couples in Stage II often despair of their relationships. A growing disillusionment with the institution of marriage is undercutting the incentive to hold to a commitment that seems to have betrayed its promise. In general, people seem to be abandoning the hope that a permanent couple relationship can be satisfying, as if that hope were a romantic illusion.

This book represents an argument to the contrary. We believe that relationships can achieve a concord that may seem prosaic but that is real and lasting and in its own way exciting.

We believe that a shared struggle through difficulties will enable them to bring their relationship to maturity; that with arduous effort, they can sustain the ardor of love.

There is no reason to expect that couple relationships will be free of the

> Knotts we doe meet with . . . daily
> Which crabbed, angry, tough, unpleasing bee.*

* John Fiske, "Upon the much-to-be-lamented decease of the Reverend Dr. John Cotton, late Teacher to the Church at Boston N.E. who departed Life 23 of 10 (16)52."

But there is good reason to trust that with realism, perspective, and intelligent responsibility, those "knotts" will mark the growth of a love that's strong, sweet, and secure.

CHAPTER 12

Stage I

FALLING IN LOVE creates an incontestable high. Our culture has affixed a peculiarly tempting invitation to the experience of falling in love, and those who respond to its beckoning find themselves filled with sweet and bittersweet emotions—with longing, passion, fondness, uncertainty—and wonder.

The delights of Stage I aren't savored by every couple, however, because not every couple comes to love each other by way of falling in love. Love between two people can grow little by little, unobtrusively knitting them into a pair. A relationship that unfolds in this deliberate fashion bypasses both the ecstasy and the angst in a full-fledged Stage I.

In fact, some people aren't willing to enter into Stage I at all. Falling in love is a risky business that requires people to deliver themselves over to the unknown and live with the awareness that they do not know how love will turn out.

Stage I unavoidably subjects people to an alarming degree of uncertainty and vulnerability. To fall in love, they must suspend many of the defenses they rely on to shield themselves from pain. Stage I forces a person to relinquish control over the experience he's involved in. The anxiety this creates can be felt as a

149

nameless, nebulous uneasiness, on the one hand, or as pangs of terror on the other.

This anxiety can take a variety of forms. Often a person interprets the uneasiness he feels as fear of rejection. 'What if she doesn't love me back,' he worries. 'What if he doesn't want me,' she fears. Stage I requires a person to make himself known to his partner, and people often dread the closeup scrutiny that closeness entails. Sharon said retrospectively, "When we were first getting together, I used to tell Jimmy all the time—if he really found out what I was like, it would be all over." To fall in love is to risk having one's shortcomings (intellectual, physical, sexual) discovered and frowned upon by the very person whose censure tells most keenly.

Stage I jitters can also manifest themselves as a fear of being swallowed up. 'Am I going to be trapped?' 'Will my individuality be blotted out?' One Disarmer said of an earlier engagement, "My fiancé was my whole identity. Nobody knew who I was. I was known as Charlie Bishop's girl friend. I don't want that to happen to me again."

An incipient Stage I can raise a person's anxiety level so high that he backs away from every potentially serious relationship. A veteran Dance-Away commented, "I've been with women who throw themselves into a thing—give up all defenses and go for the catch. It's delightful, something I'd like to be able to do. I'd like to be able to jump in like that and deal with the consequences later. Get hurt if necessary. But instead I go in with all kinds of defenses—never really getting involved, and then slide back out again at the first or second opportunity."

Fear can lead a person to barricade himself behind a wall of mistrustfulness. For example, one woman who had experienced repeated disappointments in love said, "I don't risk anymore. It used to be that men would try to get me to fall in love with them— that it wasn't just a casual thing—they really did care —that was the moment they would start pulling away.

Sooner or later they'd disappear. Gradually I closed down. I just don't let myself get carried away."

Doubting her own lovability and viewing her love for a man as a burden she foisted on him, this woman steeled herself against the rejection she anticipated. She squelched the impulse to be affectionate for fear of tipping her hand. She attempted, in various ways, to manipulate a potential partner into falling in love with her first, to ensure that she could safely fall in love with him in return. Unwittingly, this Anxious Ingenue-strategy betrayed her poor self-esteem and her desperate pessimism, thereby undercutting whatever appeal she might originally have had for a partner. When a woman is perceived as an Anxious Ingenue, a man often responds in Dance-Away fashion, by suspecting her of trying to bamboozle him and by beginning to look for an exit.

A man who's caught between a desire for Stage I and a case of insecurity about his attractiveness, is liable to look like an Anxious Pleaser to the woman he's pursuing. The more he dotes on her, the less appealing he seems. The more avidly he courts her, the more tedious she finds him. The Anxious Pleaser, in short, is experienced as a weak and slightly pitiful pest. Reluctant to hurt his feelings by telling him to go away, a woman often endures his attention until her discomfort erupts to a push-away. From this position, she can't manage a clean, clear 'No.' Instead, feeling harassed and resentful, she rejects him with a harsh, "Why don't you leave me alone?" Once set in motion, the anxious-please/push-away dynamic often rings the curtain down on an incipient relationship.

Some anxiety besets every fledgling relationship, but, needless to say, all budding couple connections aren't blighted by its effects. In fact, while certain kinds of risks and fears are built into Stage I, so are reassurances and incentives to trust. As the first traces of mutual interest ripen into mutual absorption, as touch and talk and separation and anticipation fuse into intoxication, the glow transfigures both partners. Rilke wrote of Stage I:

Oh, how my body blooms from every vein,
More fragrant, since you came into my ken.
See how I walk, more slender and upright,
And you wait calmly, and who are you then?*

Implicitly and explicitly, Stage I provides a person with proof that he is cherished. His partner's desire to be with him testifies to his significance as does her willingness to set aside old habits and commitments in his favor. The affection and approval she offers are the functional equivalents of a peal of applause—deeply comforting and deeply exhilarating. In fact, Stage I tends to act as a self-esteem escalator, which temporarily lifts a person out of self-doubt and enables him to believe that he is the truly lovable person that his partner discerns in him. Often, a Stage I couple comes to compose a kind of mutual admiration society. Entranced by the desirable qualities they discover in each other, they shrug off what shortcomings they find. Susan, a Dance-Away woman, said of her new lover, a Self-Assured Pleaser, "I respect him . . . I know he's a terrific teacher. He's sort of slow and supportive and warm. . . . It's so easy to talk to him. I feel so at peace when we're together. Everything feels right." Apropos of the debit side of the ledger, she commented, "The things that he does that I think are full of shit—like his politics—I don't care about."

Virtues arouse intense appreciation and vices appear trivial or irrelevant, a weighting that creates an extraordinarily favorable image of the other. Perceived in these flattering—perhaps fanciful—terms, the partner appears to be incapable of doing harm.

* R. M. Rilke, "Oblation."

Something said: you have nothing to fear
From those long fine bones and that beautiful
    ear.
From the mouth and the eyes set well apart
There's nothing can come that can break your
    heart.*

Stage I fosters trust; trust fosters intimacy. Susan
said, "Always before, I felt I had all kinds of things
inside me I could never let out. With Murray I feel
like I can be completely open. I'm not scared with
him. Anything that happens is okay, because there's
nothing I have to hold in."

As the couple nestles closer together physically and
psychically, they develop a growing sense of 'usness.'
Just as both focus on the other's merits and disregard
the other's defects, so both experience an overwhelming desire for closeness, which temporarily blots out
the fears intimacy might normally arouse in them.
Ambivalence about intimacy yields temporarily to the
simple childlike wish to be enfolded.

Stage I makes Pleasers of us all to some extent,
eager to bring happiness to the partner at every opportunity by every possible means. One Tough-Fragile
said of her lover, "He's so giving. I feel like I just
want to hold him, be with him, I want to do anything
that would make him feel better. Any strength I have
I would give to him."

In Stage I, people give before they're asked. They
give spontaneously and ungrudgingly. They experience their own power in terms of their ability to give
pleasure to each other, and they give, or at least they
appear to give, without keeping score, secure in the
trust that 'the more I give to him, the more I will get
back.'

Stage I inclines people to treat each other with affectionate indulgence, which defuses the impact of
whatever differences arise between them. They ex-

* Louise Bogan, "Heard by a Girl."

press their love by giving in to, as well as by giving to each other. Their overall interest in preserving good feeling takes precedence over satisfying narrower interests. For example, rather than spoil the evening, one person relinquishes his preference to see a movie and goes along without complaint to the party his partner wants to attend.

Interactions in Stage I often follow a commandeer/accommodate pattern that also minimizes conflict. One person strikes a given note, and the other chimes in to produce a harmony that's gratifying to them both. One partner, most often the man, initiates activity and takes responsibility for making a go of it. The other partner, usually the female, follows his lead, adapting her course and synchronizing her pace as closely as possible to his. Such a transaction provides him with the pleasures of dominance and affords her the pleasures of protection. The smooth mesh of the commandeer/accommodate pattern gives both the delightful sensation of being in step together practically as they're in tune together emotionally.

The instinctive teamwork of Stage I helps the couple to cope with failure as well as to skirt conflict. When one partner experiences a reverse, the other usually responds with genuine concern, manifested in one of several ways. Should one person falter in dealing with the situation, the other will volunteer a rescue if it seems to be within his power. For example, one Tough-Fragile man said of his Tough-Fragile girl friend, "She came to the relationship with a backlog of bum sexual experiences. She had avoided men for about six months, and she could hardly handle any sexual contact without freaking out. I was patient and gentle and she gradually relaxed . . . I saw myself as helping her to get freer."

When they are falling in love, people are deeply responsive to each other's needs. They often offer each other unequivocal backing, and display an inexhaustible interest in each other's feelings. The alliance between them is deepened by this interminable talk—

about what's going on in their lives and how the pair of them should deal with it.

If problems sometimes arise that are too threatening to be discussed, they are apt to be assiduously avoided. For example, one young Disarmer attempted to deal with her fiancé's impotence by ignoring it. She said later, "I never wanted to say anything, because I guess, in the beginning, I thought it would scare him away or we wouldn't get married, or something." Serious faltering elicits protective avoidance. In Stage I, people avert their eyes from each other's failures as they disregard each other's faults—to preserve their images of each other and to safeguard their hopes for the relationship.

The flip side of Stage I tenderness around each other's weaknesses is relish in each other's strengths. A Tough-Fragile said of her Prizewinner partner, "I pick on him physically; I love to tease him, grab his ass, pull on his moustache. It's my way of being affectionate. He acts like he hates it, but he really loves it. And he's great to play with in this sense because he says, 'I'll kick your ass.'" Matching wits against each other and cutting loose together, the partners can bounce off each other's high spirits.

A person who is falling in love feels good about himself, good about his partner, and good about the relationship—so good that he's tempted to believe that the relationship will realize his fantasies and transform his life. A Disarmer said, "My relationship with Martin is so beautiful, so perfect, so fulfilling . . . I can imagine being locked away with him in the middle of nowhere for the next ten years and it would be great."

But under these circumstances, a person's vision of his partner is doubly distorted. His perception is colored by his selective attention; his desire to seek out and attend to what he finds admirable in the other and to blank out whatever is discreditable.

Both partners strive to be their finest selves and

they're apt to be at their most appealing in the context of Stage I. Providers are a good bit more open and spontaneous in Stage I than they are otherwise. The Tough-Fragile looks softer and warmer, the Victim more cheerful and easygoing than they otherwise might. Stage I usually displays people to advantage because it leads them to relinquish, temporarily, many of their ill-favored defenses.

To a certain extent, Stage I also cushions individuals from external stress. A reverse at work, a spell of financial trouble, don't pinch as painfully when there's a newfound lover to kiss the hurt and make it well.

But the bleak fact is that Stage I is necessarily fleeting. Over time, satiation dilutes the intense pleasure the partners originally found in being together. Real-world obligations encroach on the relationship. As evidence of each other's shortcomings piles up, and as the relationship begins to exact visible costs, mutual idealization gives way to mutual disillusionment. With the dimming of the Stage I sparkle, any underlying ambivalence about intimacy begins to reassert itself. The Tough-Fragile becomes more hostile and distaste creeps over the Dance-Away.

"Soon done with, and yet dearly and dangerously sweet,"* Stage I inveigles lovers into the belief that the whole of their relationship will prove as auspicious as its debut. In fact, the systems of behavior which lead a couple to believe 'we get along so well' are more a function of the situation (falling in love) than they are the result of the special qualities that the partners bring to the situation.

Over the long term, the liabilities inherent in each role begin to take their toll. Conflict will arise between the partners that can't be smoothed away by means of mutual pleasing or the commandeer/ac-

* Gerard Manley Hopkins, "The Leaden Echo and the Golden Echo."

commodate pattern. Continued faltering will tax the goodwill that enables the partner to respond at first with a helping hand or sympathetic commiseration. The teamwork of Stage I is apt to shift gradually into the divisive and threatening exchanges (like blame and withholding) that characterize Stage II. Gradually, a couple discovers all the dismal reasons why they shouldn't be together after all.

Stage I can cloak a relationship in a specious plausibility, and when a person is gripped by desire, he can rationalize even the most inappropriate, ill-considered choice of partners. A commitment made on this impulsive basis may well collapse under the weight of the incompatibilities both partners originally tried to ignore. Someone who's falling in love can take serious chances—financial risks, or birth-control risks, for example—that might have consequences he's not prepared to handle. Falling in love is such a powerful and profoundly pleasurable experience that it can make more mundane activities seem empty in comparison. Preoccupied with the beloved, a person can let his life slip into a muddle of neglected duties.

Furthermore, in Stage I, a couple's desire for togetherness can be so urgent that it leads them to neglect other relationships. Intent on each other, the couple can become unavailable to the friends and family members who are used to depending on them. The onset of ardor can provoke major changes in the lovers' lives, and others may find that they can't be counted on to behave in familiar fashion. The resulting anxiety can make the bystanders critical.

When a person discovers that others are reacting adversely to the fact that he's fallen in love, he's apt to feel hurt and to discount their response as jealousy. To shield himself from their disapproval, he may retreat even further into the haven of the relationship, intensifying the threat to those who already feel displaced by it.

A person who's falling in love necessarily relinquishes some of his prudence and some of his self-control. He may profit greatly from this temporary abandon—this yielding to emotion and this sense of merging with another. Stage I offers most people the most intense intimacy they ever experience with another adult. Furthermore, Stage I means a fresh start, of sorts. To genuinely fall in love is to reach a major juncture in life; a crossroads where old commitments can be reassessed and new alternatives explored. But for best results, this willingness to take risks should be tempered with a little perspective.

One phase of a long-term process, Stage I constitutes the most romantic, but not the most enduring, version of coupled love. Stage I should be appreciated for what it is—a very special experience, and not mistaken for what it isn't—a paradigm to which all experiences of love should conform. Delightful in and of itself, a Stage I doesn't ensure that a relationship has a potential to endure or flourish.

To have gone through a Stage I bestows a valuable benefit on a couple's relationship, as well as on them as individuals. In Stage I, two people learn how to enjoy themselves together. They discover pleasures they can share and ways to spend time together that make both of them feel good. Needless to say, a couple can't survive on a capacity to have fun together, and likewise, a couple can make do without knowing how to be playful or joyful together. But a relationship that lacks this endowment is the poorer for it. Evanescent of itself, Stage I can leave a couple a valuable legacy—the knowledge that they can create pleasure together—that will help them to keep their relationship a source of satisfaction to them both.

CHAPTER 13

Sex

FOR MANY PEOPLE, having sex is like going to parties —not nearly the good time it's cracked up to be. Parties are often given and attended out of obligation, and the same sense of duty tarnishes many a sexual relationship. Nevertheless, the p.r. for both activities remains great. The cultural idealization of sex we engage in provides us with a profusion of evidence (films, books, photographs) about the heights of performance and pleasure we should receive as sexual beings. But as Carole Lombard is reported to have said about her husband, Clark Gable, when someone asked about his prowess as a lover, "Gable's no Gable." We know the scale on which we're expected to enjoy sex, and if the actuality doesn't match the anticipation, we blame ourselves or our partner for the discrepancy.

Some people are troubled by their inability to enjoy a free-wheeling sex life. The one-night stand can generate so much performance pressure that a participant can't even function, much less derive pleasure from the encounter. More numerous, though, are those who have trouble enjoying the overly familiar and somewhat perfunctory sex they have with an established partner. A Self-Assured Pleaser said about his eleven-year marriage, "We had a couple of years of happy

159

dynamic sex, but it seems like since then the curve has been down in terms of frequency and pleasurability."

The lovemaking that people are apt to enjoy most is the lovemaking that they share in Stage I. "That first fine careless rapture" can turn good sex into euphoria.

> Did each become the other in that play?
> She laughed me out and then she laughed me in.
> In the deep middle of ourselves we lay,
> When glory failed, we danced upon a pin.*

If a Stage I couple must contend with a substantial sexual problem, they're apt to minimize its significance. As Norman Mailer wrote: "A bruised apple at the foot of the tree is another reality from a bruised apple in the frigidaire." † Similarly, in the setting of Stage I, when a couple is still gamboling in the orchard they are usually willing to savor the sweetness of their sexual relationship and to overlook what would otherwise count as blemishes in it.

Solidifying the couple relationship takes precedence over correcting the sex problem and both partners ignore the difficulty to avoid jeopardizing the commitment. Usually they hope that they will outgrow the problem in time as they become more comfortable together.

Frequently, though, as the years wear away, a couple's sexual difficulties aren't eased; they're exacerbated. The passage of time can serve to entrench sexual failure and to extinguish hope that the dysfunction(s) will ever disappear. Disagreements over what's appropriate sexually are likely to tax their tolerance, and prompt value judgments like moral/immoral, healthy/perverse, liberated/uptight.

In many Stage II relationships, sex becomes a cas-

* Theodore Roethke, "The Wraith."
† Norman Mailer, *The Prisoner of Sex*.

ualty as well as a cause of stress between the partners. When they are at odds emotionally, two people often feel unable or unwilling to allow each other sexual intimacy. A Provider who had recently separated from his wife observed, "Somehow we just got mad at each other for reasons other than sex, and it invaded the sexual thing in the sense that we turned off sexually. Then sex went backward and made us lose affection for each other. By the end, neither of us felt much desire to do it."

Monotony is another antagonist an established sexual relationship must contend with, although resentment is frequently traveling under the alias of boredom with a partner's body or sexual style. "We've got the mechanics down pat," said one Ragabash. "We both have orgasms and all. But we've developed a pattern. There are certain times we do it and certain ways we do it and it's gotten kind of blah. There isn't much spontaneity or enthusiasm to it anymore."

Sometimes, dissatisfaction with sex now is based on memories of how much better it used to be. One Disarmer said of the man she'd been living with for several years, "I used to get really excited with Jerry. I used to get really turned on when we first met. That was really fun." At other times, disappointment with sex stems from the disparity between the way it is and the way the culture leads us to believe that it should be.

More often than not, reality doesn't honor the sexual expectations the media have fostered in us.

A sexual relationship that's frustrating or threatening tends to push people in one of two directions. Sometimes discouragement over a sexual relationship leads a person to recruit a new sexual partner and to share with that partner all the delights of dalliance—a short-term solution. The person who wants a long-term solution can seek help from the experts who tender their advice in books and articles and columns, or he can obtain direct professional assistance in the form of sex therapy.

The last ten years have seen major innovations in the treatment of sex problems.* However, this progress in the practical realm hasn't been matched by advances in the theoretical realm. Human sexual responsiveness is still conceptualized almost entirely within the framework of ideas that William Masters and Virginia Johnson introduced in the 1960s. Masters' and Johnson's analysis of sex problems in terms of dysfunctions and performance pressure is an achievement of truly remarkable force. But while we consider this framework of ideas necessary for an understanding of sex, we don't believe that it's sufficient to explain what goes on between people who make love. The Masters and Johnson model leaves the interpersonal—the couple—aspects of the sexual relationship largely unexplored. We prefer to address ourselves to the neglected interpersonal dimension of sex. The approach we have developed does not compete with the dysfunction-performance pressure model; we consider the two complementary.

To know that a sexual relationship is troubled by a given form of failure (or conflict or monotony) is to know something significant. To know how the partners react to such difficulty is to know a good deal more. We have addressed ourselves to this issue—to the question of what strategies couples adopt in relation to sexual power and pleasure and performance.

Take, for example, the case of Jack and Deedee. Jack was a Provider in his mid-forties who began to experience sporadic impotence. After his first few failures, Jack began to approach lovemaking with trepidation. He would waver about initiating sex, worried that "when I got there I wasn't going to have anything." More and more frequently he would find himself unable to carry through on the sex he did initiate.

* Particularly the development of women's and men's groups as effective and inexpensive formats for therapy.

"When I couldn't get it up—it would make Deedee feel she was not sexually attractive, so she would cry. And I would feel tremendously guilty, and then it was straight downhill from there. I would break out into a cold sweat when I got into bed because I was scared to death I wouldn't be able to do it." When it turned out he wasn't going to be able to do it, in Deedee's words, "We would both be very disappointed, and just go to sleep real fast to escape."

As Jack began to think of himself as a sexual failure he would "think about sex and get uptight . . ." Increasingly, he avoided mentioning sex and detoured around situations that might possibly have led to sex. On the few occasions when Deedee ventured an overture, he fended her off with one or another of the excuses used to cloak discomfort. He said, "I withdraw. I tell her, 'Leave me alone. I'm tired.' Sometimes I am. But sometimes after I do it, I'm ashamed of myself." Jack's solution to his anxiety about their sex life was characteristic of a Provider: he retreated from the problem into avoidance.

Deedee dealt with her anxiety in characteristic Disarmer fashion by protecting her husband as best she could. She hesitated to broach the topic of his impotence because, as she said, "I felt like I would be insulting his masculinity or something. Like maybe he would never be able to forgive me for it." But she was deeply hurt by his impotence, which she experienced as rejection. "It makes me feel like I'm not very desirable or not a very good lover," she said unhappily. "When his erection goes away I just feel terrible. I don't want to face the disappointment." To spare them both the pain and shame of sexual failure, she colluded with him in avoiding sex.

Mutual avoidance is often a couple's solution to sexual failure, but its short-term plausibility belies its long-term destructiveness. Couples often hope, naïvely, that *taking the pressure off* will help relieve the problem. In fact, the conspicuous absence of sex from the couple's life most of the time increases the pressure on the occasions when someone does risk initiating sexual contact.

When two people experience recurrent sexual failure, both are apt to need reassurance that they are worthwhile and desirable individuals anyway and that the love between them isn't collapsing beneath the weight of sexual misfortune. A system of avoidance ensures that this kind of reassurance can't be exchanged. The cost of avoidance isn't just sexual isolation, therefore, though it often does mean that "We never touch each other at all." The further penalty it exacts is emotional isolation.

> Talking in bed ought to be easiest
> Lying together there goes back so far . . .
> Yet more and more time passes silently . . .
>
> . . . Nothing shows why
> At this unique distance from isolation
>
> It becomes still more difficult to find
> Words at once true and kind,
> Or not untrue and not unkind.*

Over the long term, a person who engaged in protective avoidance on his partner's behalf may well end up begrudging the strain of a sacrifice that was originally made willingly. Deedee said, "For about a year and a half I was getting frustrated. About half the time I'd walk around making excuses for Jack in my mind. Because I figured that if he had a potency problem, it wasn't going to do me much good to put a lot of pressure on him. The other half of the time, I was walking around planning to leave him. But I never told him that. I thought he'd be upset and crushed by it." Deedee found herself fantasizing about a person with a "big erect penis," speculating about affairs with men who would coolly dominate her. At length she realized, "These excuses I'm making for him, this

* Philip Larkin, "Talking in Bed."

could just keep going indefinitely. I'm waiting for him; I might have to wait forever. And I feel like I can't live with the situation much longer. In other ways, we have a good relationship, but this is starting to overshadow the other aspects of our lives."

The strain on her wasn't lost on Jack. He said, "She'll be really hard to live with, and she'll act like it's other things, but it's really this." He worried that he might eventually lose her, but he still shied away from acknowledging the problem. He said, "I think she wants to face it. I want to sweep it under the carpet." Dysfunctions can't be wished away. But most dysfunctions can be remedied if the couple can bring themselves to confront their problem and secure competent professional help in treating it.

Mutual avoidance around a dysfunction is not the only bad alternative to getting help with it. A couple can also evolve into the anxious-please/push-away response to sexual failure. The anxious-please/push-away system is particularly common as a response to a woman's difficulty in achieving orgasm.

Being nonorgasmic is no longer a woman's private misfortune; this complaint has recently become a concern for her partner as well. The crumbling of the old double standard around sexual pleasure (he gets it, she goes without) can only be cheered. Fairness and practicality require that women too be able to expect that their sexual relationships will afford them arousal and orgasm.

But many couples try in vain to realize this expectation. Women's inhibitions about expressing their sexual preferences, the assumption that *real sex* means intercourse, the prejudice both men and women feel against the clitoris—all amount to a deck that's stacked against a woman's prospects for orgasm. Furthermore, performance pressure often seizes the woman who's trying to have an orgasm.

In our culture, the man who's trying to perform well attempts to prolong intercourse by delaying his orgasm. If performance pressure makes him tense, it's liable to speed his orgasm and render him a premature ejaculator. Conversely, the woman who's trying to perform well wants to reach climax quickly, usually more quickly than is easy for her. Often she feels, "It takes me longer to come than it should, so I get uptight." She worries that her partner will become weary or impatient with her, and she tries to force herself to "respond or he'll get bored. Respond!" Her anxiety blocks arousal and delays her orgasm or derails it completely.

The woman who doubts that she's capable of having an orgasm, or doubts that her partner is capable of "giving" her one, may end up faking. Faking, the conventional feminine solution to being nonorgasmic —is essentially denial of and defeatism about the the problem. A woman forecloses her own opportunity for orgasm in order to spare her partner and herself the risks of pursuing it.

Janet was a preorgasmic woman. She had never experienced orgasm under any circumstances but she had faked it, first with several lovers and then with her husband. Her frustration mounted over the seven years of her marriage, however, and exposure to a more liberal outlook on female sexuality persuaded her to try masturbating. After several weeks of secret practice, Janet climaxed for the first time in her life.

It was several more weeks before she managed to tell her husband the news. She was mortified to have to confess her deception, and her husband, Herb, was mortified to discover the real state of their sex life. Both hoped, however, that her new skill could be transferred easily to him.

Herb was unaccustomed to giving a woman clitoral stimulation, though, and his hands seemed clumsy to them both. Janet said later, "I kept telling him 'Softer. Softer. That real hard stuff really turns me off.'" But although she tried to show him what to do and he struggled to "get it right," her body refused to respond properly. She remained situationally nonorgasmic, which meant in her case, able to experience orgasm alone, through masturbation, but not in her partner's presence or through his touch.

As their lovemaking became progressively more tense and awkward, Janet began to react adversely to Herb's sexual attentions. She complained that he rubbed her too hard and left her sore, that his elbow was pulling her hair, or the weight of his body was squeezing the breath out of her. She registered annoyance that he began intercourse too soon and kept at it too long. She became convinced that Herb was an inept lover, and that his incompetence was to blame for her unresponsiveness.

In fact, sexual stimuli trigger a process which involves a person's attitudes and emotions as integrally as his nerve endings. Although the authority of the body in this respect is rarely challenged, responses like arousal and aversion don't represent raw sensory data; they are conclusions shaped by the interplay of psychology and physiology. In Janet's case, performance pressure made it difficult for her to relax and enjoy sex. Anxiety converted Herb's touch into an annoyance to her and she would snap, "That feels terrible. Let me alone!" She began to push him away, sexually and emotionally.

In response, Herb intensified his anxious-pleasing, with the usual unfavorable consequences. His desire to bring Janet to orgasm registered on her as a demand for her to climax. Herb acknowledged, "If she doesn't have orgasm, I feel so incredibly bad and guilty that it really makes it worse for her, and it makes it more tense the next time." More tense for both of them, because as Herb said, "When she doesn't have an orgasm, I guess it's that I tell myself that I'm not very good in bed."

The sexual Anxious Pleaser falls prey to his own version of performance pressure. He tries to figure out how to turn his partner on and watches for signs that she likes what he's doing. Janet said, "If I'm passive, if I'm not moving my hips or something, he has a feeling nothing is happening . . . A lot of times he'll say 'How is it?' and it's hard for me to be honest. Because if I say I'm not feeling anything, or it doesn't feel good, then he gets upset." Herb added, "I just want her to *enjoy* it. If I don't feel like I'm making her happy or pleasing her, the whole thing is totally meaningless for me."

What would have made Janet happy was to be swept off her feet by an aggressive self-confident man, and she scorned her partner's sexual hesitance. Locked into an anxious-please/push-away system around sex, the couple gradually became alienated and antagonistic outside of bed as well as in it.

Frequently, resentment about other aspects of the relationship ends up contaminating a couple's sex life. Sometimes one partner deliberately uses sex as a weapon against the other. More often, though, strain elsewhere in the relationship seems to be involuntarily converted into disinterest in sex. "I just feel like I can't relate to her sexually if I can't relate to her in other areas." The result is often a demand/withhold system around sex, such as operated in the lives of Eleanor and Sam. Eleanor was a thirty-year-old Disarmer stuck at home with two children who kept her busy but not happy. Sam was a Provider, and when he got home he usually settled down with the paper or watched TV. This lack of sociability bothered her, and she said, "I feel really bad when he hasn't spoken to me all day and then we go to bed and he wants to have sex. I don't feel loved then, I feel used. Sex should come out of closeness, not be the only contact there is."

As a Provider, Sam found it easiest to make an emotional connection via sex. Sex reassured him that he was loved and wanted and ideally would have conveyed the same reassurance to Eleanor. For her, however, sex lacked this penumbra of positive significance and her simple physical pleasure in it had never equaled his. She said, "I have to feel loved in order to feel sexual." Increasingly unhappy about the state of their relationship, Eleanor did not often feel loved and did not often feel sexual. She didn't consciously punish Sam with a sexual cold shoulder, but her resentment against him did contribute a good deal to her lack of desire for sex with him.

Sam said, "I feel rejected most of the time when she doesn't respond. One part of it is simply frustration. Sometimes it's almost like—in my mind—like I'm really hungry and she says, 'No, you can't open the refrigerator.' And I say, 'Why not? I'm really hungry.' It feeds itself. It gets worse and worse. So what I do, in effect, is walk out of the kitchen. I'm sitting there thinking of radial tires or when my next report is due —trying to completely remove myself from the situation." But he didn't succeed. He said, "For a long time I've tried to say to myself—just because Eleanor doesn't want to make love with me—I shouldn't feel rejected . . . But I begin to feel bad, constantly pursuing her and her always backing off."

Eleanor's withholding hooked Sam's doubts about his attractiveness and made him question how much she really cared for him. Frustrated and threatened, Sam began an anxious demand for sex. "I guess I've become rather insistent about it," he said. Hopeful that perhaps she would yield to his entreaties if she realized how much it mattered to him, Sam coaxed and pestered and complained.

In response to this badgering, Eleanor dug in her heels. She said, "I feel pressured to have sex, and when all that pressure is on me, it just makes it worse . . . I feel like there's something inside me telling me, 'Don't do it, just don't do it.' " Withholding made her uncomfortable. "I feel guilty and uptight saying no," she said. But she was also angry. "No matter what I do, it's not enough. He wants something more immediately."

The demand/withhold system can become functionally autonomous, a process which perpetuates itself independent of the conflicts which originally caused it. Sam said, "I keep asking, and she keeps saying, 'No.' The more I ask, the more she says 'No.' So, sometimes I think the thing to do is stop asking."

But breaking out of the system is not so easy. Eleanor said, "I know several times you've said, "I'm not gonna pursue her anymore. I'm sick of getting rebuffed. I'm just going to wait and let her do the initiating.' But the minute that happened in your mind, I knew it. I knew that you were just sitting there thinking, 'I'm waiting.' And the more you waited, the more I thought, 'Screw it! I'm not going over there. He's expecting me to. I don't want to be expected!' "

Withholding usually cuts a person off from his own desire for sex and his own satisfaction in sex. Periodically, Eleanor would succumb to feeling guilty about not wanting sex. "So I think, 'Well, okay.' Then I don't enjoy it." Like resentment and anxiety, this kind of guilt is an antidote to pleasure, and another disagreeable episode of sex reinforces the withholder's belief that what she really wants is to be spared the whole business.

Withholding sex is traditionally a feminine strategy, but increasing numbers of men now seem to be turning to it. In many respects, male withholding is exactly like female withholding, but often male withholding seems to have more serious consequences for a couple. The role demands that a man be sexually aggressive, and a woman sexually submissive, are apt to make him very uncomfortable if he's withholding and her very uncomfortable if she's put in the position of demanding sex for herself.

A couple's choice of sexual strategies can interlock to their benefit as well as to their detriment. The conventional way to ensure sexual harmony is the commandeer/accommodate system. One partner (typically the male) exercises the initiative, and the other partner (typically the female) acquiesces in the preferences he displays. One partner assumes the assertive role, the other the adaptive role, and the complementarity of the resulting system forestalls conflict between them. Especially if this system is flexible—if both partners are willing to lead at times and follow at other times—the sex that results can be satisfying to them both.

Mutual pleasing can create the same agreeable results. When both partners devote their imagination and their skill to enhancing each other's pleasure, each can soak up enjoyment vicariously as well as directly. Each feels willing to give because each is aware that the other will give back—reciprocity fosters generosity. But both mutual pleasing and the commandeer/accommodate can break down if either member of the pair becomes dissatisfied with his share of the pleasure proceeds.

A man who is locked into commandeering and a woman who is habitually accommodating can run into trouble if their lovemaking doesn't bring her sufficient pleasure. If he doesn't know how to bring her to orgasm (or doesn't realize she isn't getting there), and she's too uninformed or too inhibited to guide him, then sex may eventually become a chore to her. The accumulation of her resentment may eventually make her unwilling to comply with his sexual desires. In this event, the commandeer/accommodate system is apt to shift into a demand/withhold system. Alternatively a man can feel burdened by the responsibility of commandeering. He can experience passivity in his partner as a demand to "do it to me." Sex on this basis can seem to the uncertain man like being forced to give a speech instead of being allowed to have a conversation. His retreat from this performance pressure can lead to partial or complete avoidance of sex. A third unfortunate ending for the commandeer/accommodate system is a man's resentment of his partner's sexual-do-nothingness. One Self-Assured Pleaser complained of his wife, "From the time we got married, sex was not a mutual thing. It was my responsibility. I had to make the approaches. She decided whether or not to accept. Sometimes her attitude was 'it's okay'; sometimes 'it's kind of a chore'; sometimes it just didn't happen." Although this couple often experienced simultaneous orgasm (for many the definition of sexual satisfaction), "She still never made any approaches to me, or let me know she was turned on to me, or got actively involved. It was a passive involvement. I really started withholding a lot because I felt that she wasn't being fair. She would accept my attention—accept all I could give her—but she wouldn't give me anything back, or say, 'You're okay. Our sexual thing is good.' " The original commandeer/accommodate system between these two evolved, over a period of years, into mutual withholding.

A sexual relationship requires a person to deal with power and pleasure, intimacy and anxiety. He often responds to these issues in the same fashion whether they are raised in the narrow context of sex or in the broader context of the whole relationship. But is there any predictable connection between particular sexual dysfunctions and the roles one adopts in a relationship? Which female role is most commonly associated with anorgasmia? Which male stance is most prone to impotence? The answers are inconclusive at best. The reason it is so difficult to posit connections between particular roles and dysfunctions lies in the complex etiology of sexual problems. There are many different reasons why men become impotent or lose ejaculatory control; and women's lack of sexual response is likewise complexly determined. Similar symptoms can be very differently derived. Both a Prizewinner and an Anxious Pleaser may ejaculate prematurely, but the Anxious Pleaser's obsession with pleasing his partner is the likely source of his distress, while the Prizewinner falters when he is trying to be a sexual superstar. A number of professional athletes we have seen have been premature ejaculators for this reason. Compared to the Anxious Pleaser who keeps trying, the Prizewinner is more apt to shy away from failure, avoid sex, and thereby make a bigger deal out of fewer occasions.

By and large the roles suggest how individuals will be likely to deal with a sexual dysfunction if they have one, not whether they will have one. Sexual strategies may well prove to be a metaphor for the role one assumes in the rest of the relationship. For example, aversion, saying as it does, "I don't want any; go away and leave me alone," is a classic push-away maneuver. The counterdependency inherent in the aversive stance is most characteristic of Tough-Fragiles, Victims, and Dance-Aways. When the Dance-Away feels he must move on because the initial rush of infatuation has faded, the claim apt to be made is, 'You just don't turn me on anymore.' Fragiles and Anxious Ingenues, on the other hand, almost never feel aversive or withhold sexual favors. 'It won't seem to come out of my mouth to say no!' The desire to possess the partner and the fear of losing him make them sexually accommodating no matter what. The exception to this universal accommodation occurs when the Anxious Ingenue or the Fragile receives the overwhelming attention of an Anxious Pleaser; then they reject him just like everyone else.

Disarmers, Anxious Ingenues, and Fragiles are least at ease with assertion. Even if pressured by a partner to take initiative and ask for what they want, such women are uncomfortable directing. Receptivity is their strong suit. Passivity may be their downfall: if they don't know what they like and their partners can't guess, these are likely candidates for the nonorgasmic class. Unlike Tough-Fragiles, these women don't take their sexuality into their own hands. Their strategy is to wait patiently: "Someday my prince will come and so will I."*

* A. J. Nelson, "Personality Correlates of Female Orgasmicity." (Master's Thesis, University of California at Berkeley, 1974.)

In considering the etiology of sexual dysfunction, it is important to note the crucial differences between simple sexual dysfunctions and couple-generated sexual problems. The former usually antedate the relationship and arise from anxiety, inhibition, and misinformation. In the latter, the sexual sphere has been invaded by the power struggles of the couple system. Withholding is almost invariably a sexual symptom of a disturbed couple system. Situationally nonorgasmic women (women who reach climax in some situations and not others) may be exhibiting the simple sexual dysfunction of lack of information, or be acting out the withholding half of an anxious demand/withhold. Tough-Fragiles and Victims are often able to achieve orgasm through masturbation, while they have long since stopped having (or never experienced) orgasm with their partners. Used to controlling their partners through withholding, they'll agree to make love but complain, 'You're not doing it right.' To express anger, they withhold their own pleasure. The Provider may also express anger indirectly by withholding sex. Men who are uncomfortable with anger are likely candidates for impotence as well.

Frequently, characteristic roles and sexual strategy do seem to fit together like a hand and glove, but many other variables besides a person's role shape sexual behavior. One relevant variable is the level of sexual self-confidence. The higher one's sexual self-esteem, the greater his tolerance for failure—in himself or in his partner—and the less he is susceptible to the kinds of defensive strategies or dysfunctions we've described.

The other major variable that figures into the equation is what purpose sex serves. A person's sexual strategy reflects whether he uses sex to express his anger, or to establish distance in the relationship, or to serve as a surrogate for affection.

Our analysis of sex focuses primarily on the strategies that individuals pursue and the system that their behaviors create. We believe that a couple's relationship cannot be understood without a grasp of the stage

of that relationship and the sexual systems that structure it. A Disarmer who uses sex to establish intimacy
in Stage I may begin using it to express her anger as
State II descends. A system like mutual withholding is
almost invariably a symptom of Stage II. Often then, a
couple's sexual relationship serves as a kind of micro-
cosm for their entire relationship.

Improving a sexual relationship is apt to be a
more difficult business than the sex manuals imply,
even if that relationship is reasonably good to begin
with. From a practical standpoint, any attempt at im-
provement must address a troubled relationship on the
system level as well as on the level of dysfunction. If
a man's impotence is cured, while the system of avoidance that grew up around it isn't dismantled, the
couple is likely to slip right back into their old pattern.

Whether they work together with or without the assistance of a therapist, two people who want to improve their sexual relationship must each learn to take
responsibility for their own sexual pleasure, to ask
for what they want, and to exchange information
about what is pleasurable and what is not. They must
learn to stay in touch with pleasurable sensations and
to acknowledge anxiety openly when it interferes with
that pleasure. The most constructive response to anxiety is usually to slow down in deference to it, to fall
back to some more general kind of pleasuring and allow the tension to dissipate.

The simplest way for a couple to heighten their
arousal and increase the intensity of their orgasms is
to tease each other. Teasing, the slow seductive gather-
ing of pleasure, is an easily accessible, nonprescription
aphrodisiac that will enliven almost any sexual relationship.

But no matter how fully functional, cooperative,
and varied a long-term sexual relationship is, it can't
consistently deliver the same ecstasy that a sexual
Stage I can offer. People tend to envision an ideal sexual relationship as a perpetual Stage I. No lasting
relationship can fulfill that hope, a hope at once com-

mercial and romantic. Sexual pleasure can, however, outlast novelty and euphoria and can become a deep, shared, and knowing satisfaction, one that strengthens the affection and trust necessary for true, and truly mature, intimacy.

CHAPTER 14

Stage II

STAGE II of a couple relationship begins in disappointment. Conflicts and failures pile up, the letdown settles in, and a couple begins to realize that their relationship is not bringing them the fulfillment they'd hoped for. Instead, "The reality of living with her—it isn't good. It isn't working. We haven't been getting along for a long time," said one man of his wife of eight years. "It's really getting me down."

> And it was in vain that tears blotted the contract
>   now, because
> It had been freely drawn up and consented to
>   as insurance
> Against the very condition it was now so efficiently
> Seeking to establish . . .*

the couples' mutual unhappiness.

As attraction gives way to alienation, and optimism yields to pessimism, people express their anxiety and their resentment in characteristic ways. The Victim retreats into "thunderous and oppressive gloom"; the Tough-Fragile becomes ever more hostile and quarrelsome, and the Provider withdraws into emotional isolation. Given their different patterns of response,

* John Ashbery, "Clepsydra."

couples are prone to different versions of Stage II's distress.

A Provider and a Disarmer are likely to turn to silence. "She gets mad at me over something. Then she clams up. Then I clam up, so that makes things worse, and we don't talk to each other for two or three days." There's no overt anger and no disruption of routine, but under the surface "We freeze each other out."

The Provider and the Tough-Fragile are likely to end up with him "withdrawn into stony defensive silence, and her lashing into him with bitter invective." A Tough-Fragile and a Self-Assured Pleaser are likely to wind up fighting pitched battles. "We're constantly at each other's throats," said one Tough-Fragile. "The things that would have caused little fights between us have gotten 'way out of hand, and we're having huge screaming battles." Estrangement comes in these and other forms, all unanticipated and all unwelcome.

In Stage I, a couple has the pleasure of discovering agreeable likenesses between them and likable aspects of the differences between them. In Stage II, however, as they try to integrate their values and their habits, a couple must come to grips with the differences which truly divide them. For as William Godwin wrote, "It is absurd to expect the inclinations and wishes of two human beings should coincide through any long period of time. To oblige them to act and to live together is to subject them to some inevitable portion of thwarting, bickering and unhappiness."*

They discover, for example, that in his enthusiasm for a given pair of friends, "He wants to see them Friday night, Saturday afternoon, Saturday evening, and Sunday afternoon." But as for her, "I don't have such a smacking wonderful time over there." Or she realizes that, "Doing the same thing every morning— getting up, making coffee, feeding the cats, eating

* William Godwin, *Political Justice*, quoted in Frederick L. Beaty, *Light from Heaven*.

granola—I kind of like that. It regulates my day. Every morning the same thing; it gets me going, where I think it gives him the doldrums." It did.

Such differences over what a couple finds enjoyable and comfortable often feed into differences over what they see as reasonable. For example, one Tough-Fragile man said of a conflict with his wife (a Victim who suffered recurrent aches and pains), "I remember one time she was in the bedroom and she wanted me to plug in the electric pad for her. Just plug it in—a normal electric pad in a regular outlet. I was really tired, and I was sitting in the living room, and I said, 'I'm really tired. Plug it in yourself.' She was right there. All she had to do was lean over to plug it in. And she said, 'No, I can't. It's too hard.' We got in a real big argument about it."

In Stage II, every couple discovers that there are crucial ways in which their operating procedures do not mesh, and crucial features of each other they find neither "creditable nor lovable."* The question then becomes, "What do I do about all those things about him that I don't like, things he can't change—his jokes, his values . . . ?"

Usually the partners find it difficult to reconcile themselves to the liabilities inherent in what originally counted as assets. The Prizewinner's partner finds that "to admire a strong person and to live under that strong person's thumb are two different things."† The Disarmer's partner finds that behind her feminine yieldingness lies a reluctance to assume responsibility —even when he needs her to.

There are discoveries that are even less welcome than these, however. Infatuation is compounded partly from ignorance and partly from denial. Stage I doesn't usually elicit displays of cruelty, dishonesty, irresponsibility, or the like. To the extent that a person

* Virginia Woolf, quoted in Quentin Bell, *Virginia Woolf, A Biography.*

† George Bernard Shaw, "Pygmalion."

glimpses such faults in his partner, he's likely to see their brunt falling on others and to discount their relevance to himself. Sooner or later, however, he finds himself forced to contend with the worst propensities in the person he's chosen, because those propensities are now directed against himself. Stage II therefore involves a gradual and disturbing discovery of the "slipperiness of the soul"* of each partner.

It is difficult to be subjected to someone else's flaws and limitations without questioning the wisdom of the commitment to that person. It can also be difficult to keep from using such discreditable discoveries about a person as weapons against him. For example, one Ragabash told his Tough-Fragile wife, "It hurt me a lot when you said I was weak. It came from all those times I let you know I felt weak. That bothers me. Why should I want to tell you where I'm at if you're going to use it on me?" Since disillusionment is a painful process all around, Stage II usually entails defensiveness about one's self and disenchantment about one's partner.

Stage II means mutual disapproval, the more painful because it's unexpected. The most concentrated dose of approval people usually get comes when they're falling in love. A major proof of the rightness of a new relationship is the fact that the partner 'makes me feel so good.' But gradually, the appreciation turns to criticism. One Provider said, "A million times she's made me feel like I never made the mark and I never would." She rejoined, "In a lot of ways, I don't respect my husband. Am I supposed to lie about it?" It's difficult for most people to maintain their self-esteem in the face of such intimate, informed disapproval, and the characteristic Stage II complaint becomes, 'You make me feel so bad.'

The anxiety and the resentment that mark Stage II often provoke people to behavior they have trouble

* Virginia Woolf, quoted in Quentin Bell, *Virginia Woolf, A Biography*.

accepting in themselves. One woman brooded, "I've become a bitch. The more he doesn't listen to me, the more I yell. And I don't like it. I'm always screaming —I'm sick of myself."

Usually a person holds his partner responsible for the unappetizing changes that have been wrought in him. This woman invoked the fact that "I don't get into scenes like that with anybody else" to reassure herself that the fault for them lay with her partner.

The issue of who's at fault obscures the fact that people almost invariably behave badly in Stage II. One of the reasons they do so is because they have realized that their couple relationship is never going to give them the things they truly want. In Stage I, optimism and goodwill sweeten what sacrifices were necessary. The satisfactions a couple didn't obtain from their relationship were deferred ('it will happen sooner or later and I can wait till then') or discounted ('it doesn't matter, I can go without').

This is more easily said than done over the long term. In Stage II, a couple must come to grips with the fact that 'there are so many things that aren't there' in their relationship and that the sacrifices it exacts are not just painful, but are hardening into permanence.

One man said, "I wake up in the morning and feel 'Aaagh, what's the point in getting up?' and I want to turn to somebody to feel close, to feel excited about my life. But she can't come across with what I want . . . excitement, passion. I don't feel she's really excited about me in the morning either." Sometimes what the relationship doesn't offer is passion. Sometimes what's lacking is consideration, or closeness, or security, or room to breathe.

In the aggregate, such unsatisfied needs assume crucial significance. They seem to foreclose the possibility of happiness. A Disarmer who is married to an Anxious Pleaser said sadly, "I can say I have these needs I shouldn't have, but my desire is still there, for someone who is like a lion, somebody who will be strong and turn me on and knock me off my feet . . . I just don't think I can adjust to not having that."

Worse perhaps than a partner's inability to fill needs is his seeming unwillingness to fill them. One woman said of her husband, "I don't know if I have too many needs that he can't meet or that he doesn't want to. It comes through to me that he doesn't want to. He knows I need love and affection; he just doesn't want to give it . . . He knows what this does to me."

A Stage II relationship creates a profound sense of helplessness. Caught between his own neediness and his partner's unresponsiveness, the person usually resorts to the kind of defensive controlling strategies we have described in earlier chapters.

The anxious demand is one hallmark of Stage II. Eileen, a young Disarmer, said to her husband, Fred, "I want attention and I don't get it. You ignore me. I'm sort of there to fill in the time between whatever else you want to do. I have to ask you all the time to spend time with me. And I'm getting tired of it." She couldn't enjoy the attention he did give her because she knew it was prompted by her pestering and not his own preference. The drum roll of the anxious demand creates resistance instead of overcoming it. Fred began to spend progressively more of his free time away from home. He said, "Do I want to spend sufficient time with her, in her eyes? No. I work hard all day, and there are things I like to do at night, and I want to rebel against being told that I have to just sit home with her every night." Predictably, her anxious demand provoked his withhold.

Another way a person often tries to get his needs met in Stage II is to blame his partner. A Self-Assured Pleaser who faced a financial crisis wanted more warmth than usual from his wife. His response to not getting it was to blame her for being unhelpful. "I don't feel like I'm getting any support anywhere along the line. I'm practically having ulcers trying to figure out how to make enough money to keep our family going . . . I work pretty long hours and I'm having a hard time and I don't see you doing anything constructive."

Blame that focuses on a solid grievance is usually threatening and blame that dwells on a flimsy grievance is annoying. Either one is likely to provoke counterblame. In the above case, it did. The Pleaser's self-righteous blame made his wife feel guilty and provoked her to blame him back, rather than yield to him.

Pushing away is another response to unmet needs. Rather than experience himself as incapable of getting what he wants, a person denies that he wants anything anyway. Frequently, a person resorts to pushing away after other strategies have failed him. One man who had engaged in an unsuccessful anxious demand for sex said, "I felt bad about being rejected over and over. So my response has become—I won't give a shit. Then I won't have to deal with a rejection."

To acknowledge one's needs means admitting dependence on one's partner. That partner's unresponsiveness can seem to turn this from a weak position into an ignominious position. A woman said of her fiancé, "It makes me so angry. I look at him as the man I want to be with for a long time, and there are these things I'm not getting from him. It just makes me so angry. And I think—what I should do is stop caring. He won't give me this, therefore I won't care. I'll make sure I never ask for anything . . ."

Withholding is the other major Stage II response to being denied. The withholder says, in effect, 'I'm not going to give to you if you're not going to give to me.' Often the witholder is not aware of his noncompliance, but he 'can't find time,' or just 'can't,' or, more simply, 'won't come through' for his partner. For example, one Provider felt that his wife was denying him sex, and his response was to begin withholding affection from her. He said, "The only way I can put pressure on her [to have sex] is by not giving in some other area of the relationship—just withdraw—not be very outgoing or very warm . . . I'm using it for leverage."

Withholding, pushing away, blaming, and anxious demanding are all forms of coercion, ways of trying to force a partner to respond to needs he won't meet voluntarily. But under pressure to give, the partner often turns stubbornly stingy. One male Dance-Away said of his partner's depressions, "When she's down I get into a 'here we go again' mentality. I get exhausted before we even start. My reaction when I see she's depressed or having a bad time—my reaction is 'Grow up, Cecile.' "

When the Stage II coin is thrown into the air, for some people it comes down heads, 'You don't give me enough'; for some people it comes down tails, 'You ask for too much.' Often a person's sense that enough isn't coming in feeds his resentment about what he's being obliged to put out. He begins to perceive his partner as a burden, a liability. For one Provider, his wife's demands became "wearying, wearing. It's a constant drain. She's always coming after me. I'm always being pushed to meet some need of hers."

Given that the first major issue in Stage II is how people deal with their own unsatisfied needs, the second major issue is how people deal with being asked for things they don't want to give. The motivation to refuse can differ from one situation to another. Sometimes a person's 'No' means 'I don't want to do that.' Sometimes it means 'I'm scared to do that.' Sometimes it means 'I want to punish you.'

A refusal is often ambiguous and one or both partners can be confused about what's meant by it.

The whole transaction is complicated by the fact that most people feel too guilty to offer a simple straightforward 'No.' Instead, discomfort leads them to blame. 'Why can't you . . .' A refusal comes as rejection. 'Get off my back! Leave me alone. Why can't you do something for yourself for a change?' The partner isn't just turned away, he's pushed away.

Withholding offers a covert means of refusal. The withholder rarely says 'No' out front, but he never

quite delivers either. One woman pressed her husband
to do repairs around the house; he responded by
spending a year painting his way across the back of the
house. The withholder doesn't cause a scene, he simply
doesn't come through.

In Stage I, each partner believed or hoped that he
could trust the other to respect his wishes and respond
to his needs. In Stage II, it's hard to keep this faith.
No longer entirely confident of each other, or of the
love between them, the partners take care to protect
themselves, resorting to strategies which feel defensive
on the inside but look offensive from the outside. The
person on the receiving end of such measures often
finds his self-esteem, his trust, or his sense of autonomy
jeopardized by his partner's maneuvers. Each feels
wronged, and each feels

> I gave sugar for sugar
> Now I give salt for salt.
> You don't like it, baby,
> And I guess it's your own goddamned fault.*

The classic Stage II systems are mutual blame and
mutual withholding. Mutual blame tosses the onus for
a couple's unhappiness back and forth between
them like a hot potato. Couples that consist of a
Tough-Fragile and a Pleaser are most prone to this
complaint. For example, as one such couple got ready
to leave for a dinner party, she fussed with her hair,
changed her clothing, and finally turned to her husband wailing, "I look awful." Beverly's concern about
her appearance was largely a symptom of her anxiety
about the evening ahead, but Henry interpreted it
quite literally. As he saw it, he came to her aid by suggesting, "Why don't you put on your blue pants suit?
That dress makes you look like a secretary."

"Oh, I see," she said coldly. And from there on it
just started to snowball. She blamed him for insensitivity, and for failing to offer her the reassurance ('You

* Traditional Blues.

look great, honey') she felt she deserved. And she resented his criticism. He maintained self-righteously that he had acted from excellent motives ("I want her to feel good"), had offered useful counsel, and that she had picked a fight out of spitefulness.

Beverly said, "What we were fighting about is not just that one thing, but what it means to both of us, what it reminds us of—all the things we dislike about each other and all the things we disagreed about in the past." Old injuries were dredged up and stock accusations were exchanged and the battle escalated. The more wronged each felt, the more ruthless he became.

Each blamer believes himself wholly innocent and believes the other to be completely at fault. Each tries to vindicate himself by forcing the other to admit the truth of his interpretation, but what looked like harsh facts to the one seemed like distortions and aspersions to the other.

The indictments are painful, however, even when their validity is contested. "I keep telling myself—he's angry and he's trying to get me. He doesn't mean what he says." Nevertheless, a system of mutual blame eats away trust. "When I see the hatred and contempt she has for me—I just feel like it's hopeless." The other's abuse is frightening because it provokes the doubt, 'How could he possibly love me if he sees me like that?'

A fall-apart can sometimes break the spiral of blame. At other times, exhaustion sets in. But making up after a fight can be as tricky as avoiding a fight in the first place. The conciliatory impulse often doesn't strike both partners simultaneously. And one person's attempt to lay the dust can send a partner who's still angry off into a fresh fit. Or, alternatively, a couple doesn't agree about how to patch things up. He wants to forget about it, and she wants to talk it out; she wants affection for reassurance, and he wants sex.

Both, however, are apt to want a sincere apology. A Ragabash said, "I don't know what I want when I'm angry. I guess I want acknowledgment for the hurt—

that it happened—and I never get it." Mutual blame makes both parties balk. Neither wants to admit that his accusations were unjustified and both are too threatened to acknowledge their wrongdoing. So resentment 'continues to hang in the air after an unpleasantness.' One woman said sadly, "We quarrel and we don't make up, or we say it's over and it's three weeks before we crawl into bed together."

If 'the hostility gets to be too much,' a person can withdraw from a system of mutual blame. "I can't take it day after day after day," said an Anxious Pleaser. "I've been told what a dumb son of a bitch I am so often that I'm just not going to expose myself to it anymore." He withdrew into silence and absence.

If the disengagement is bilateral, the result is mutual withholding. A Disarmer said of her twenty-year marriage, "We're not close anymore. We've had too many destructive fights. One or the other of us has pulled down the shade and said, 'I'm not ever going to bring that up again,' or 'I'm not going to put myself into a position to be hurt again.' " But, withholding hurts too. For example, a Prizewinner and a Disarmer in their late twenties struggled over his unwillingness to offer excitement and her unwillingness to engage in sex. Shelley complained that she not only had to inspire and arrange their social activities, she practically had to drag her husband out of the house to participate in them. Jim admitted, "I by and large get my entertainment all day. I don't need that when I come home . . . The thing I most want on weekends is to spend time with my kids. The thing Shelley wants is to spend time with me." Shelley lost. He denied her impromptu evenings and romantic gestures—he simply didn't initiate them. He remarked defensively, "I'm not going to play games like that. I did that. We're married now. We're grown-up—she's going to have to realize that." Shelley's response was, "I don't feel very sexy at night if I've just been bored all day. If there is an emotional high or sensual high . . ." But lacking that, she was rarely willing to make love.

Jim said, "At this point, I'm reluctant even to approach her sexually. I know she's probably going to reject me." Likewise Shelley said, "There's a limit to how much you can ask without feeling manipulated. If I have to ask all the time, I feel like a fool." To minimize their vulnerability, therefore, both of them abandoned their anxious demands and dug into their withholding.

A system of mutual withholding usually evolves slowly and covertly. Each person is conscious of his unmet needs and the other's negativity. But neither can see how his own behavior perpetuates that negativity. Each believes 'I've been putting out, but there hasn't been anything coming through to me.' Each feels the other is intentionally thwarting him, and each waits for the other to redeem himself by making the first move.

If someone does step forward, however, his gesture is often discounted as an attempt at manipulation. If Jim took Shelley out to dinner she assumed, "He just wants to go to bed with me," and resented the obligation she incurred. He said likewise, "I've always got this suspicion that if she does agree to make love with me that she'll tell me the next day that she was doing me a favor." Withholders balk at giving because it feels like giving in. They become unable to accept with pleasure what they in fact want the other to offer and eventually, too proud to ask for what they want and having lost hope of getting it, they lose touch with wanting it. The consequence is "There are these long periods of tension where we're just not even willing to deal with each other."

A Stage II couple can alternate between mutual blame and mutual withholding but on a deeper level the two systems reinforce each other. Blame provokes withholding, "I'm not going to give her anything if she treats me like that," and withholding supplies grist for the blame, "You're not willing to do anything for me. You're totally preoccupied with yourself. And what I think and what I feel and what I need don't mean a piece of shit to you."

Mutual blame is a kind of hand-to-hand combat; mutual withholding is trench warfare. And warmth is one of the principal casualties of both. Neither partner considers the other entitled to support or approval and neither experiences the other as a source of pleasure.

> Now no joy but lacks salt,
> That is not touched with pain,
> And weariness and fault.*

In the depths of Stage II, a relationship may seem hopeless. Each person usually perceives the problem as the product of the other's unwillingness to change. In fact, both are trapped by their common unwillingness to examine or alter their behavior. Each feels his strategies are survival measures, innocent because they're essential.

Even if one partner sees the destructiveness of what he does, he usually feels unable to change it. For example, one Tough-Fragile woman said, "If I feel bad, I know there are other ways to say it. But every way that comes to me sounds bitchy. I fall back on what I've done for years . . . I know I'm driving him away. I'm always afraid tonight will be the night he won't come home. But I don't know how to change. I don't know what to do."

Often, all that a person can think of to do is leave. At a point in time when many people don't believe in commitments of 'forever' proportions, the thought that Stage II usually prompts is—maybe it would be different with somebody else. Maybe 'she's bad for me,' or maybe 'we're not right for each other,' and maybe all the misery is a symptom of some fundamental unworkability in a relationship.

In fact, lasting couple relationships don't work any
* Robert Frost, "To Earthward."

other way. Stage II follows Stage I with the relentlessness of death and taxes, no matter who the participants in the relationships are. Stage II means a certain amount of misery, and the experience of that misery is likely to make victims of us all.

A little perspective may help to take some of the edge off that misery. The troubles a person experiences in Stage II do not necessarily have prognostic significance; they don't necessarily mean that he's made a bad choice of partners or that he won't be able to relate successfully to someone else. Furthermore, these troubles should not be allowed to obscure the bearable or the agreeable aspects of the relationship. There are ups and downs within Stage II, and it's possible, with persistence and goodwill, to reach "a place beyond resentment," a place where concord is not banality, and where harmony is not the simple absence of discord.

CHAPTER 15

Affairs

THE PROMISE of open marriage has appeared in our lives like an emotional credit card arriving through the mail. Just as limitations of a monthly paycheck need not inhibit us from acquiring a new color TV, so we now feel able to surmount the constraints of monogamy which limit us to a single sexual and emotional partner.

A credit card, though, does not augment a person's buying power in any lasting way. His financial means don't stretch elastically to fit the dimensions of the installment payments that fall due, and likewise people's emotional capacities often don't expand to meet the demands of the multiple relationships they involve themselves in. The fact that on an intellectual level people embrace the concept of emotional pluralism no more equips them to deal with the repercussions of an affair than a BankAmericard brochure prepares a person to deal with the retribution a collection agency exacts.

The impulse to philander seems straightforward. Under certain circumstances it may even be straightforward. But more often it's not. A Dance-Away woman said, "It's the forbidden dangerous route that seems to excite me the most. The more I have to lose at either end and the less sense the whole thing makes, the more I want it, and the more sexual pleasure I obtain."

Affairs are often begun and continued for complicated and uncomfortable reasons. One unacknowledged purpose an affair often serves is avoidance. Oscar, for example, was impotent with his wife and his response to his incapacity to perform sexually was to back away from her altogether. He never initiated sex with her and rarely responded to the invitations she sometimes gingerly tendered. He began, sub rosa, to experiment with one-night stands. Ironically, with other women he could perform quite well. His outside relationships offered him a refuge from his marital failure.

The Avoidance Affair is common among graduate students. For example, under increasing pressure to finish his thesis, Matt fluctuated between frenetic activity and immobilizing anxiety. His wife urged him to work so that the thesis would get done and the couple could resume life on a regular basis. Feeling anxious and pressured and resentful of the pressure, Matt fell suddenly and tempestuously in love with a fellow graduate student. The student almost never makes a casual connection between his anxiety and his sudden passion for a new lover, but the result is a classic example of nonsublimation: the energy that could have been channeled into work is instead diverted into sex.

Paul was a salesman in his mid-forties who had repeatedly been put on notice by his employers that he'd be fired if his sales record didn't improve. He said, "I couldn't quite live with what was happening. To make life livable my outlet was running around and screwing with other women. I think my wife kind of knew, but it was on the sly."

A person often enters into an affair as a kind of self-administered tonic for low self-esteem. Linda, a Disarmer, was minimally possessed of a husband who had been dancing away from her ever since their marriage four years earlier. She had felt inferior to him to begin with, stacking her one year of junior college against his master's degree in landscape architecture; her humdrum work as a secretary against his prestigious career as an urban design consultant. Ralph exacerbated her self-doubt by engaging in a number of barely concealed affairs that left her feeling worthless and sexually undesirable. When a man who worked in her office began to ask her out for lunch, Linda responded gratefully to his interest in her and within several months they had become lovers.

Finding favor with a new love is as close as many people (women in particular) come to achieving a sense of personal significance. An affair is a way of gaining the recognition a person is too frightened or too ill-equipped to obtain in the outside world.

The Frustration Affair is prompted by a person's conviction that his marriage denies him experiences he wants. A woman who gravitates into an affair is often looking for an intimacy her marriage doesn't offer her. Alternately, she can be seeking the sexual gratification that is the traditional male motive to philander.

Francine, for example, was a young Disarmer who loved sex, but was married to a man who was a premature ejaculator and a reluctant and inhibited partner in lovemaking. She complained, "He makes me feel like I'm oversexed. One night I went to bed and said, 'I feel like a two-bit whore because I have to ask for love.' Well he got really mad, but that was the way I felt. Every night I was going to bed and having to touch him and being turned down. I felt cheap and wrong." Mark admitted, "I don't require the—I don't know what you call it—the sexual part of making love that much. In other words, it isn't nearly as often as Francine. If I'm not in the mood I do have to force myself a little to do it because I know she wants to make love more than I do."

An affair is often a way of communicating with the original partner and the nature of the message is usually threatening. 'I'm not happy with this relationship, and I'm not sure whether I want to stay with you or not.'

A person can use infidelity to punish his partner or to distance her. One woman said, "I have used George (her lover) to cut myself off from Paul (her husband). It's like 'See what I have here? It's much better than what I have with you.'" Taking a lover can say 'You don't own me' and it can serve as a way of reasserting the autonomy that the ongoing relationship seems to have undercut.

An affair can be a way of legitimizing leaving a relationship or a person can use an affair—or, more likely, a string of affairs—to force his partner to leave him.

Conversely, a person's affair sometimes is intended to revive a flagging relationship. A woman who doubts her husband's attachment to her may involve herself with another man to jar her husband out of his apparent indifference. Her attachment to her lover and her pleasure in the affair remain subsidiary to the effect she hopes her infidelity will have on her husband. Her lover is a test of her partner's love and her hope is that the latter will reclaim her jealously.

The question of why a person has engaged in an affair may well have a complicated answer that is not well understood by the participants. Most affairs seem to "just happen" and discreditable motives pass as legitimate ones—e.g., avoidance masquerades as discontent with an inadequate partner. The "why" of an affair is often too hot for a couple to handle objectively. The one partner is likely to be so threatened and resentful, the other so guilty that discussion between them is likely to consist of nothing more than rhetoric and mutual blame, which embitter the situation and obscure its real meaning.

Probably the two most crucial aspects of an affair are the scope it's given in a person's life and the bearing it's permitted to have on his marriage. The Recreational Affair entails minimal involvement. This kind of affair is essentially no more than a one-night stand. Sex without emotional concomitants (beyond simple friendliness), and wholly without commitment, the Recreational Affair can nevertheless be devasting to a spouse. One case of a Recreational Affair involved a young couple who'd been together five years. Gloria said, "We've had problems, but I never had cause to doubt Lenny and his love for me." He made some friends, however, who were involved in the singles bar scene and "One night he came home and hit me with this bombshell. He really wanted to go out with other people. He said it wasn't that he didn't love me. He wanted to be free and he felt like I was tying him down." She cried, but, "he kept going out at night and I was upset because he didn't want me to go . . . I have this horrible imagination . . ."

Gloria finally went to visit a friend for a week to "try and get myself together" and when she returned Lenny told her that he had dated a couple of girls in her absence and had slept with one of them. "I kept asking him 'Who was she?' 'What was it like?' And he said, 'Physically I had a better time with her than I do with you. I don't know if it was because it was a new experience or because I haven't slept with anybody else since we got married or what.' " Gloria became hysterical. For several days she was distraught and Lenny responded with affectionate consideration.

The resolution of the situation was less satisfactory, however. Lenny told Gloria that she was too dependent on him and that she was being uptight and unrealistic about what a marriage meant. Nevertheless, he was clearly disturbed by the pain he was causing her. On the one hand Gloria felt guilty about her unliberated demand for exclusivity. "I was thinking about it, and I don't want to get so upset about his going out with somebody else because it's not what counts." On the other hand, she told him, "I know myself and I know if you start going out I just can't handle it and I'll leave."

Lenny yielded to her threat and agreed to return to the old monogamous basis of their marriage, with substantial bitterness that she should "box me in like that." Her relief was tinged with fear that she had asked too much of him and that she would lose him in the future by clutching him too tightly in the present. His brief adventure introduced a disquiet into their relationship which their pledges of mutual love couldn't quite dispel.

In the Supplementary Affair, the stakes are higher. The connection to a third person is both sexual and emotional and the affair may have considerable duration, but the Supplementary Affair is intended to augment, not replace, the primary relationship. The involvement with a lover may be intense but it does not jeopardize the person's loyalty to his or her original partner. Thomas, a Self-Assured Pleaser, said of the several lovers he had taken over a period of a few years, "Initially I wanted to know what sex would be like with other people and I think I was looking for friendship and personal validation, but I don't think I was looking for substitute partners. I've never felt I wanted to choose other people over her, and those other relationships didn't affect my desire for Vicky or my commitment to her."

The Supplementary Affair is rarely acceptable to the original partner. Vicky said of the first affair, "I just about lost my mind. I've always been really jealous of him, afraid he would see somebody else and leave me for her. I couldn't see how he could be turned on to somebody else and still love me."

The aboveboard Supplementary Affair requires both original partners to believe that erotic and emotional involvement with a third person can be controlled by an exercise of will and that the affair will remain safely contained. Few people are capable of this act of faith in the face of a partner's Stage I with somebody else.

Threatened and hurt by Thomas's affair, Vicky gradually withdrew from him. She said, "I was spending my whole time dwelling on that business. Then I just sort of pulled away from him it seems like. I decided I had to get my own life together so I began to make some friends of my own and I got a job . . ."

She also got a lover, which brings us to the third level of affair, the Even-It-Up Affair. One woman, for example, began an affair with her husband's tacit consent, as a way of compensating for the frequent absences from home his career entailed. Jealousy extinguished his original tolerance, however. He proceeded to take a mistress. His wife became enraged; in her mind, her lover had represented a functional equivalent to her husband's career; it had made things equal between them. He retorted, "If you are going to go out with another man, I cannot stay home by myself." From his point of view, his lover equaled her lover, so *that* made things equal. The justification, if not the impetus, for such an Even-It-Up Affair is the belief that 'It's only fair.' The anger that provokes such an affair is usually more obvious to the person it's directed against than to the person it motivates.

People who open their marriages a crack to permit Recreational Affairs often find the opening widens progressively until the door is standing completely ajar and one partner is decamping through it. This outcome, the desire to run away with a paramour, is the defining characteristic of the Escalating Affair.

Although the individual usually didn't embark on an affair with the intention of changing partners, the affair gathers momentum, expands beyond its original Recreational, Supplementary, or Even-It-Up boundaries, and becomes a serious threat to the original relationship. One woman said of her husband, who had long been involved in extramarital relationships, "He had all these other women, but ultimately he never cared a whole lot about them and all of a sudden this new lady comes along and this is different. This is it. He wants to marry her. He wants to have a baby with her, and as for me and the kids . . ." Affairs are often unpredictable and difficult to control and the Escalating Affair usually has serious consequences for the relationship it challenges.

One husband and wife in their late forties suddenly shifted from mutual withholding to bitter mutual blame when he discovered she had been having affairs for about two years. He confronted her and soon after began an affair with her best friend, a divorcée. As these two fell in love, the spouses' quarrels increased, and a year later he moved in with his lover. He rationalized his departure by telling his wife, shortly to be his ex-wife, "Well, you started it."

The most threatening type of affair is the Out-the-Door Affair. A person initiates an affair of this sort with the realization that it will jeopardize his marriage. Either the affair will provoke his spouse into leaving or the new lover will provide the extra incentive and the emotional support necessary for a person to make the break himself.

For example, a Disarmer who had been married for twelve years separated from her husband shortly after she fell in love with another man. Nadine said, "I wanted a divorce for years. I've just never had the guts to do it. But now I know that I want to be with Jim, and I'd be hurting him if I stayed with my husband."

A new lover usually brings pleasure, but not immunity to pain. Nadine said several weeks later, "Every time I see Peter he's crying and telling me he loves me. It just breaks me up. I can't take it. He says he'll change, but if I went back to him it would just be to make him happy and I can't do that. I don't love him, but I don't want to hurt him. I see that sad look on his face and I see the tears and my head starts spinning."

People often embark on an affair in the ingenuous hope that it will perk up their lives, the same naïvete that has led other couples to have another baby as a way of propping up a sagging marriage. As solutions for couple trouble, they're probably equally ill-advised.

The benefits of "open relationships" have been widely touted and the penalties they exact have been generally ignored. In an objective moment, the authors of *Open Marriage* conceded,

> While some benefits were noted for those involved in extramarital relationships which included sex, it was observed that by and large these experiences did not occur in a context where the marital partners were developing their primary marriage relationship sufficiently for this activity to count as a growth experience. Frequently this involvement became an avenue of escape, intensified conflicts and actually obscured problems in the primary relationship.*

The media discussion of multiple relationships rarely depicts the discouraging aspects of how they actually affect people's lives. Private discussions of the topic are apt to have a similar positive bias. The issue of open marriage tends to be discussed more in the abstract than in the particular; 'People should be able to' . . . , rather than 'this is how it worked out for us.' The fear of seeming excessively moral or old-fashioned inhibits some people from expressing the reservations their experience has suggested. The worry that an adverse experience with affairs reflects one's personal inadequacies rather than the difficulties inherent in the phenomenon deters others from sounding a somber note.

Affairs now occupy the position sex did one hundred years ago. People have affairs and know that other people have them, but there is very little forth-

* Nena and George O'Neill, in *Beyond Monogamy*, ed. by James R. Smith and Lynn G. Smith.

right talk about them and consequently there is wide-spread ignorance about the impact they have on people's lives.

To account for the frequent conjunction between a couple's affairs and a couple's divorce, people often conclude that the marriage must have been bad to start with or there would have been no cause for the partner(s) to go outside it. As we have seen, however, people can resort to an affair for a number of reasons, some—but not all—of which stem from the faults of the relationship per se. The whys and wherefores of affairs are too complicated to permit a simple back-ward leap from the effect: an affair, to the cause: a defective relationship. Indeed, the evidence seems to point the other way, to suggest that an affair of-ten places such heavy strain on a relationship that it collapses.

This is not apt to be welcome news. The fact that an affair usually has a damaging effect on a relation-ship is no more agreeable than the fact that a person will have to walk three miles to burn up the calories in a brownie. People are sometimes inadvertently, but of-ten willfully, oblivious to the consequences they invite by indulging themselves in a lover or two.

Under some circumstances an individual can profit from an affair. Many women discover through extra-marital liaisons that sex is pleasurable, and men can also learn that sex can be more imaginative and less inhibited than routine intercourse with their spouses has led them to believe. A person who has taken the blame for a sexual dysfunction may discover that with a lover he doesn't suffer from the same difficulty.

A new lover can introduce a person to other experi-ences which enrich his life. Stage I of an affair can create an upsurge of energy, which has a kind of ripple effect throughout a person's life, creating positive re-sults as an indirect rather than a direct consequence of his affair. An affair can also give a person perspective on his spouse's real merits since a lover sometimes proves to be a lemon in comparison.

Personal growth, however, is not the simple linear phenomenon its popularizers would have us believe. More often than not the 'changes' a person makes through the aegis of an affair prove to be temporary, or they erode instead of enriching the marriage.

A person who wants an affair may rationalize it by telling himself or his spouse 'I need it. It'll make me feel better. And if I feel better it will make me a better partner.' A lover does provide reassurance, at least at first, that a person is sexually desirable and possesses a personality that someone can find endearing.

Jane, for example, a mother of three in her late forties, had been married for twenty years to a Prize-winner who completely overshadowed her. Her husband ran a department store and thrived on the hectic pace and pressure of his life. He had little time to spend with his wife and little inclination to increase their togetherness. She said sadly, "Why doesn't he want me very connected to him? I guess he doesn't need my love, or as I see it, a real closeness. And I have wanted it. I have really wanted it."

In fact, the crucial issue for Jane's self-esteem was the lack of work in her life that she could value. As her children grew up, she found herself without a function and without a meaningful connection to the outside world. Rather than grapple with the frightening question of how she should use her time, she retreated into the escapism of an affair. For the first three months of that affair she rejoiced in a new sense of self-worth and her marriage seemed to improve a bit as well. But the affair soon petered out and this new experience of rejection intensified her insecurity. In short, affairs are not the Yellow Brick Road to self-esteem.

It's usually difficult for people to incorporate changes they make with a lover into their relationship with a spouse. For example, Trudy initiated a secret affair primarily because she wanted to widen her sexual horizons. She succeeded, but her new knowledge made her all the more disparaging of her husband's limited sexual repertoire. "You're always flat-backing me," she told him dourly.

She complained about him but she couldn't change her sexual behavior with him. She was constrained by the apprehension that he would wonder where she had come by these new ideas all of a sudden. She was also deterred by the fear that he would disapprove if she suggested activities beyond missionary-position intercourse. "He'd say I was trying to be a sex-pot and that I should act my age," she said.

An affair often increases alienation. Although it is possible for married couples to explore together an avenue that one partner's affair has opened up, it requires energy, courage, and persistence to change a relationship and too often defensiveness or defeatism means that the effort isn't made. Instead of struggling to incorporate into the marriage the changes an affair prompts, people use what they've learned as ammunition against their spouses, as fuel for the flames of discontent within the marriage.

If it's difficult to make an affair a constructive force in a relationship, it's even harder to prevent it from becoming a destructive force. The first major danger is the witchery of Stage I of an affair. With a new lover, a person may call in sick at work and for the first time in his life spend the whole day in bed, luxuriating in the sensuality and the illicit leisure. Infatuation holds a double temptation. It beckons a person into a wider and deeper involvement with a lover. If a limited relationship is good, then a full-fledged relationship would be better, a person's happiness prompts him to conclude. Stage I of an affair gives him a tantalizing sample of his lover, and a person is often hard put to resist the inclination to go with his feelings and commit himself completely to the wonderful person he's discovered.

Stage I of an affair also provokes comparisons. One

woman contrasted her affair of two months with her marriage of eight years. "The relationship I have with Ted (her lover) is so beautiful. It's like the first time in my life I've been willing to give absolutely everything. I feel so at peace with him and I never feel that with Walter (her husband). With him I'm always agitated and itchy and uncomfortable. It's easy to talk to Ted. Most of the time we're together we just talk. But I never have anything to say to Walter. Whenever he says something, it pisses me off and I just go down inside myself and get miserable and frustrated."

The difference in thrust between a burgeoning romantic love and a settled domestic love often seems like proof that the former is true love and the latter merely habit or a kind of emotional security blanket. When a spiffy Stage I relationship is stacked up against a shopworn Stage II relationship, it requires real wisdom to remember that in the natural course of events the former will end up looking very much like the latter.

A person is prone to like himself as well as to like his partner better in the context of an affair. "She makes me feel like I'm real interesting," one Provider said of his lover. He had found himself talking to her far more openly than he ever did with his wife and suggesting the kind of afternoon picnics and evenings out that had ceased to be part of his marriage some years earlier.

In the setting of an affair, a Provider often shifts into a Pleaser. Since he can't express caring for his lover by offering her security or respectability, he offers her more of his inner self instead. He can relax into behavior with his lover that's more spontaneous and expressive than he feels comfortable showing with his wife, and the result is apt to be that the affair is a good deal more intimate than the marriage. The man usually attributes the agreeable change in himself to the different effects the two women have on him.

The new lover has a good effect. The old partner has a bad effect, or so it seems.

That "bad effect" deserves closer examination. In fact, "it's really hard to deal with having feelings for two people at the same time." Usually a person feels guilty about his disloyalty to his original partner and about whatever deception the affair has involved. The person in the middle is apt to feel an obligation to give his original partner attention and affection and sex, and often he finds it hard to enjoy doing so. His discomfort in the situation may lead him to dance away from his original partner—to lose touch with all warmth for her and to perceive her as demanding and clingy.

Alternatively, the situation can make him resentful. Like a Tough-Fragile, he may convert uneasiness into hostility toward his partner. His concern makes him feel controlled by her and he shifts the burden of blame for what's happened to her. Feeling caught between his lover and his partner, he grows colder and more critical toward the latter.

Even if an affair is secret, one partner is likely to be threatened by subtle changes in the other's behavior. She may begin an anxious demand—'Is something wrong? Is something bothering you?'—that he'll brusquely fend off. "When under pressure, I lie. I'm embarrassed about it, but there it is." The strain of the double-dealing may lead him to avoid his original partner, to minimize the chance of revealing himself.

Many people have acknowledged that affairs don't work "if you're doing it on the sneak," but they continue to argue that affairs can work "if you do it on the up-and-up." It's painful, though, to watch a partner carrying on with a new lover. Thomas said of Vicky's affair with a mutual friend, "It's like we're all together in the evening in our house and pretty soon it's late and I go to bed and Vicky and Bill stay up talking into the night. I would hear her voice talking to him in a way that she's never been able to talk to me—a low-key, mellow, warm, comfortable thing. From the beginning we've had a history—when I would want to talk to her she would get uptight and nervous and either not respond or act kind of silly, giving me the message 'that's too dangerous or too close.' So we never had much in the way of easy conversation—intimate conversation—and it bothered me that . . . it was a really kind of painful thing to hear this interaction going on with another person that I would really have liked and never got a chance to have."

It usually causes the onlooker deep hurt to see his mate "behaving with somebody else the way she never behaved with me." Even more sadness and resentment arise from seeing a partner act with a new lover the way he used to act with you and no longer does.

What's more destructive is the anxiety that an affair creates. The threat of being displaced can lead a person to fall apart, or to sink into depression and self-pity. The old partner wants to be reassured he's still the best, but he is apt to mistrust any reassurance he's given. He asks for more by complaining that he hasn't been given enough. Feeling not just wronged, but intolerably wounded, he blames reproachfully, 'How can you do that to me?' When his partner does move toward him, his resentment pours out, 'What do you mean you love me? You couldn't love me or you wouldn't put me through this'; and in time, both partners may be persuaded that this is true.

The partner's affair may be a serious blow to a person's self-esteem. "He doesn't like what he's got at home so he's out looking," one woman said of her husband. Another woman said of her husband's mistress, "I don't want to be told how beautiful she is, how great she is in bed. I don't need that."

For many people, anxiety and humiliation are metabolized into wrath. To protect themselves from a partner who no longer seems trustworthy, they harden themselves. "I felt like I didn't want him to know that I was hurt," one woman said.

Insecurity fosters jealousy. The fear of sexual and

emotional rivals led one woman to feel that she had to fight for her husband against a crowd of amorous females, ". . . a giant quivering Medusa, the composite vagina of their desire turning into a huge jellyfish that seemed to devour me."*

Wanting and needing someone who's moving away from her, a woman often finds it difficult to accept the diminished quota of affection she's offered. She's too resentful to share warmth with her partner and too anxious to be honest. The way that remains of making contact is through anger. To remind them both that she matters to him, she attacks him, usually for breaking the rules. "It's not that I'm jealous," said one Tough-Fragile woman of her husband's affair, "it's that he never comes back on time from being with her."

Apprehension can make her suspicious and touchy and temper tantrums can begin or become more frequent and more uncontrolled. The affectionate lover begins to seem ever more desirable in comparison to the frantic, blaming spouse.

The Tough-Fragile is ashamed of her jealousy and afraid that the situation makes her powerless. She usually feels caught between the compulsion to punish the partner that's caused her such pain and the awareness that her outbursts further alienate the man she's in fear of losing.

The Prizewinner has no such ambivalence about his jealousy or the authoritarian stance it prompts him to take. For example, one Prizewinner suggested to his wife that she stop complaining about his lover and start taking care of herself. When she found a lover of her own, he reacted to her beatific glow by telephoning the man and threatening to shoot him. He commanded his wife never to see or speak to her erstwhile lover again, and she folded into submissive tears under his brow-beating.

Tolerance is another possible response to a partner's affair. For example, Thomas (the Self-Assured Pleaser

* Hannah Tillich, *From Time to Time*.

described some pages back) reacted calmly to the beginning of Vicky's affair. He said later, "I knew how I felt about you and I knew from my own experience that my relationships with other people didn't have anything to do with our relationship." He operated on the reassuring assumption that her loyalty to him was equally unswerving and he denied whatever was upsetting him in her relationships with other men.

He didn't impose restraints on her and didn't complain to her—behavior that he saw as selfless, but that Vicky found peculiarly disturbing. She said, "It used to blow my mind. He would always say that it didn't bother him that much that I was seeing somebody else." But more important, she construed his forbearance as evidence of his indifference to her.

Some people believe that an absence of possessiveness indicates a shortage of love. One woman told her husband point-blank, "I wish you would tell me that you didn't want me to see him, that you want me just for you."

The person who ventures more deeply into an affair can place himself in double jeopardy, responsible for a lover as well as a spouse. The deeper his involvement with the lover, the more divided his loyalties. The person in the middle is responsible and is likely "to go around feeling guilty all the time because I'm always hurting them both."

In some fundamental sense, most affairs are a no-win situation. Either the lover or the spouse is lost in the end. If it's the former, then

> There is always some weeping
> Between us   and someone is always checking
>
> A wrist watch by the bed to see how much
> Longer we have left. Nothing can come
> Of this   nothing can come
>
> Of us:*

* James Dickey, "Adultery."

Even couples who sanction each other's adulteries are likely to run into trouble if she's happier with her lover than he is with his, or vice versa. Since jealousy is notoriously attuned to these niceties, one spouse is apt to become anxious and to begin causing trouble. Or one affair will collapse, leaving its participant feeling lonely and aggrieved until he succeeds in hustling up a new affair. Or one spouse will be more prone to jealousy than the other, so the arrangement will not inflict suffering evenhandedly, and there will be hostilities on that score. Setting up a system of plural relationships is like trying to balance a table by sawing off the bottoms of the legs. The legs are never quite even and the results are never very stable.

The truism about multiple relationships is that someone once heard of a person who had a friend who knew of a couple who said they had talked to some folks who claimed it worked for them. We have yet to see any couple make it work over the long term and we've seen a great many marriages fail to withstand this stress.

Some do survive, of course, despite the odds. If both partners relinquish their lovers and reaffirm their commitment to each other their relationship may take on new value for them both. One man said, "Her affair really got me much closer to Audrey. I feel love that I've never felt before." Newly reconciled, these couples begin to enjoy and appreciate each other in a way they may have forgotten, or perhaps never experienced, and their relationship warms up to a kind of pseudo-Stage I.

The couple is apt to interpret this pleasant development as proof that they've "really worked things out" between them. A couple that's making a "fresh start" usually does have more goodwill and more flexibility than a couple stuck in the depths of Stage II. The partners can use this opportunity to make constructive changes in their relationship, changes that genuinely reduce their anxiety and their antagonism and bring them closer to Stage III.

But a post-affair honeymoon is usually even more transient than the post-courtship honeymoon. If a couple doesn't make genuine changes in their relationship, they're likely to find the old stresses surfacing again a year or two later. The problems that prompted affairs before may prompt them again and reconciliations gradually lose their credibility. An affair is often the "digitalis of failure" administered to a relationship. But over the long term, few relationships are cured by it, and many are undone altogether.

CHAPTER 16

Splitting Up

STAGE II PROVIDES most folk with ample motivation to quit a relationship if they care to. Just as people attribute the exhilaration of Stage I to their partner's virtues, so they assign their partner the blame for Stage II. Any experience of mutual falling in love is apt to be sweet; any experience of long-term commitment is going to be trying, painful, sometimes demoralizing. Often the only way up seems to be out.

For one thing, there are the solid and legitimate grievances against the partner that Stage II supplies to everyone. There's the realization that "we are so different. I think both of us would be happier with more compatible people."

A person who is eyeing the door can fortify himself with arguments like: "We got together for bad reasons in the first place." Or he can impugn the relationship on the charge of dependency. Judy said of her marriage, "I have no confidence. I think I'm staying with him because I'm scared to go out and be on my own. If I was healthy, I would get rid of him."

Often, there's support from others for the notion that there's better to be had. Friends may observe sympathetically, 'He doesn't appreciate you,' and urge warmly that, 'You should find somebody who'll be

good to you.' The impulse to leave is often buttressed
by ideology as well. The loose aggregate of groups that
comprises the human potential movement has preached
that a person's fundamental commitment is his duty to
his own identity. The need to grow and develop, to
find the greatest possible joy and fulfillment in life are
the crucial priorities, they assert. The human potential
movement fosters the illusion that love should come
naturally, effortlessly, and that if it doesn't it can't be
'forced' and the two individuals in question are better
off going their separate ways, each 'doing their own
thing.'

Abandoning a relationship gets coded, not as a failure, but as a positive step in a healthy process—the
striving for full self-realization and the achievement of
a complete relationship with another. The stigma is
removed from departure, and it becomes, instead, evidence of integrity, perhaps even idealism. In various
ways the human potential movement authorizes an escape from struggle.

The women's movement, conversely, issues a call to
struggle. It declares that women can't achieve happiness and health in our society without wholehearted
struggle against the destructive system of sex roles
that prevails against us. It provides an analysis of relationships that both aids a woman in formulating her
grievances and underwrites the legitimacy of her complaints.

The women's movement provides a woman with
rhetoric (oppression, sexism, and so on) and supplies her with allies, with sisters. It also infuses her with
a sense of urgency. She must stop molding herself to
fit the contour of the man she's with, and develop a
sense of who she is. The women's movement has
addressed one of the crucial injustices of the time. Its
long-term effects are bound to be constructive, but it is
equally inevitable that, in the short term, the women's
movement should cause trouble. A woman who's decided to begin initiating sex can find that her asser-
tiveness precipitates impotence in her partner. The

housewife who decides to go back to school can find her husband is dead set against it. A woman can feel guilty when she demands that her husband do the dishes because part of her still believes that the kitchen is a wife's responsibility.

Ambivalence and anxiety are apt to make a woman defensive in this position, and in her defensiveness she's apt to blame her partner, in the rhetoric of liberation, cloaking her own internal conflicts. Unfortunately, recrimination about chauvinism polarizes a couple at the very point when they need an alliance most.

The women's movement raises expectations and doesn't prepare people for the difficulties involved in attempting to realize them. It posits an ideal—mutual support and total equality—that no actual relationship could achieve. While it's more admirable than the romantic fantasy it challenges, this egalitarian fantasy is equally unrealizable, equally likely to foster disillusionment with and escapism from the real-life relationships that necessarily fail to measure up.

When a woman recognizes that her couple relationship is oppressive, her empathy with her partner is likely to diminish and her antipathy toward him is likely to increase. She's likely to despair of the possibility of transforming their relationship. Ingrained habits seem immutable, and the only hope may appear to lie in a new alliance, which could be set up properly from the beginning. A new love, she hopes, will offer her the chance to square her consciousness with her daily life that she believes is ruled out by her present circumstances.

This growing discrepancy between the aspiration and the reality is one way to account for the fact that the member of a couple who leaves is increasingly apt to be the woman. Women, who have traditionally fostered couple commitments, are becoming increasingly willing to challenge them.

Their motivation is partly hope. To leave an established couple relationship often seems like a way of making a fresh start. Frequently a woman's departure has this kind of symbolic significance to her. Separating from her partner becomes the crucial change that will trigger other changes she wants: an increase in her self-esteem and her self-sufficiency, a clarification of who she is. She declares to herself and to others that she wants to leave because 'I want to be free. I want to be me!'

Usually, she believes that the relationship has made her unwholesomely dependent on her partner. Meredith said of her husband, "He's loved me more than anybody in my life, and I've loved him. So I've completely turned myself over to it, and kept nothing of my own. I've just become an extension of him."

Her conclusion is apt to be the 'I need my own space' strategy that we call developmental separatism. "I feel like I need to be by myself for a while, and get some things worked out. I want to be a different person than I've been inside the marriage. And I don't think I can change if I stay with him."

Leaving often seems to promise relief to men and women. One Provider said, "I just wanted to be free of the hassles when I got home every night." Leaving spells freedom. "I want to be able to stay out and have a good time, without having to come home and answer to Roberta." It means a chance to fall in love again, or to begin a new life.

The desire to start over can strike anyone. We now see an increase in divorce among older couples whose children have grown up and whose judgment of their relationship is, 'It isn't good. It's not a good life.' This sense of deadness often conceals pervasive unexpressed anger.

Resentment about the past often infuses a person's departure with the kind of animosity epitomized in this note from a James Thurber fable: "I have gone away with Bert. You will find some arsenic in the medicine chest."

On the other hand, there's also apprehension about the well-being of the partner who's being forsaken. A man said of his wife several months after they'd separated, "She's gaining all kinds of weight. She just stays home and watches TV. I wish she'd get a hold of herself."

But there's more to it than just anger. A Disarmer said of her husband, "I've thought sometimes 'I wish he would die.' But I don't want to hurt him. I see him go through all this hurt. He walks in the room, and I'll be sitting on the couch. He'll get down on his knees and I'll look up. It reminds me of the little puppy that you're ready to take down to the pound. That's just the look in his eyes."

The desire to leave a relationship is usually conflicted. The person who's heading toward the door feels a good deal of apprehension: fear of discovering, 'The loneliness is enough to wipe you out.' Fear of deciding later, 'That maybe it was a mistake.' One man said shortly before he moved out, "I'm afraid to forfeit all I have with Judy. And then realize later—that was a good deal. She was a good person. And I was such a schmuck to get out of something like that when I could have worked at it." Intermingled with these emotions, there's almost always some (perhaps unexpressed) affection for and desire to remain with the partner and some recognition that parts of their relationship are satisfying and valuable.

Sometimes people consciously experience this ambivalence. One young woman said of the lover she'd been living with for several years, "Some days it just comes over me that I have to leave. I have to get out —and I have every reason down perfectly, and I feel great. Then I look at him, and it's all shot. I can't remember one reason. It's driving me bats. I feel strongly both ways—that I do and don't want to be with him."

More often, the person who's leaving gets locked into either a dance-away or a tough-fragile state of mind, convinced either that 'I just don't love you anymore' or that 'I don't need you and I can't get anywhere till I'm free of you.'

A dance-away exit is characterized by the desire to disappear. There's little anger toward the partner, only an overwhelming desire to get away from her. Her appearance and her mannerisms become progressively more unappetizing; her presence becomes progressively more disagreeable. Affection seems to have turned to indifference. "I feel so cold and hard. I just care nothing for her." Unable to enjoy himself with her, he becomes reluctant to be with her or make love with her, and most particularly, reluctant to talk to her about what's going on.

He wants to avoid the tears and pleas and recriminations that would exacerbate his guilt. So, he often won't acknowledge to his partner that he wants to leave her, and the double message increases her insecurity. One woman in this position said, "I'm at my wit's end trying to figure out what happened. And I can't get an answer from him." To fend her off, he turns distant. "I just don't want to see her," one man said of his girl friend. "It'll just be another horrible bummer. I don't want to deal with it. I wish she'd vanish in a puff of smoke and leave me in peace."

A person who's dancing away wants to escape. In fantasy, he disappears in the night, leaving a note pinned to her pillow. "You're a wonderful person, I have to go. Love." Anyone who wants a trauma-free disengagement is apt to choose the dance-away strategy.

A person who wants to confront his partner chooses the style of the Tough-Fragile, the push-away strategy. He provokes confrontation, in order to engage in a battle, seeking victory. His fantasy is to win by a knockout.

The person who engages in an angry, heated process of rejection wants splitting up to give her vindication, proof of some kind that she mattered more to her partner than he realized, and proof that he repents his mistake in letting her go. She also wants to establish that she's not to blame for the demise of their relationship. She attacks her partner with hostile blame, partly to clear her conscience, partly to punish him, partly to test his love, and partly to test his strength. Some part of her wants him to remain unshaken by her assault, to declare unequivocally, 'You're not going anyplace. You belong with me.' If he's kind of wishy-washy, then her own ambivalence is apt to make her harsh.

The Disarmer or the Provider who wants to exit is apt to dance away—to turn distant in an effort to avoid scenes. The Tough-Fragile and the Prizewinner are apt to push—to become angry and belligerent.

Blame is almost invariably a part of the process of splitting up, and that blame frequently focuses on issues that have more rhetorical value than real significance. For example, one Tough-Fragile woman stormed at her husband, "I want to be loved for being an important human being, not for being a pretty little girl you come home to after your important day at the office and fuck any time you want to." She framed a grievance (his chauvinism) that would divert her from the real problem (her low self-esteem).

Sometimes the terms of the confrontation are designed to protect the partner who's being rejected. For instance, Madeleine, a Disarmer, was married to a feckless Provider named Charles. He had lied to her consistently about his income, and had never been able to deliver on promises of a home, a second car, life insurance, or the other appurtenances of financial security. She was bitter enough about the deceptions and the anxiety to decide to leave him, but she was afraid to confront him with the truth of her feelings. "I don't want to tell him I don't respect him. It might crush him forever."

Rather than broach the real issue—his failure to support his family—she resorted to a false issue, his suspicions about her fidelity. Madeleine was a beautiful woman who attracted, quite intentionally, a great deal of attention from men. Charles' jealousy became the pretext for her departure. She told him, "I've lived for years with a bony finger being pointed at me. I can't stand you not believing in me." Charles colluded with her in establishing this as the central issue in their relationship. He repented. "I've tied her down. I've jailed her. I've been wrong. I didn't give her the freedom a woman deserves. I know she needs that trust between herself and myself."

In truth, she needed trust between them in quite different ways, but getting close to their real troubles made both of them extremely anxious. It frightened Madeleine to think that she and her children depended on so unreliable a man, and it made her feel foolish to realize how she'd deluded herself about their finances. As a Disarmer, though, she was reluctant to expose her husband. As a Provider, he was frightened of standing revealed as a ne'er-do-well. If she began to press him about money matters, he would deter her by falling apart. "I'm shaking. I'm nervous. I'm trembling." She would then hastily abandon her attempt to get information out of him.

Alternatively, he would shift the grounds of the discussion by dredging up the scarlet-woman charges. She would cooperate by beginning to defend herself, thus perpetuating the myth they had fabricated: that Charles could be trusted to take care of business, but Madeleine couldn't be trusted to behave herself.

Blame can also serve a defensive function. 'I'm leaving because I can't stand your bullshit' might well be the line with which a Self-Assured Pleaser exits from a relationship. Ron, for example, was a Self-Assured Pleaser who experienced a strong internal demand to be patient and helpful toward his wife and felt guilty about "selfishly" taking care of himself. No matter how miserable the marriage made him, he could justify leaving it only if he could persuade himself that he had absorbed intolerable abuse already and had made immense efforts to remedy the situation. The real function of 'I can't stand your bullshit' is not to attack his partner, it's to square his leave-taking with his value system. The self-righteousness of his stance doesn't reflect an inner sense of moral superiority. Quite the opposite, it's an index of the guilt and anxiety that flood the Self-Assured Pleaser when he's put in the position of terminating a relationship.

Whatever the explanation for the exit—'I don't love you anymore. I love somebody else'; 'I love you but I can't put up with the terrible things you do'—the person who utters it usually refuses to allow himself to experience warmth for his partner. One woman said perceptively about her husband's chilliness, "It's too dangerous to feel good about me now." He often reinterprets love for his partner as mere dependence on her, and he clings to his anger or his coldness as safeguards against the possibility of being sucked back into the relationship. One Tough-Fragile man said, "Just caring is no reason to carry on a relationship. I don't want to get talked into accepting this relationship, and carrying on, and letting it be satisfying if it can be. I don't want to get drawn into something because I feel sorry or guilty or even because I care." He's usually unwilling to expend effort in order to improve the relationship. "I don't want to work it out. Something in you that wants to fix things dies."

The act of deciding 'I'm leaving' frees people to get in touch with resentment that they've buried for years. The experience of being left, on the other hand, often prompts a wave of longing and love. For example, one Dance-Away Lover had contracted a marriage, several years earlier, to a woman he'd never loved with any passion. He'd philandered flagrantly and had twice tried to leave, but the sudden discovery that his wife had a lover and wanted a divorce was intolerable to him. "It's the hardest thing I've ever had to go through," he said. Suddenly, his partner's presence became critical to him, their marriage the whole basis on which his future rested. "I'm having a real hard time living with knowing that she's off someplace with that guy." He lost fifteen pounds in one month and couldn't sleep through the night. Being on this end of the process of splitting up usually teaches you that

> At midnight tears
> Run into your ears.*

As she watched her husband's car back out of the drive, his suitcases in the trunk, Shirley said she had felt "Like I was going to go under, like I was going to crack up. He was leaving to be with somebody else, like he's erased me out of his life. I couldn't stand it." Being left behind brings many people as close as they ever come to panic.

Trouble functioning, loss of appetite, drinking, accidents—the fall-apart that people often experience when they're left is both an involuntary and an instrumental reaction. On the one hand, it's a surrender to devastation, when there seems to be no possible way a person can hold himself together. On the other hand, it reflects the person's hope that his partner will respond to his misery by relenting. He offers his emotional disintegration as proof of how much she matters to him. 'I can't stand to be without you' is a threat as well. In leaving, a person incurs the risk that his partner will go off the deep end, and he'll be responsible.

The fall-apart rarely succeeds because it inspires guilt and distaste rather than compassion. When Charles told Madeleine, "I feel like a banana that's been peeled," she was repelled by this display of pitiableness. "He just stands there and is scared to death of any life without me. He cowers." His weakness makes her feel superior to him, a superiority with which she's completely uncomfortable. It relegates him even more irrevocably to the status of a liability.

Unfortunately, someone who is falling apart seems particularly undesirable just at the moment when he most wants to be appealing. The perverse reality of relationships is often, "I care about her more when the probability of having her is less." As he feels his part-

* Louise Bogan, "Solitary Observation Brought/Back from a Sojourn in Hell."

ner pulling away from him, he reaches out to reestablish closeness. Eagerly, he moves toward her, and the mechanics of ambivalence are such that she, uncomfortably, edges away.

Rejection breeds desperation. The person who's being discarded begins to grasp at his partner, trying to extract attention or affection. The anxious demand, 'Please love me. Please don't leave me,' becomes a wearisome refrain.

Equally self-defeating is the Anxious-Pleaser strategy. The lover who's being left behind hopes that solicitude will persuade his partner to reconsider. He floods her with attentiveness, with gifts, with compliments. The rejection he's experiencing throws him off center and makes him doubt his own judgment. So he asks his partner for instructions on how to win her back. She construes docility as a pitiful capitulation. She finds his desire to be with her all the time suffocating instead of satisfying, even if her old complaint was about his excessive absence from home. He wants to please her to keep her in the relationship. She resolutely refuses to be pleased for exactly the same reason: she doesn't want to be inveigled into staying. She discerns the frightened attempt at manipulation beneath his thoughtfulness and discounts the love that prompts it. And given the anger or coldness that is felt by the person who is leaving, it is usually impossible for her to find satisfaction in the new solicitude. "You want to make me happy? Take a walk," is apt to be her response to his insistent attentions.

The corollary to 'I'll *do* anything to keep you' is 'I'll *be* anything you want.' When Meredith tells David she's leaving because he's "chauvinistic" and "bourgeois," his reaction is earnest: "I'll change." His implicit message is, "You don't like who I am? I'll be something different, then." Since his identity has failed to secure her love, David retreats, instead, to the promise of metamorphosis. But she discounts both his avowed intention to change and his averred ability to change, with a sour, "So how come you haven't changed up till now?"

Such skepticism is both natural and blind. In fact, a person's actions and feelings often can change when a vital relationship is jeopardized. But even visible changes can lack credibility for the leave-taker. Sarah said of her husband, "Before, Michael would tell me that he cared, but there was a lot in his behavior that didn't indicate he loved me. There was a lack of affection, and he didn't show much interest in me. So I figured he didn't care very much for me. Now I'm getting a different feeling, but it's hard for me to trust it because I've gone for so long seeing it the other way. It's strange to be responded to so differently." Often the leave-taker wonders, suspiciously, "How long would this last if I gave in and went back?" attributing his partner's reform to panic, rather than to an enduring change of heart, and assuming that the old habits will reassert themselves when the crisis is past.

Someone who wants to leave is careful to avoid being duped, while the one who is being left cannot afford the luxury of such caution. In his eagerness to forestall his partner's flight, he's willing to put up with anything.

Donna described her year-and-a-half-long effort (ultimately fruitless) to keep her husband: "I really tried, I tried in every way. I always tried to be cheerful. I put up with so much, and I was walking on egg-shells the whole time. I was always afraid that something I would say or do would trigger him off, and he'd be gone." She did not complain no matter how badly she was treated, wouldn't say "No" no matter how roundly it was deserved.

More than one spouse has signed the divorce papers, hoping that his cooperation will win his partner back. She, however, sees his compliance as spinelessness. His fear of imposing any limitations on her (lest she deliberately step across the line to prove her independence) becomes unpalatable evidence of his neediness. Convinced that it's 'you or me,' the person who wants to leave is apt to abjure all responsibility for the partner she wants to shed. She becomes unexpectedly capable of saying and doing things that would previously have been unthinkable to her. She flaunts her new lover, or treats her old partner contemptuously, making herself feel guilty, and, as a result, even more anxious to leave.

The person who's being left often becomes apologetic about the past the couple has shared. When, for example, Meredith told David, "You never loved me; you've just been using me," he accepted her accusation as accurate. Part of him hoped that shouldering the blame for the past would convince her of his regret about what had happened and his sincere desire to change. Part of him feared that a struggle with her over who did what would complete her alienation from him. And part of him came to believe that the fault was truly his. He began to think that maybe he had been exploiting her—sexually and emotionally. Guilt over the actual injustices and cruelties he had done her (common and inevitable occurrences in any relationship) ballooned into the inflated guilt that the whole relationship had foundered because of his misdeeds. He adopted a 'guilty white-liberal' position, knowing that in the past he had been culpable on certain counts, but accepting guilt on all of them because he could not sort out the valid charges from the crooked ones.

By assuming this intensely painful position, moreover, David exacerbates the anxiety he brings to the present. For the person who has assumed the posture of retrospective guilt, every action becomes potentially suspect. Does he want to sleep with his wife out of selfish male lust, or does he desire sex with her because he loves her and wants to bring them closer together? His belief in himself erodes, and he becomes ever more dependent on her for approval, approval that she, prickly with resentment, is unlikely to provide.

A partner who dons the dunce cap and goes obe-
diently to sit in the corner obliges his partner to forgive
him. But the person who is leaving usually has ware-
housed too much resentment to be able to exchange
absolution for repentance. If she continues to heap
blame on her repentant or cringing partner, she
looks unreasonable, and she feels guilty. So, she can
neither smother nor discharge her anger. Partly to legitimize those ugly feelings, and partly because a sudden
conversion always arouses suspicion, she is apt to accuse him of insincerity. "He's just trying to buy me off."
She suspects he has usurped the good-guy position
with his plaint of mea culpa and has thus, deviously,
regained control of the situation. She feels reduced to
impotence again, and her fury adds to her determina-
tion to leave him.

The second adverse effect of assuming all the blame
for all manner of harmful acts and destructive motives,
is that it distorts the past, thereby preventing essential
change. A person colludes with the leave-taker's
sense of her own innocence. The partner who is exon-
erated is never brought to terms with the part he
played in creating his own unhappiness. For example,
Meredith blamed her husband for treating her like a
child. She, in fact, had sought the benefits of a childlike position—the freedom from responsibility, the
comfort of knowing her husband would protect her.
He sought power in their relationship, and she gave it
to him voluntarily.

The version of the past, which exonerates her and
convicts him, simply perpetuates the myth they shared,
that he is powerful and she is helpless. This view of
herself as helpless is to a great extent what incapaci-
tates her. For her husband, however sincerely, to sub-
scribe to this is a crucial disservice to her. Alternatives
were available to Meredith in the past, and her own
ambivalence about adulthood and power and responsibility led her to make the choices she did. To take

responsibility for those choices, and to recognize their harmful consequences, is the key to resisting the temptation to make those same seductive choices again in a future relationship. Truth and psychological health both require that she be able to recognize that the enemy is both within her and in him, and that getting rid of him will not get rid of the propensities in herself that made her old role so attractive.

A final tactic for someone who's discarded is the optimism born of nostalgia. "You used to love me. You can love me again," is the refrain. "We could be really happy together . . ." But landing on the optimistic side of the ambivalence about your future as a couple throws your partner onto the pessimistic side. When Meredith assailed David with, "The whole way we deal with each other is completely wrong," and he replied, "We can work it out," he only confirmed her conviction that he had no sense of the gravity of the situation, no real understanding of her unhappiness.

The mere decision to leave will often seem a final, not preliminary, act of dissolution. The one who leaves becomes an instant adversary, no longer an ally. He finds it hard to tolerate any agreement with his erstwhile partner. He defines himself in contradistinction to the other. His sense of what he wants often goes no further than his clarity about not wanting what the other wants. Just as a teen-ager rejects his parents' values to establish his own autonomy, a woman who's emerging from a dependent, subordinate position in a relationship often denounces her husband's goals and life-style despite the fact that she has, as yet, no clear idea about how she herself wants to live.

In fact, all she's clear about is that she won't resume her old position and that the possibilities for change within her old relationship are too meager to be adequate. Her husband is left double bound. If he avows, "This is who I am," she responds, "Yes, and that's why I don't want you." If he proposes that they change together, then she rebuffs him because the whole starting point for change, in her mind, is dispensing with him.

A person who's being left behind has his own forms of ambivalence. In part, he wants to revive the old relationship, whatever it takes. But, in part, he wants to protect himself from pain and punish the person who is inflicting that pain. One defense against rejection is withdrawal. Frank, a Provider, distanced himself from his wife, Penny, who'd been threatening departure for several months. When she attacked him, he said, "I've got nothing to say," instead of the more accurate, and productive, 'You're making me feel terrible and I don't know how to deal with this mess.' Withdrawal can be fatal if, as in this couple's case, the standing complaint has been lack of connection and communication. However, it doesn't have the same suffocating and supplicating effect of the other strategies we have described, so it can be a less destructive alternative.

Alternatively, a person who's being left behind can escalate to anger. Particularly if he's made extensive efforts to conciliate his partner, the failure of these attempts may leave him furious. One Self-Assured Pleaser said, "I've tried to work it out. But the more I try to move toward her, the more I seem to chase her away. I'm tired of feeling like a puppet on a string."

He has grievances of his own about the relationship, but he's afraid of the consequences of expressing them. "She's put me through the wringer. I have a right to be angry, but all the anger I feel will only drive her away."

That anger is most likely to surface on the occasions when his partner shows some desire to be close. A departing spouse will often feel a need, at times, for the kind of support and help she's been used to getting from her partner. She turns to him when she needs a helpful ally to deal with the kids, or for financial relief when the money won't stretch far enough, or comfort when an affair with a new lover peters out.

At moments like these—when he's being sought out—the person who's being left behind is apt to feel a kind of momentary security that allows him to get angry. Usually, he experiences the anger as outrage that his partner should expect to be given to after treating him so badly. Her temporary willingness to depend on him gives him access to her emotionally, and his suppressed resentment leads him to lash out at her. This confirms her belief that the love he avows is a fraud, and that she cannot trust him in the future any more than she could in the present.

Nevertheless, a partner's anger (particularly a man's) is usually less alienating than a collapse into pathos, and anger is often to be preferred to its anxious alternatives.

When anger swings completely into the ascendant, the person who's being left behind may become rejecting in turn. Ironically, rejecting a person who's outward-bound may be the most effective way to persuade him to stay. The mechanics of ambivalence come into play again. Initiative is bound up with rejection, so by beginning to reject his partner, a person begins to deprive him of much of the power in the situation, and frees him to get in touch with the warmth, nostalgia, and hope for a joint future which will enable him to pull for a reconciliation. This process, however, has its very great dangers. When partners take turns rejecting each other, then ambivalence keeps them seesawing up and down—perpetually out of kilter—but never quite able to part.

Some people will experiment with trial separation as a solution to their couple troubles, hoping that altered circumstances will give them new perspective on each other and give the relationship a new lease on life. Randy explained about the trial separation he and his wife had agreed on. "We love each other, but we can't live together without making each other miserable. We can't change things while we're living together, but maybe we'll be able to come back together after a while and renegotiate." A little absence is invoked to stimulate a waning fondness. In fact, the same couple system that damned their marriage will usually blight their separation. The husband who was financially irresponsible probably won't provide regular child-support payments. The wife who protected her husband, rather than take care of herself, will probably perpetuate this misguided benevolence.

Not only does the open-ended trial separation fail to solve the original problems, it usually imposes additional strains on the relationship. Anxiety about a nebulous future, the financial strain of supporting two households instead of one, the advent of new lovers, all increase the friction between partners until reconciliation becomes unthinkable.

Without doubt, some relationships ought to expire. In some cases, a man and a woman genuinely can't fulfill each other's needs and don't have the flexibility to make the fundamental changes and compromises that a life together would require. In cases where one or both persons simply refuse to bow to a revealed necessity for change, then splitting up is a reasonable step. If both partners have honestly worked to change their relationship and have failed, then they too may be justified in calling it quits.

The important criterion in the survival of a relationship is double-edged: Love must coexist with the willingness to change. But in the absence of that willingness, it is important to remember that you can love someone and be, nevertheless, unable to live with him. To decide you must leave him does not oblige you to conclude that you do not love him.

It must be said, however, that in the preponderance of cases we've seen, couples have split up over issues they might well have struggled through. Leaving is more often an avoidance of change than an instrument of change. The pain of parting misleads people into thinking that they have not chosen the easy way out.

In Ibsen's play, *A Doll's House*, written nearly a hundred years ago, Nora left her husband and children with the declaration,

> I must stand quite alone, if I am to understand myself and everything about me. It is for that reason that I cannot remain with you any longer.*

But the self can be explored and strengthened inside of the relationship as well as outside it. And certain kinds of growth can only really occur in the context of a relationship.

A woman, for example, who has learned to defer to men and to mold herself to suit them, can only really divest herself of these tendencies by struggling to overcome them. To retreat from a relationship with a specific man, or with men in general, is apt to be simply that, a retreat from the problem rather than a way of coming to terms with it. On her own, a person may well learn to cope with the problems of independence. But the skills she masters will not necessarily equip her to deal with a partner more soundly.

When seized by the urge to leave, the best solution is to disobey the injunction to 'follow your feelings.' "The desires of the heart are as crooked as corkscrews," Auden wrote.† And at junctures like this, those desires become particularly tortuous. One consideration to weigh is the part outside circumstances may be playing in the relationship. Energy for a new lover may arise from frustration with a job. Tension about a stretch of penury may be translated into an indictment of a marriage. A person's desire to separate may have more to do with feeling bad about himself than feeling bad about his mate. Problems of self-esteem are better dealt with directly than obliquely through separation.

The strongest response to a partner who wants to leave is,

* Henrik Ibsen, *A Doll's House*.
† W. H. Auden, "Death's Echo."

If you don't want my peaches
Don't shake up my tree.*

"This is who I am. I love you, and I want you. But if you don't want me or the life I lead, then leave and don't plan on coming back." This is a high-risk, high-gain strategy that requires pretty solid self-esteem for underpinnings. A person must feel he is worthwhile and lovable. In other words, he must keep from getting hooked by the rejection he's experiencing. This strategy requires that he stay in touch with his love, and it requires clarity about what kind of relationship and what kind of life he wants for himself.

Nevertheless, a partner who has left and who does want to come back usually deserves a hearing. His experience of splitting up, of being alone, of being with another lover may have produced that motivation to change that he lacked earlier. To despair of change before attempting it is a costly species of defeatism. A relationship can survive a great deal of change, and bitter memories can fade. The couple who can stop dwelling on their grudges about the past, and focus instead on what they want from a future together may find that,

> The cracked glass fuses at a touch
> The wound heals over, and is set
> In the whole flesh, and is not much
> Quite to remember or forget.†

* Traditional Blues.
† Louise Bogan, "The Changed Woman."

CHAPTER 17

Stage III

> Romance has no part in it.
> The business of love is
> cruelty *which*
> By our wills
> we transform
> to live together.*

ROMANCE usually does have a part in it, and not just at the beginning. But it is not the "Romance" of the romantic illusion. And cruelty has a much larger part in it than it's comfortable to remember. What a lasting couple relationship requires is that by an effort of will and all other possible means, romance and cruelty be transformed into a love that is stronger and greater.

A Stage III couple has brought their expectations for their relationship into some kind of equilibrium with their everyday lives. Frustrations and anxieties don't stop, but these no longer trigger doubts about their future as a couple. That's settled. Each knows, and knows the other knows, that they're here to stay. Beth, a Disarmer in her mid-thirties, said of her thirteen-year marriage to George, "Even those times when I'm angry with him, I have confidence. There's a reliability there that it's going to get better and it's going to be good. We've seen too many good times not to live through the bad times."

* William Carlos Williams, "The Ivy Crown."

In raw statistical terms, a Provider and a Disarmer probably have the best chance of a long-term survival as a couple. Our culture has clearly spelled out their respective obligations. One Provider put it this way, "My responsibility was to earn a living and support my family. As hard as I worked, she worked just as hard at her job with the family, taking care of the house first class, and that's important. She took her responsibilities as seriously as I took mine."

Their principal common objective is to maximize the family's security. On this basis, he chooses what seems to be the appropriate course of action and she falls in beside him, supporting his approach and trying to smooth the way. Reflecting on his thirty-five years of marriage, Al said, "Earlier in our marriage when it was touch and go with my business and I was deeply disturbed, she sensed my mood and she could say the right thing or touch me in such a way that strength flowed from her to me. Our whole marriage has been that way."

Theirs is a complementary relationship which virtually eliminates competition and forestalls conflict between them. Both of them feel most comfortable if it's apparent that he is, in all relevant aspects, slightly taller than she is.

In the Provider-Disarmer model, responsibilities are divided up tidily: he pursues a career and provides an income, she tends to the home and children. But caught in the throes of socioeconomic flux, many couples simply can't look to the Provider-Disarmer formula for a solution anymore. Clearly, if both parents work a forty-hour week outside the home, the allocation of duties within the home must shift. But what part should a Provider play in housework and childrearing? And who's responsible for seeing that he fulfills it?

In many ways, both psychological and practical, the Provider-Disarmer model has ceased to seem either appropriate or desirable. In the course of the 1960s and 1970s, many women have allowed their expectations for their lives to grow beyond the boundaries the Disarmer customarily accepts. Responding in part to the women's movement, they have begun to long for achievement of their own, for independent standing and direct involvment in the world outside the home. They have begun to feel, 'I want a turn.' Accordingly, the expectations of the Disarmer seem to them too static and too confined. Yet, often, these were their own expectations. As Beth put it, "I was my parents' little girl who did everything that was expected of her. The 1950s child. I got married, I had children, I had a house. Then I looked at my life at the age of thirty and said, 'Where the hell *am* I and *where* am I going? This is ridiculous! I don't have enough, even though that's all I ever wanted out of life.'"

Women for whom accommodation has lost its allure often become angry. They have concluded that it is better to fight for what you want than to forfeit it through gratuitous acceptance and unexamined complacence; and in the ensuing conflicts, they have become increasingly willing to put their couple relationships on the line.

No longer a vital form of protection for a woman, a couple relationship, especially a couple relationship that isn't working very smoothly, can begin to look like a barrier to independence. So, her response to serious troubles with a partner is either to challenge her partner to leave or to threaten to leave herself. The upshot is that many women, especially young women, have rejected what they see as the dependent aspects of the Disarming role and have developed the expectations and the responses that are characteristic of the counterdependent Tough-Fragile.

Correspondingly, some men have begun to defect from the ranks of the Provider and the Prizewinner, although this process has been much less dramatic and much more diffuse than the female analogue. Some men have turned into Pleasers, and others into Ragabashes, both in order to avoid the emotional straitjacket which they see buckled around the Provider and the Prizewinner. Beth's husband, George, said, "I'm sometimes amazed at the difference I perceive in my own attitudes. I used to be a very high-achieving person and material things were very important to me. I get my good feelings out of doing different things now, like relating to other people and being outdoors."

Thus many women, and some men, have become unwilling to follow the traditional Provider-Disarmer guideline, adopting instead stances that seem to them to offer more freedom and greater chance for fulfillment. As George put it, "It's been sort of like throwing a light down into the depths of a completely dark cavern and lighting it up inside. Before this all started I had no conception of what Beth wanted to achieve. I had her basically categorized as a mother, the role my mother had as a mother within the family, and that should be her happiness. When that started to become unhappy for her, then I couldn't handle it. I couldn't understand why anybody wouldn't be happy being a housewife. My mother was happy being a housewife."

The question then becomes: What are the consequences for a couple relationship when a Provider-Disarmer break their mold? The Provider and the Disarmer inherit a carefully worked-out scenario for a couple relationship; couples who play different roles are forced to improvise. And with improvisation there's far more potential for conflict and a much greater likelihood that this conflict will jeopardize their commitment to each other. How are they going to deal with the competition that's apt to crop up between them, or with the centrifugal pull on the relationship that their outside involvements are likely to create? How will the drudgery get distributed, when it's a symbol of status as well as a chore? How can decisions get made if both of them feel entitled to prevail? They're apt to have stormy times. But does it follow that such couples are bound for an endless Stage II, or an eventual divorce?

Not if they're willing to venture the kind of change which is more arduous than the change implicit in revised expectations and standards. For a relationship to reach Stage III, changes on the level of behavior and feeling are invariably necessary. Most frequently, couples breaking free from the Provider-Disarmer model find themselves locked into the Pleaser-Tough-Fragile struggle. In this case, she has to learn how to control her anger, especially when frightened, and he has to outgrow the posture of self-righteousness to which he retreats when his "goodness" doesn't get him his way. She has to come to realistic terms with her deficit of self-esteem, and he has to round off the sharp edges of his arrogance. He has to stop taking so much responsibility for her, and she has to learn not to drop her troubles in his lap. Both of them need to become more tolerant of their own vulnerability. All of these changes are desirable for them as individuals as well as valuable to them as a couple.

In order that their relationship may flourish, a couple must relinquish threatening strategies like mutual blame—and they must learn some way of responding helpfully to each other's needs. As one Tough-Fragile said, "Instead of placing demands on my husband, instead of saying, 'Why can't you do this?' or 'Why can't you do that?' from the point of view of a judge, I decided that I was going to go out and see what it was like in the business world. That was a big step. Instead of blaming him for my problems I determined that I was going to change the situation myself."

But changes in practical strategy must not remain the mere artifice of enlightened accommodation. They must reflect, as well as stimulate, the capacity for emotional change. Changes on the level of feeling are as necessary as changes on the level of behavior. This suggestion is apt to go against the grain. The same feelings that prompt revised expectations have become sacrosanct and, paradoxically, a new obstacle to deeper change. A client who's been dancing away from his wife says, "I want to spend more time getting my head straight about some stuff and I have to do that by myself and I just feel that in my gut." His assumption is that if he feels an emotion, it must be 'true.' While the verdict of the intellect might well be unreliable, feelings are not simply trustworthy. They are now beyond question.

Certain schools of popular therapy urge people to 'get in touch with your feelings' and 'go with your feelings.' We agree that this is often apt advice, appropriate, for example, for a Provider, one who admits that he can "go for long stretches of time without really feeling anything." Unfortunately, however, these too often exhort people to turn up the volume on feelings they've been indulging pretty freely all along.

We suggest a different tack—that people should probe their feelings a bit because their emotions may be altogether more complicated and equivocal than they realize. Feeling something doesn't make it so any more than believing makes it so. Like beliefs, feelings are biased in characteristic ways we're not usually aware of. And like cognition, affect should be eyed with a little healthy skepticism.

Kenneth Burke wrote, "A way of seeing is also a way of not seeing." Similarly, a way of feeling is a way of not feeling. Almost any situation can arouse a range of different emotions. For example, if a person discovers his partner has been unfaithful to him, he can be dismayed or outraged or even intrigued. An emotional response is a choice among alternatives, not necessarily a conscious, deliberate choice but a choice nonetheless.

People tend to make relatively consistent and characteristic emotional choices, choices structured by assumptions about what is appropriate and what is safe to feel. Each of the stances we have discussed authorizes certain emotional possibilities (anger, for the Tough-Fragile; helplessness, for the Fragile) and forecloses others (resolution, for the Ragabash; self-regard, for the Victim). People by and large do not question the limitations of their emotional range. Thus, a role creates a kind of emotional tunnel vision. It never occurs to the Fragile to get angry herself—the risk it would entail automatically disqualifies it as a possibility.

Usually it isn't obvious that certain emotions have been exercised because other emotions are pressed into service as substitutes for them. For example, when a situation makes the Tough-Fragile fearful, she responds by getting angry. The surrogate emotion—anger—is neither comfortable nor productive, yet it's far more acceptable to the Tough-Fragile than apprehension. Certain emotions, therefore, are forced to do double or triple duty, standing in for other emotions that are too threatening to be experienced or expressed straightforwardly.

A feeling can serve a person as defense against other, more alarming feelings, serve as a way of disguising to himself and others how precarious his position is. Most important, when a feeling becomes a form of psychic camouflage, it obscures the real meaning of the situation for both partners. If a Tough-Fragile gets angry under stress, and neither she nor her partner realizes that she's actually anxious, then she won't ask for and he won't think to offer her the reassurance that might relieve that anxiety.

It follows, then, that what a person 'feels' can be a very unreliable guide to what's going on. Emotion can't always be taken at face value. A feeling can be a straightforward reaction to a situation or a strategic response to it, or somewhere in between. As Imogen Cunningham, photographer and feisty nonogenarian, used to say, "If you want to get angry, you can always find reasons for it." She knew whereof she spoke.

Whatever the validity of an emotion, it forms one element of a larger response pattern. Usually affect, cognition, and behavior are interdependent and mutually reinforcing aspects of a reaction, so no one dimension of the response (the feeling, for example) can serve as proof of the appropriateness or the inevitability of another dimension (behavior, for example). All are equally credible or equally suspect.

This gets us into an apparently complicated distinction between 'real' feelings and feelings which are, in some sense, bogus. But this is not so esoteric a distinction as it might seem. And it is a distinction characteristically made, and necessarily made, by partners in a Stage III relationship. People who know each other well have usually learned to spot the clues (she's not really angry, she's upset . . .). And this technique, learned through experienced love and practical compassion, is one hallmark of a Stage III intimacy. Nor is it merely the province of one partner in his scrutiny of the other. Each must perform this role for himself, learning to recognize himself and thereby making himself available to another.

It's difficult but not impossible for a person to learn to tell the rings from the sixpence in his own emotional life. Attention is of the essence. A person can learn to watch for the bias which is inherent in his own stance. Someone who's primarily a Tough-Fragile, for example, should examine his anger with particular care. He should consider whether a given situation might have provoked other more accurate feelings such as disappointment, or jealousy, or fearfulness, feelings which might at once account for his agitation and open awareness to productive, because accurate, remedy.

Second, a person who is subject to vehement emotions can learn to exercise control over them instead of being controlled by them. An angry Prizewinner said, "I'm so mad at her. I saw her looking at another man. And I don't know what to do. I could let rage erupt, but that isn't the end of it . . ." The Prize-winner usually believes that the only way out of his anger is to prevent it until it's gone. It's not only possible, however, but useful, for him to learn how to turn it off. Freewheeling temper tantrums inevitably weigh heavily on his partner, and the couple relationship runs more smoothly if the Prizewinner learns to work the brakes as well as the accelerator on his temper.

The most difficult step for a person is to allow himself to experience emotions which he previously denied or avoided. It's extremely frightening for the Provider to be open about his anxiety, or for the Fragile to get angry, or for the Ragabash to feel powerful. These are fundamental changes contravening habit and belief, and they're never made quickly or easily. But they can and should be made. The more candidly a person's emotions reflect his real state of being and his real needs, the more effectively he can answer to these needs and allow another to answer to them too.

Simply stated, we believe that a Stage III relationship requires that people take responsibility for their emotions, and emotion is, in part, a psychic expedient. Often, a person's emotional response to a situation is shaped by his internal needs (such as self-protection) more than by external factors. The less his emotional choices are controlled by defensiveness, and the wider the repertoire of accurate feelings he can choose amongst, the better he serves himself and his partner.

Changes in behavior and feeling must ultimately be accompanied by further changes in expectations. The person who asks his couple relationship to fill the conventional romantic bill is guaranteed the disappointment that awaits the person who says,

And when the milkman comes leave him a note in the bottle
Penguin dust, bring me penguin dust, I want penguin dust—*

A person can only accept and find satisfaction in a long-term relationship if his expectations for it are realistic. The relationship will continue to be more comfortable in some ways than in others, and at some times than at others. And a couple relationship alone can't ensure a lifetime of happiness. Furthermore,

* Gregory Corso, "Marriage."

couple trouble is often merely the visible symptom of problems in other areas of the partners' lives. Often, "some of my discontent with the relationship is discontent with myself," one Ragabash said.

If that's the case, the best tonic may be to stop focusing so intently on a relationship's deficiencies and to undertake the kind of independent activity that will make each partner's life more satisfying.

It's easy enough to describe the kinds of changes that are usually helpful. It's far harder to actually venture these changes. The person who consciously tries to change often finds himself feeling awkward and artificial. If, as is very likely, his partner doesn't give him a great deal of credit for his efforts and doesn't respond with changes of the same magnitude, the whole business is likely to seem futile, or worse yet, exploitative. Despite their good intentions, couple after couple end up at a 'you first' impasse. "I'm not going to change unless you're going to change." "Well, why should I change if . . ."

The process of change is almost never very speedy or very dramatic. For most couples, it's two steps forward, a step back, and a spell of foot-dragging. People get perspective and lose it again. A Stage III relationship can relapse into a Stage II under the brunt of external stresses, like illness or financial reverses. But the same combination of realism, responsibility, and desire that enabled the couple to achieve an equilibrium in the first place can enable them to restore the balance to their relationship.

In some quarters, aspirations are high for reaching Stage III: coupled love is the solution that will bring meaning to an unsatisfactory life. In other circles, optimism is low. Betrayed by their hope for a happily-ever-after marriage, some couples have begun to question the whole notion of a commitment to love someone 'forever.' The cynicism is in many ways a reaction against the romanticism, and in many ways it's a constructive development. Couple problems are discussed far more frankly now than they were twenty years ago. And people are no longer as isolated in their disillusionment. But shared disillusionment may foster the conviction that a lasting couple commitment inevitably contracts into a dim business of obligation and resignation. We believe that an altogether different outcome is possible.

We believe it possible to affirm that love "lasteth till 'tis old." But Stage III is an achievement, almost never a happy accident. Stage I can be a product of good fortune, but Stage III is a product of good work. A couple has to struggle to overcome the disillusionment and the mistrust that relationships often create. They have to believe that "there's a place beyond resentment" and persist in their efforts to reach it despite discouragement over the lack of change or the slow pace of change in their relationship.

But although they are essential, persistence and good intentions are not sufficient to reach Stage III. The essence of Stage III is mutual acceptance, the knowledge that with one's partner there's "no need to hurry, no need to sparkle, no need to be anybody but one's self." * The partners trust each other and feel at home with each other. Beth expressed it this way. "Part of the success of our marriage is that the family is a kind of safety valve where you can act out in a way and manner you can't someplace else."

Stage III also means mutual accommodation. Beth's husband explained, "Ten years ago, or even five years ago, I would have been less happy with her slumps. It's a pain. It's so visible in her, in the way the house looks, in everything. It's striking. But now I'm better about saying, 'Well, I'll pick it up, I'll do it.' I can wait till her mood goes away without getting too upset. Basically we're more sensitive to each other."

One of the prerequisites for survival of any couple is enduring mutual attraction. Al puzzled over how he maintained such an attraction over the years. "I say to her, 'How can I be in love with a sixty-year-old woman?' But I am. So she excites me and I'm grateful

* Virginia Woolf, *A Room of One's Own.*

for it and I'm grateful that life has dealt me the cards that I can stay excited." As Al pointed out, "We have always been able to have a good time together, just the two of us."

For their relationship to survive over the long term, a couple must not only share a lively interest in each other, they must also share the inclination to seek each other out for pleasure. This demands, of course, the ability to remain curious about what is familiar, and to recognize the unfamiliar where it steals in. This kind of lasting involvement—mental, physical, and emotional—creates a deep mutual knowledge that enlightens both partners.

> Now that I have your heart by heart I see.*

The Stage III couple has learned to accept themselves as lovable people. And they have also learned to embrace each other as,

> Mortal, guilty, but to me
> The entirely beautiful.†

Known, and appreciated, a person is free to become most fully himself or herself. He can trust his partner, and the slow accumulation of trust over the years spent together enables the Stage II couple to share an unrivaled intimacy, an intimacy not of illusion, but of achieved, earned knowledge.

A lasting couple relationship requires that a balance be struck between a couple's individual and joint pursuits, between autonomy and interdependence. This is, and should be, a fluid equilibrium, affected by change, change either in the partner, or in their external circumstances.

The desire for 'security' has taken some hard criticism of late. It has become synonymous with a lack of vision or a capitulation to anxiety. But in fact, men

* Louise Bogan, "Song for the Last Act."
† W. H. Auden, "Lullaby."

and women who are secure—who love and know they're loved in return—are apt to be far more venturesome and spontaneous than those whose emotional footing is insecure. Beth spoke to the point when she said, "We needed to be married to go ahead and do the rest of our lives. We needed that reassurance from each other. That part of our lives had to be sound. Then we could go out and develop the rest of our lives. I needed that successful relationship to be successful elsewhere."

The security of a Stage III relationship accomplishes an indispensable function for the couple. They have each other to rely on, and the strength they exchange reassures them and reinforces them for their struggle through life. But, best of all, that exchanged strength enriches their experience of life.

We began this chapter on fulfilled love by admitting that "the business of love is cruelty," and that "Romance has no part in it." That is not the poet's last word on the subject. Nor is it ours. For the poem, like love itself, continues:

> Sure
>   love is cruel
>   and selfish
>   and totally obtuse—
>   at least, blinded by the light,
>   young love is.
>   But we are older,
> I to love
>   and you to be loved,
>   we have,
> no matter how,
>   by our wills survived
>   to keep
> the jeweled prize
>   always at our finger tips.
> We will it so
>   and so it is
>   past all accident.*

* William Carlos Williams, "The Ivy Crown."